AF543182

Mystery Behind Maoists

Mystery Behind Maoists

K.N. Sinha (Dy Coll.) (Retd.)

PRASHANT PUBLISHING HOUSE
DELHI-110094

Published by :

Prashant Publishing House

C-34, 28 Foota Road, Gali-3,

West Karwal Nagar, Delhi-110094

Phone : 011-22963970, Mob. : 9810396373

e-mail.: prashantpublishinghouse@gmail.com

Mystery Behind Maoists

Reserved

First Published 2013

ISBN 978-93-80565-35-4

No part of this book may be reprduced or transmitted in any form or by any means, electronic or mechanical, Including photocoying, recording or by any information storage and retrieval system, with-out permission in writing from the Publishers.

PRINTED IN INDIA

Published by Mr. R.K. Jha M/s Prashant Publishing House and Published at H.S. Offset House Press, Delhi.

Preface

The Maoist's revolutionary strategies were very important in many insurgent movements, especially in the middle of the 20th century. However, currently their role is less important than it used to be and the changes described above significantly contributed to such a situation. In order to better understand what the role of Mao's views on insurgency has on contemporary insurgent movements it is necessary to analyse its basic assumptions and than compare them to the current situation and the insurgent movements of 1970-1990s.

Administrative heads and senior officials of 12 States, including Chief Ministers, Home Secretaries and Directors-General of Police, met in New Delhi under the auspices of the Union Home Ministry and decided to set up inter-State joint task forces to "facilitate coordinated and synergised anti-naxalite operations across State boundaries" and "strengthen intelligence networks" for this mission. Home Minister Shivraj Patil announced that "these forces would be made functional quickly", in the context of the developing situation in various naxalite-affected States. A number of politicians and security officials who attended the meeting rated the decision as historic, essentially because the "Union Home Ministry had for the first time accepted the need to raise a special joint task force that can operate across State borders to counter the naxalite threat". Even as the "historic", albeit somewhat contentious, decision was being circulated and officials of the administration and security agencies were working out the details of its implementation, Home Departments of various States received reports about scores of naxalite conventions across large tracts of forest land, stretching from Andhra Pradesh in south India to Orissa and Bihar in the east.

The basic problem with the conceptual framework of Maoism as has been elucidated by the Indian Maoists lies in their inability to come to grips with the need for evolving with the changing situation and grasping the concrete situation in the society where they are working. Thus the basic analysis of the Indian State of the 40 year old CPI (ML) programme in the wake of the Naxalbari movement is retained by the Maoists, failing to draw any lesson from the complete splintering of the ultra Left movement into myriad factions and groups.

The CPI (M) understands that the Indian ruling classes consist of an alliance between the bourgeoisie and the landlords which is led by the big bourgeoisie. The big bourgeoisie, in turn, increasingly collaborates with international finance capital. At the same time, the CPI (M) recognizes that the Indian bourgeoisie, as a whole, has a dual character. On the one hand, being part of the world capitalist system and seeking to develop capitalism in India, it collaborates with imperialism and international finance capital. On the other hand, in order to preserve and expand its economic domain from being encroached upon by global capital, it also has conflicts with imperialism. Such conflicts, however, get resolved not by confrontation but through compromise, pressure and bargain.

As the book addresses this crucial issue quite deftly, it is hoped that it would prove to be a source of great information for the reader.

—Editor

Contents

1

Behind Maoists

The frustrated Nepali Congress leaders as well as other anti-insurgent political groups often ask question such as "who is really behind Maoist terrorism?" The favourite past time among the Nepali ruling elite have been to see foreign hand whenever they fail to manage the country and the political situation goes out of their hand. A section of hyper nationalists, who exist inside all political parties, see India behind "Maoist terrorism", although they fail to provide convincing argument. Why would India, which itself is biting a bullet from Maoist insurgency in Bihar, Madhya Pradesh and Andhra Pradesh, would support Nepali Maoists? Their only argument is that India enjoys in political instability in Nepal and hence does not want to see strong and stable Nepal, an argument without an iota common sense.

Arguments lacking common sense abound regarding Maoist insurgency in Nepal. Former Prime Minister Krishna Prasad Bhattarai once blamed the United States for fanning insurgency when he was reported to have said that the Maoist leader Dr. Baburam Bhattarai was sheltered by the American Embassy in Kathmandu. Why would the United States, a staunchly anti-communist and a global status-quo power, whip-up Maoist insurgency in a land, which is geo-politically so far away and has little day-to-day interests? It may be noted here that the United States had withdrawn the office its military attaché a few years back indicating the declining strategic value of Nepal.

This leaves China as a potential destabilizing force. Here, too, it does not make any sense to blame China behind Maoist war because China is not a Maoist state any more. Further, it is not in the interest of China to antagonize India and Western powers under normal circumstances by politically and militarily messing in Nepal.

In this context, it does not make any sense for Americans or Indians to fan communist rebellion in Nepal even for the purpose of temporary expediency. Maoist war is thriving in Nepal thanks mainly due to the internal environment of poverty buttressed by repressive policies of incompetent and corrupt leaders. Foreigners will certainly watch the developments to protect their day-to-day interests but it is absurd to say that they are doctoring the Maoist political and military events.

Strategic Choices for Regional Actors

In the past, both India and China have sought and competed for influence in Nepal. Nepal, in the past, had tried to maintain a relationship of equidistance (some prefer the term "equi-proximity) between the two regional heavy weights. How would these two antagonistic neighbours react to the growing instability in Nepal? What are their strategic choices? There are people in Nepal who think India would not let Maoists come to power. They argue that if Nepal government fails to disarm the guerrillas, New Delhi will not hesitate to step in with its armed forces to flush out the guerrillas. In that event what will China do? Will it stay as a spectator? Perhaps, not. What are the choices for India? Prolonged instability in Nepal is not definitely in India's interest. But sending the armed forces to quell Maoist insurgency will not be a prudent decision on the part of New Delhi either. India has already learned a painful lesson in Sri Lanka when its armed forces entered the island-nation but failed to disarm roughly 6000 Tamil guerrillas. Similarly, tens of thousands of military personnel had to be deployed in Kargil to flush out less than one thousand militants. Fighting against guerrillas in Nepal's mountainous terrain will prove highly costly, a fact already experienced by the British in 1814-16 war.

India will have to do cost-benefit analysis before deploying its force even if the beleaguered government of Nepal requests for the same. Will India's relation with Maoist Nepal be worse-off than what it is presently? Will India lose anything in Nepal in the event of a Maoist take-over? One of the 40-points of Maoists is the scrapping of the 1950 Treaty of Peace and Friendship. This is nothing new for India as all other political parties, too, have sought a new treaty and New Delhi has agreed for a comprehensive review of the treaty. In this context, New Delhi has nothing to lose, in strategic terms, from a change of political system in Kathmandu. On the other hand, if India enters Nepal in arms, the ongoing insurgency will take the form of national liberation war in which India will get nothing but international condemnation. It will only hasten the Maoist take over. The topography is clearly in Maoists' favour and existing wide spread anti-Indian sentiment also will rally behind the Maoist guerrillas.

The growing Maoist insurgency with its link with India's People's War Group (PWG) and Maoist Coordination Centre (MCC), however, appears to have heightened India's security interests which is reflected in Uttar Pradesh, Bihar and West Bengal government's recent decision to establish additional police posts along Indo-Nepal border. Indian Defence Minister George Fernandes recently has said that his ministry is actively considering setting up of army camps along Indo-Nepal border in Bihar to check infiltration and subversive activities against India allegedly being carried out by Pakistan's Inter Services Intelligence (ISI) from the Himalayan kingdom.

Although not openly declared but certainly one of the factors behind the decision to establish additional police posts and the contemplation for the deployment of armed forces along India-Nepal border appears to control cross border linkages between India's PWG and MCC. It is a well-known fact that the supporters of Free Tibet Movement based in India have used Nepal as a conduit to transfer men and propaganda materials into Tibet. The government of Nepal, despite the request of Chinese government authorities not to allow anti-China activities from Nepali soil, has failed to stop Free Tibet Movement activists from sending men and propaganda materials into Tibet through the only Arniko highway (previously called Kodari highway) connecting Nepal to Tibet. The flight of Karmappa Lama into India in the winter of 2000 through the territory of Nepal has made Beijing unhappy with Kathmandu The Arniko highway (120km) was constructed in 1962-64 period with Chinese assistance despite India's objection. The then King Mahendra had argued to silence the Indian critics by saying that, "communism does not come by taxi cab." The construction of highway was the opening of the first Chinese gateway to South Asia. The Arniko highway has remained a militarily strategic point for both India and China while Nepal has considered it as politically important in its policy of balancing the neighbours.

POLITICAL PARTIES AND THE PEOPLE'S WAR

After the restoration of democracy several parties began working in Nepal. Among them seven parties have representatives in parliament. The Nepal Communist Party does not hold any seats in parliament but at 7% of the vote has become a national party. There are four kinds of political forces in the country: the Liberal Rightist force, led by Nepali Congress; the Non-Liberal Rightist force, led by the former Panchayat system's successor, the Rastra Parjatantra Party; the Communal force, led mainly by the Nepal Sadvawana Party; and the Communist force, led by many parties. Expect for the Maoists, all parties participated in the 1999 election.

The Nepali Congress does not have a clear view on the Maoist People's War. Some of its leaders consider it to be a terrorist group and the problem one of law and order. That is the official line. However other members consider the Maoist problem a political issue that should be solved politically. The Rastria Parjatantra Party and Nepal Sadvawana Party do not have clear-cut views on but consider the war a political problem. All communist parties consider it a political problem, but sometimes condemn it for terrorist activities. There are slight differences in views between communist parties on the Maoist People's War. The Nepal Communist Party [UML] and Nepal Communist Party [ML] want to change society by peaceful means. The other communist parties consider armed struggle necessary for revolution, but argue that the situation is not ready to start armed struggle.

The Maoists mainly target the Nepali Congress workers. Many of them have been killed, abducted and injured. They also target Nepal Communist Party [UML] cadres, and other parties' workers. According to the Maoists they only punish those who are class enemies. They claim to not punish people because of their political ideology, but punish only exploiters, spies and enemies of people. There are always controversies as to whether victims were actually exploiters or enemies of people or just political opponents. In some events the Maoists have accepted that they have made mistakes against innocent people.

The Government and the People's War

All governments have had the same attitude regarding the Maoist People's War. All major parties have had the opportunity to form government. Governments typically consider the Maoists terrorists and the problem one of law and order. However they have different attitudes while they are in opposition. The government has never considered the Maoist problem a political problem and has never recognized the Maoists as a political force. The government has tried to solve this problem by using the police and army. Sometimes they talk about dialogue with the Maoists, but they do not take it seriously.

Governments have launched internal security and development programs in Maoist areas. They have also formed victim associations. Two commissions have recommended solutions to the government, but these have never been implemented. The government has enacted the Internal Security Law and established the Armed Police Force to control Maoist activities. These efforts have not made any progress towards solving the Maoist problem. After Sher Bahadur Deuwa became Prime Minister, both sides declared a cease-fire. For the first time the government gave recognition to the Maoists as a political party. Now both sides are trying to make an atmosphere suitable for peace talks.

The Monarchy and the People's War

Theoretically Maoists are republican. In the beginning of the people's war, the Maoists did not have a direct view on the monarch, however they considered him to represent the feudal system. Surprisingly, they had a soft attitude with regards to former King Birendra, as they considered him a nationalist. In the words of senior Maoist leader Dr. Babu Ram Bhattarai: Birendra also stood his ground against expansionist Indian powers. He introduced democracy and took a keen interest in the well being of our country, for which extremist reactionaries assassinated his whole family. We should not consign him and his values to a footnote in history. Nepali history cannot afford to discard him.

However, in the 40 demands they demanded that "All the special rights and privileges of the King and his family should be ended." After the Royal Palace incident of 1 June 2001, the Maoists changed their attitude on the monarchy. In that event all of King Berendra's family was killed. So the Maoists argued for the birth of a republic out of the incident. Dr. Babu Ram Bhattrai again: A modern day KOT PARBA took place in Narayanhiti Darbar on the night of 1 June this year. Not only did this incident destroy the entire dynasty of Birendra Bir Bikram Shah Dev, it also unexpectedly gave birth to a republic in this country. It is but natural, then, for the issues of constitutional monarchy and the birth of a republic to become an issue to be debated. He further states that Birendra's whole family was wiped out and now it is the duty of all nationalist Nepalis to help in the establishment of a republic. It is the bitter truth. If what has been said about Dipendra [Son of king Birendra] is true, it only proves that the monarchy is outdated and it is time to discard it. There is no point in carrying on with a system that has outlived its purpose. What has been proved is that it was not Dipendra who committed this act but the reactionaries, expansionists, fascists and imperialists. All this proves that anyone crowned king will only be a puppet in their hands.... From any point of view traditional, feudal monarchy is dead and the birth of the republic has already taken place.

Bhattrai has also accused the present king [brother of King Birendra] Gyainendra of organizing the massacre and has called for his overthrow.

Nepal has had a constitutional monarchy since 1990. The king has not had an active role in day to day politics. The executive/ government makes all the political decisions. So the monarchy does not have any view on Maoist directly, but indirectly has concerns regarding the Maoists. As head of state the former king directed the government to solve Maoist problem. The present king states that there should not be any conditions set while holding dialogue between the government and the Maoists regarding the constitutional monarchy and the multi-party system.

MAOIST INSURGENCY IN NEPAL: REGIONAL DIMENSION

A five-year old Maoist People's War in Nepal has quietly been capturing the hearts and minds of villagers and urban intellectuals, and has been growing more rapidly than anyone had ever imagined. So potent is the Maoist rhetoric of revolution that even if the insurgency fails, it may change the entire complexion of the country in just a few years. The Maoist People's War in Nepal is entering into sixth-year on February 13, 2001. In the last five-year Maoist guerrillas have captured many successful headlines, both at home and abroad. A recent article published on January 4, 2001 by Stratfor.com, an US-based intelligence consulting firm, has made an assessment on Nepal. In an alarming note to the ruling elite as well as to the strategic thinkers of regional and global powers, the article writes: "Nepal is likely headed toward even more difficult times with the probable change of its entire political system, from multiparty democracy to communist state… China's presence in Nepal would also complicate positions of the U.S. Navy in the Indian Ocean.....India will be forced to counter Nepal's apparent slide toward Beijing through other means, perhaps increasing contacts with Bhutan, another buffer state in the region."

The so-called intelligence assessment appears to be exaggerated. For example, Maoist take-over in Kathmandu will not necessarily slide Nepal towards Beijing. It all depends on how India will react to developments in Nepal. Maoists have no governments in the world as their natural ideological friends. That being the case, the Maoists will have to define the framework of their foreign policy based on *realpolitik*. Further, the Maoist leadership is very critical of Chinese Communist Party whom they describe as "revisionists." So, Maoists have a tight rope walking and will have to follow the policy of equi-proximity with both India and China.

Regional Instability

A close study of the insurgency gives one the impression that the guerrillas have clearly entered into the strategic stalemate from the strategic defensive phase of the Maoist People's War and are only one more phase away i.e. the strategic offensive. While the insurgency has already exhausted the state and has shaken the internal stability of multi-party political system in Nepal, it also has a potential to raise the level of instability in regional balance of power. Nepal occupies a strategic position between India and China, two nations that have unresolved border disputes and have even fought a war over it in 1962. China still occupies a section of the Himalayas claimed by India. Since the fall of the Soviet Union, China has focused more on reinforcing its southwestern border by moving troops and constructing military infrastructure. Both India and China have historically treated Nepal as a buffer state. Although Nepal is economically dependent on India, but it is relatively free of military ties to either India or China.

NEPAL: NEW 'STRATEGIC PARTNER' OF CHINA

There has been a major shift in China's foreign policy towards Nepal since the Maoist ascendance to power. China had earlier adopted a policy of 'non-intervention' in the internal matters of Nepal and largely stayed out of Nepalese internal politics. However, the demise of the monarchy and the ascendance of political parties have forced China to reshape its Nepal policy. Moreover, frequent protests by Tibetans in recent months alerted the Chinese to the possibility of the China-Tibet border being misused. Consequently, China has sought to engage Nepalese political actors at all levels, primarily to secure the border with Nepal. With the Maoists in power, China also hopes to use its ideological commonalities to suppress the Tibetan movement in Nepal.

When the Maoists emerged victorious in the April 2008 elections, China adopted a wait and watch policy because it was unsure of their intentions. After all, the Maoists were backed by India and were catapulted to the political centre stage only after a comprehensive peace agreement in which India had played a substantial behind the scenes role. However, media reports reveal that after several interactions with Maoists leaders, China has begun to feel quite comfortable with the Maoist-led government. The Maoists' ideological linkages with China and their keenness to neutralize India's influence in the region have also made them an obvious choice for engagement.

It has been reported that in interactions with Chinese the Maoist leaders gave the impression that the future of democracy in Nepal could be guided by the example of the Communist Party of China. Indeed, there are many in Nepal who argue that persistence with the Maoist tag in the party name despite joining competitive politics indicates that the party may work towards a single party system in the future, given that dictatorship of the proletariat has prime of place in the Maoist lexicon. In fact, some hardline leaders of the party have suggested a people's republic similar to that of China on a number of occasions even after Maoists joined the political mainstream. These ideas might have encouraged China to attempt to consolidate its position in Nepal by continuously engaging the Maoists at the political, economic, military and social levels, and thus secure its strategic interests in the region. In fact, twelve high-level Chinese delegations, including two military teams, visited Nepal in the course of 2008-2009.

During these visits, China has repeatedly assured economic, technological and military aid to Nepal. The Maoist-led government was also asked to adopt a 'One-China' policy, not to allow Nepalese land for anti-China activities, take strong action against Tibetan refugees and grant special facilities for Chinese investments in strategic sectors. Beijing has also initiated Track-II diplomacy with Nepal and invited Nepalese scholars to undertake visits to Chinese think tanks. Some of the important visits from China to Nepal were:

- 25 February 2009: Assistant Chinese Foreign Minister Hu Zhengyue led a 14-member delegation.
- 19 February 2009: Liu Hongcai, Vice Minister of the International Department of the central committee of the CPC led a delegation to take part in the inaugural ceremony of the 8th convention of the UML in Butwal.
- 10 February 2009: A high level Peoples' Liberation Army (PLA) delegation, one of the largest delegations in two months, arrived in Nepal.
- 06 December 2008: Lieutenant General Ma Xiaotian, deputy chief of General Staff of the PLA headed a ten-member delegation. China agreed to provide US $2.61 million worth of security assistance to Nepal.
- 01 December 2008: China's Foreign Minister Yang Jiechi visited Nepal.
- 24 July 2008: Chinese Vice-Minister for Foreign Affairs, Wu Dawei, visited Nepal. He pledged a grant assistance of 100 million yuan as economic and technical cooperation.
- 04 March 2008: Assistant Minister for Foreign Affairs of China, He Yafei, undertook a three-day visit to Nepal.

Nepal's engagements with China have also increased manifold with the visit of delegations both at State and non-state levels. Apart from visits at the official levels, private visits by political leaders, journalists and academicians are also sponsored by China as part of public diplomacy. During these visits Chinese authorities have reportedly assured all kinds of support to the Maoist government in its efforts aimed at laying the foundation for a 'New Nepal'. For the Nepalese Maoists, growing Chinese engagement is a win-win situation in line with their 'policy of equidistance', which has been deliberately adopted to counter-balance India's influence in Nepal.

The increasing level of bilateral engagement also indicates that China is wooing Nepal as a new strategic partner. This has been confirmed by the statements made by various Chinese officials. For example, on 16 February 2009, Chinese Foreign Minister Yang Jiechi said in Beijing that China would prefer to work with Nepal on the basis of a strategic partnership. In fact, Vice Minister of International Department of the Central Committee of Communist Party of China, Liu Hongcai said in Kathmandu in February 2009 that "we oppose any move to interfere in the internal affairs of Nepal by any force." Similarly, on November 04, 2008, Liu Hong Chai, International Bureau Chief of the Chinese Communist Party, stated that "China will not tolerate any meddling from any other country in the internal affairs of Nepal- our traditional and ancient neighbour."

China has also submitted to Kathmandu a draft Sino-Nepal friendship treaty. The draft states that China will not attack Nepal and would respect Nepal's sovereignty and territorial integrity. Nepal would recognize 'One China' policy and not allow its territory to be used for "anti-China" activities. The draft treaty in fact looks more like a strategic one that is tilted highly in favour of Chinese security concerns. China needs this agreement because it does not have confidence in the democratic arrangements and future governments in Nepal, and wishes to consolidate its position while the Maoists are in power. China has penetrated the Nepalese political system by gaining the confidence of hardline communist leaders both in the CPN-UML and the CPN-Maoist. China is also known to have played a major role in facilitating the alliance between the CPN-UML and the Maoists. Prior to Jhala Nath Khanal becoming UML Chief, a four-member Chinese delegation visited Kathmandu on May 10, 2008 and met Khanal and other Maoist leaders. A senior delegation from the Communist Party of China led by vice Minister Liu Hongcai was also in Kathmandu in February 2009 to attend the inaugural ceremony of the 8th national convention of the UML. The victory of Khanal as chairman of the UML, who is close to Prime Minister Prachanda, has been crucial for the survival of the Maoist-led coalition government.

The nature of Chinese engagements in Nepal goes beyond the political domain. They might also be aimed at influencing the process of drafting of the new constitution to ensure that China's long-term interests are served, particularly in hydropower and other strategically important projects. China has also assured Nepal help in the modernization and integration of registered Maoist guerrillas into the Nepal Army.

Considering the strategic and economic interests Beijing has in Nepal, in terms of energy from hydro projects and as a transit country between China and India, China may expand its state level engagements by entering into long-term agreements at various levels. The proposed new friendship treaty marks the beginning of this process. Moreover, the treaty may enhance the bargaining power of the Maoist government vis-à-vis India to resolve some of the long standing disputes between the two countries.

2

Maoist Theory

Unlike the earlier forms of Marxism-Leninism in which the urban proletariat was seen as the main source of revolution, and the countryside was largely ignored, Mao focused on the peasantry as a revolutionary force which, he said, could be mobilized by a Communist Party with their knowledge and leadership. The model for this was of course the Chinese Communist rural insurgency of the 1920s and 1930s, which eventually brought the Communist Party of China to power. Furthermore, unlike other forms of Marxism-Leninism in which large-scale industrial development was seen as a positive force, Maoism made all-round rural development the priority. Mao felt that this strategy made sense during the early stages of socialism in a country in which most of the people were peasants.

Unlike most other political ideologies, including other socialist and Marxist ones, Maoism contains an integral military doctrine and explicitly connects its political ideology with military strategy. In Maoist thought, "political power comes from the barrel of the gun" (one of Mao's quotes), and the peasantry can be mobilized to undertake a "people's war" of armed struggle involving guerrilla warfare in three stages.

The first stage involves mobilizing and organizing the peasantry. The second stage involves setting up rural base areas and increasing coordination among the guerrilla organizations. The third stage involves a transition to conventional warfare. Maoist military doctrine likens guerrilla fighters to fish swimming in a sea of peasants, who provide logistical support. Maoism emphasizes "revolutionary mass mobilization" (physically mobilizing the vast majority of a population in the struggle for socialism), the concept of New Democracy, and the Theory of Productive Forces as applied to village-level industries independent of the outside world. In Maoism, deliberate organizing of massive military and economic power is necessary to defend the revolutionary area from outside threat, while centralization keeps corruption under supervision, amid strong control, and sometimes alteration, by the revolutionaries of the area's arts and sciences.

A key concept that distinguishes Maoism from other left-wing ideologies is the belief that the class struggle continues throughout the entire socialist period, as a result of the fundamental antagonistic contradiction between capitalism and communism. Even when the proletariat has seized state power through a socialist revolution, the potential remains for a bourgeoisie to restore capitalism. Indeed, Mao famously stated that "the bourgeoisie [in a socialist country] is right inside the Communist Party itself", implying that corrupt Party officials would subvert socialism if not prevented. This was the main reason for the Great Proletarian Cultural Revolution, in which Mao exhorted the public to "Bombard the [Party] headquarters!" and wrest control of the government from bureaucrats (such as Liu Shaoqi and Deng Xiao Ping) perceived to be on the capitalist road.

Mao's doctrine is best summarized in the Little Red Book of Mao Zedong, which was distributed to everyone in China as the basis of revolutionary education. This book consists of quotations from the earliest days of the revolution to the mid-1960s, just before the beginning of the Cultural Revolution.

MAOISM INTERNATIONALLY

From 1962 onwards the challenge to the Soviet hegemony in the World Communist Movement made by the Chinese Communist Party resulted in various divisions in communist parties around the world. At an early stage, the Albanian Party of Labour sided with CPC. So did many of the mainstream (non-splinter group) communist parties in South-East Asia, like the Burmese Communist Party, Communist Party of Thailand, and Communist Party of Indonesia. Some Asian parties, like the Communist Party of Vietnam and the Workers Party of Korea attempted to take a middle-ground position.

In the west and south, a plethora of parties and organizations were formed that upheld links to the CPC. Often they took names such as Communist Party (Marxist-Leninist) or Revolutionary Communist Party to distinguish themselves from the traditional pro-Soviet communist parties. The pro-CPC movements were, in many cases, based amongst the wave of student radicalism that engulfed the world in the 1960s and 1970s.

Only one Western classic communist party sided with CPC, the Communist Party of New Zealand. Under the leadership of CPC and Mao Zedong, a parallel international communist movement emerged to rival that of the Soviets, although it was never as formalized and homogeneous as the pro-Soviet tendency.

After the death of Mao in 1976 and various power-struggles in China that followed, the international Maoist movement was, in rough terms, divided into three. One portion supported — although not necessarily with great enthusiasm — the new Chinese leadership under Deng Xiaoping. Another portion denounced the new leadership as traitors to the cause of Marxism-Leninism Mao Zedong Thought. A third portion sided with the Albanians in denouncing the Three Worlds Theory of the CPC.

The pro-Albanian category would effectively start to function as an international tendency of its own, led by Enver Hoxha and the APL. That tendency was able to amalgate most of the groups in Latin America, such as the Communist Party of Brazil. The first category was extremely heterogenous.

The new Chinese leadership had little interest in the various foreign factions supporting Mao's China, and the movement fell into disarray. Many of the parties that had been fraternal parties of the Chinese government before 1975 either disbanded, abandoned the Chinese entirely, or even denounced Marxism-Leninism and developed into non-communist, social democratic parties. What is today sometimes referred to as the "international Maoist movement" evolved out of the second category- the parties that opposed Deng and claimed to uphold the legacy of Mao.

During the 1980s two parallel regroupment efforts emerged, one centered around the Communist Party of the Philippines, which gave birth to the ICMLPO, and one that birthed the Revolutionary Internationalist Movement, which the Shining Path communist guerrilla group and the Revolutionary Communist Party USA played a leading role in forming. Both the International Conference and the RIM tendencies claimed to uphold Marxism-

Leninism-Mao Zedong Thought, although RIM was later to substitute that ideology with what they termed 'Marxism-Leninism-Maoism'.

Today the Maoist organizations grouped in RIM have their strongest hold in South Asia, and are at the forefront of the armed struggles taking place in Nepal, India and Bangladesh. There are also lesser struggles going on in Peru and Turkey.

In the Philippines, the Communist Party of the Philippines, which is not part of the RIM, leads an armed struggle through its military wing, the New People's Army.

The largest Maoist group in the USA is the RIM-affiliated Revolutionary Communist Party, USA. In Germany the ICMLPO-affiliated MLPD is the largest Maoist group in the country.

MAOIST: THEORY OF ETHICS

What *makes* something good or bad, right or wrong? This is a question that people have discussed and argued about for at least 2,500 years. They have come up with dozens, perhaps hundreds, of different and conflicting answers. This might suggest that the question is very hard, or perhaps even unsolvable. Many have thought so. But actually, the answer is fairly simple. Even *proving* that this answer is correct is not tremendously difficult (though here, as elsewhere, any proof will be rejected by those who fail to comprehend its soundness).

The first roughly correct answer was discovered by the thinkers of the French Enlightenment several hundred years ago. A more precise answer, fully appropriate to contemporary class society, was discovered and elaborated on by Marx, Engels, Lenin and other Marxists. But still, this fairly simple, elegant and extremely compelling explanation of morality has by no means been widely adopted. Most people, indeed, have never been exposed to it at all. One obvious reason for this is that the capitalist ruling class always goes to great lengths to keep dangerous Marxist ideas away from the people. But it must also be admitted that we Marxists ourselves have so far not done a good job in putting forward our views on ethics, clearing up confusions and misconceptions, and replying to objections that have been put forward by bourgeois apologists. And many Marxists themselves have been quite confused and mistaken about ethics, arguing for all kinds of views such as those of Kant or the Bible—in the name of Marxism —or arguing that Marx rejected all morality. What *makes* something good or bad, right or wrong? That is the most basic question in ethics. Of course there are many other questions as well, such as:

- Why does morality exist among humans in the first place?
- When and how did morality originate ?
- How come there are different opinions about what is right or wrong?
- What is a person's conscience, and what is its relationship to morality?
- Why don't people always do what they think is right?
- Does morality, what is right and wrong, change from time to time and from place to place?
- Is there such a thing as moral progress ?

And of course there are specific questions about various human actions, such as:

- Are such things as lying or killing other people ever justified? If so, when?
- Is abortion right or wrong?
- Are wars ever morally justified?
- Is revolution morally justified? Even if it involves widespread loss of life?

Questions like these in this second group are questions of *morality,* that is, specific questions about what is right or wrong, good or bad. When you collect everything that one person has to say about all such questions, or what one group says, or one social class, or one whole society (i.e., the dominant views in that society), you have a specific *moral code. Ethics,* however, concerns itself not with directly answering these sorts of specific moral questions, or directly with constructing any moral code. Instead, it deals with the theoretical questions behind morality— such as what the real essence of moral codes are, how they arose, how they can be justified or discredited, the rational basis for choosing between them, and so forth. Of course most people who talk about morality either present ethical views at the same time, or at least imply them. And most of those who talk or write about ethics also present some of their specific moral views as well.

HISTORICAL MATERIALISM AND MORALITY

Historical materialism is the science of society. It is the result of the application of Marxist philosophy, dialectical materialism, to the history of society. An extended exposition of the tenets of historical materialism. However, there is no better brief summation of it than that given by its discoverer, Karl Marx, in the Preface to his 1859 book, *A Contribution to the Critique of Political Economy*:

In the social production of their existence, men enter into definite, necessary relations, which are independent of their will, namely, relations of production corresponding to a determinate stage of development of their material forces of production. The totality of these relations of production constitutes the economic structure of society, the real foundation on which there arises a legal and political superstructure and to which there correspond definite forms of social consciousness. The mode of production of material life conditions the social, political and intellectual life-process in general. It is not the consciousness of men that determines their being, but on the contrary it is their social being that determines their consciousness.

At a certain stage of their development, the material productive forces of society come into conflict with the existing relations of production or—what is merely a legal expression for the same thing—with the property relations within the frame-work of which they have hitherto operated. From forms of development of the productive forces these relations turn into their fetters. At that point an era of social revolution begins. With the change in the economic foundation the whole immense superstructure is more slowly or more rapidly transformed. In considering such transformations it is always necessary to distinguish between the material transformation of the economic conditions of production, which can be determined with the precision of natural science, and the legal, political, religious, artistic or philosophic, in short, ideological, forms in which men become conscious of this conflict and fight it out. Just as one does not judge an individual by what he thinks about himself, so one cannot judge such an epoch of transformation by its consciousness, but, on the contrary, this consciousness must be explained from the contradictions of material life, from the existing conflict between the social forces of production and the relations of production.... The bourgeois relations of production are the last antagonistic form of the social process of production— antagonistic not in the sense of an individual antagonism but of an antagonism growing out of the social conditions of existence of individuals; but the productive forces developing in the womb of bourgeois society simultaneously create the material conditions for the solution of this antagonism. The prehistory of human society therefore closes with this social formation.

The agency which arises in capitalist society and which is destined to destroy it is of course the working class, the *proletariat*. In summing up the experience of the 1870 working class insurrection known to history as the Paris Commune, Marx added another tenet to the theory of historical materialism, namely that the proletariat could not simply seize the existing bourgeois state but must destroy it and establish the dictatorship of the proletariat over the bourgeoisie to prevent their comeback. The proletarian dictatorship must exist throughout the period of transition from bourgeois society to communist society. Like every scientific theory of any scope, historical materialism has been further developed over the years, most notably by Lenin and Mao Zedong. But the points discovered by Marx remain as its foundation.

The aspect of historical materialism which must command our present attention is its theory of ideology. Although not specifically mentioned by Marx in the above passage, on other occasions Marx and Engels insisted that morality must also be considered as ideology and hence part of the superstructure of society. Ideology' means, in its most general use, the totality of people's ideas, views, and concepts. In class society these ideas, views and concepts are divided along class lines; ideology becomes the ideology of definite social classes, and reflects their interests. Although ideologies are reflections of the socioeconomic relations of production, they are not merely passive reflections but react in turn upon the economic base, and either serve to advance or hinder the further development of society depending upon which class they represent. And although ideologies do reflect the material interests of one class or another, and hence the economic relations which exist in society between the various classes, this relationship is not always completely straightforward or mechanical. Particular ideologists are sometimes the product of conflicting class influences, and in addition to this, many specific ideologies have a historical development of their own which is not necessarily directly relatable in all its particulars to the overall development of society.

Let us then apply the general point of view of historical materialism to the question of morality. We obtain the following principles:

1) Morality changes over the course of history.
2) Morality changes in accordance (more or less) with the changes in the socioeconomic form of society.
3) Each class in any society has its own system of morality.
4) The dominant morality in any society is that of the ruling class (at least once it is firmly entrenched).
5) Each class morality is based, in the final analysis, upon the collective interests of the members of that class, primarily their material, economic interests.

These conclusions of historical materialism with respect to morality are of course compatible—in fact identical—with some of the basic tenets of the MLM theory of ethics. As scientific evidence in favor of MLM ethical theory (or at least part of it) because historical materialism is in my opinion a valid scientific theory, and moreover a much more general and powerful scientific theory capable of entailing more particular conclusions. This will carry absolutely no weight with those who do not accept historical materialism as correct. The other arguments in favor of the MLM theory of ethics which will come later. But there are people who *have* claimed to accept the basic theory of historical materialism—people such as Eduard Bernstein, Nicholas Berdyaev (in his younger days), Georg Lukács and Herbert Marcuse, to name a few—who have nevertheless opposed the class interest interpretation of MLM ethics and have put forward instead ethical theories inconsistent with historical materialism. It is therefore not a trivial thing to point out the compatibility between historical materialism and the class interest theory of ethics.

MARXIST ETHICAL THEORIES

Let's return to the most basic question in ethics once again: What *makes* something good or bad, right or wrong? What are some representative answers to this question which have become popular or fairly widespread? I'll just briefly mention a few of the most prominent.

God's Fiat. One very popular view among religious people is that whatever God says is right *is right,* and whatever God says is wrong *is wrong—just because God says it is*. Murder and cheating are wrong, these people apparently believe, *only because* God supposedly says they are wrong. If God hadn't said these things are wrong, they wouldn't actually be wrong! If God were to change his mind, presumably they then wouldn't be wrong any more! These are just a couple of the many severe difficulties with this theory.

Another rather obvious difficulty with it, for many of us, is that *there is no God,* just as there is no Santa Claus or Easter Bunny. There is certainly no scientific evidence for the existence of any gods, and actually there are compelling scientific reasons to believe that all gods are simply pre-scientific fantasies which linger in a society that is only now finally beginning to get clear on their inherently impossible attributes. Even agnostics, those who claim not to know for sure whether or not there is a God, would seem to have insurmountable difficulties with any God-based ethical theory.

And even those who believe in God should still have some major problems here (if they were to actually think the matter over for a few minutes). Just how do you *determine* what God is supposedly saying is right or wrong? Should you wait until God speaks to you directly? What if he never does? Or should you accept the word of somebody else—maybe some mentally deranged stranger on the street corner?—who *claims* God has spoken to him about what is right and wrong? (Just why is it, do you suppose, that sensible people these days conclude that the making of such claims is in itself enough *to demonstrate* that a person is mentally deranged?! It is now known that many religious people with schizophrenia are prone to misinterpreting the voices they hear in their head as the voice of God.)

What most religious people do is accept the word of some old book like the Bible, which has a variety of conflicting things to say about right and wrong (such as Thou shalt not kill [Exodus 20:13] and Thou shalt not suffer a witch to live [Exodus 22:18]), along with various other sundry matters. It never seems to occur to these religious people to question the reliability, rationality, veracity, and perhaps even the sanity, of those who wrote their holy book in the first place!

Moreover, the Bible is by no means the only such old book which claims to present what God has to say about ethics and morality. Other religious people pick the Koran instead, or the

Torah, the Talmud, the Avesta (of Zoroastrianism), the Upanishads, the Bhagavad-Gita, or the sayings of Buddha or Confucius or some other guru—among many other holy scriptures. How does a person, even a religious person, rationally choose between these conflicting authorities as to what God has to say about morality (and other matters)? Well, obviously, rationality never has the slightest bit to do with it. In fact, most religious people simply adopt the holy book that they were *brought up to believe* is the True word of God. The relatively few who get converted generally just jump from one old book to a different old book.

In other words, while most religious people *claim* that they are following what God says is right or wrong, in actuality all they are doing is following their own family or cultural tradition on the matter. They just haven't got the sense *to see* that that is all they are doing.

There is at least one other major problem for religious people with the notion that God's fiat determines what is right or wrong: It means that it makes no sense (or is completely vacuous) to say that God himself is good! You can hardly commend a person (or entity) for having correct views, if those views are *deemed correct* simply because they have them! More sophisticated religious people, such as Thomas Aquinas, recognizing this problem, have themselves rejected the theory that God's fiat *determines* what is right or wrong. But, of course, most religious people—even Catholics, who nominally follow the teachings of Aquinas—are completely ignorant of such difficulties.

The Golden Rule. The Golden Rule is the precept that you should treat other people the way *you* wish to be treated. This is an extremely popular ethical theory among both religious and non-religious people. It is one of many conflicting ethical theories that are explicit or implicit in the Bible, which quotes Jesus as saying in the Sermon on the Mount: Therefore all things whatsoever ye would that men should do to you, do ye even so to them. One of the ethical theories in the Bible that is inconsistent with this is that of an eye for an eye : And if *any* mischief follow, then thou shalt give life for life, Eye for eye, tooth for tooth, hand for hand, foot for foot, Burning for burning, wound for wound, stripe for stripe.

Although my grandmother once assured me that the King James version of the Bible was God's own language, these days you usually hear the Golden Rule expressed something like this: Do unto others as you would have them do unto you. Incidentally, the Golden Rule is not exclusively (or even originally) a Christian precept. It has been a common theory in many diverse cultures, going way, way back. Confucius, for example, said What you do not desire, do not effect on others (even though that principle conflicts with some of his other principles).

It is amazing how little sense the Golden Rule makes when you actually *think* about it critically. (Of course hardly anybody ever does! They repeat it *without much thinking.*) You should treat people the way you wish to be treated… OK, what if you really wish to be treated as *boss,* or *king?* Should you then treat all other people as your boss or as kings, bowing and scraping in abject obedience? Or consider a slave master: He would have others (his slaves at least) treat him as master, while he treats them as slaves. In light of the Golden Rule, should he start treating his slaves as his masters, and encourage them to treat him as their slave? (This might be poetic justice, but it would still hardly be the ideal moral society!) Or what about masochists? Should they inflict pain on others just because that's the way these totally screwed up people themselves want to be treated? Or what about someone who expects, and even wants, others to be cheats and crooks, because he figures he is better at it and will come out ahead in any completely dog-eat-dog world? There are people like that, you know. (We live in a capitalist society, after all!) Does he then have a moral license to proceed with his chicanery and fraud?

George Bernard Shaw wrote "Do not do unto others as you would that they should do unto you. Their tastes may not be the same." He was putting it in a humorous fashion, but there is some real truth behind his statement. Schopenhauer put it even better: *"Don 7 do to others what you wouldn 7 like done to yourself.* This is, perhaps, one of those arguments that prove, or rather ask, too much. For a prisoner might address it to a judge."

The basic problem with the Golden Rule is that it *assumes* that people are already moral, or basically so—which is very far from always being the case. *If you* are a good, fair and reasonable person, you will want good, fair and reasonable things done to you. And *in that case* it is indeed generally reasonable to say that you should do to others as you would have them do unto you. *But if you are not already a good, fair and reasonable person,* you may *not* yourself wish others to treat you in a good (moral), fair and reasonable way. And *in that case* it is very wrong for you to treat others as you would have them treat you. This is such an obvious point that it is really astounding that all the champions of the Golden Rule never seem to have even an inkling of it! Insofar as it is a coherent ethical theory at all, the "Golden Rule" might actually amount to little more than a variety of ethical relativism.

Hedonism: Maximizing Pleasure and Minimizing Pain. Another very common ethical theory is that pleasure is the greatest good, and pain the greatest evil. Therefore, morality consists in striving to maximize the amount of pleasure for everyone, and striving to minimize the amount of pain. Like most ethical theories, this sounds fairly plausible at first, but cannot withstand even a cursory critical examination.

For one thing, human beings have many other needs and interests besides pleasure and avoiding pain, and far more than just those two things goes into making the good life. Suppose some society could be constructed where everyone (or at least most people) were both very happy and as free of all pain as could reasonably be arranged. But suppose this society was also an authoritarian dictatorship, where people had no political freedom, no control over their own lives, were severely exploited, and so forth. Perhaps this might be some sort of fascist society where the people were nevertheless psychologically happy because of both extreme indoctrination and the liberal availability of hallucinatory drugs. Obviously this would be a nightmare society, and not at all a moral society. Even a somewhat milder version of this sort of thing, such as is pictured in Aldous Huxley's *Brave New World* (1932), is a horrible nightmare.

The roots of this ethical theory, too, go way back. Epicurus (341-270 BCE) held that the practical goal of philosophy was to secure happiness (or at least to avoid all discomfort), and that pleasure was the sum total of happiness. The modern theory of promote pleasure, minimize pain, however, derives primarily from the utilitarians (most of whom would be better called hedonists, if that did not have such negative connotations). Jeremy Bentham (1748-1832), in particular, is responsible for giving utilitarianism its hedonistic twist. Utilitarianism, as its name suggests, was originally concerned more with utility or usefulness, but critics raised the question of useful for *what?*, and that led Bentham, John Stuart Mill, and other utilitarians into this very one-sided hedonist perversion of what was originally a much more sensible ethical theory.

Experiments have been done on lab rats that clearly demonstrate that there is a whole lot more to the good life than merely experiencing even the most intense feelings of pleasure. In the brain of all higher animals (and perhaps many of the lower ones as well), there is a region known as the pleasure center. Tiny wires have been inserted into this region of a rat's brain, and things set up so that when the rat pushes a lever, its pleasure center is stimulated. The pleasure is so intense that the rat keeps pushing the lever over and over again, until it is physically totally exhausted and unable to continue. It may not even eat, drink, or do anything else. And eventually it dies. Human drug addicts are sometimes perhaps in a similar situation, although they generally still have the sense to at least pull away for some food, water, and sleep once in a while. Nevertheless, it should be obvious from examples like this that the simple-minded theory that happiness and the avoidance of pain are all that matters cannot reasonably be considered to be the sole basis of either the good life or of any sort of morality.

Kantian Ethics: the Categorical Imperative. The various elements of Kantian ethics are not widespread among the masses, in the way that the ethical theories mentioned above are. But Kant's ethical ideas are still fairly popular among intellectuals, either as a whole package, or in part.

The most central and famous part of Kantian ethics is the notion of the Categorical Imperative. This doctrine has many formulations in Kant and by his followers, but probably the best known version is as follows: Act only on the maxim through which you can at the same time will that it be a universal law. The idea here is that nothing should be a moral maxim (or guide to moral behavior) unless it always applies, and unless it applies to everyone.

Antonio Gramsci noticed that there has to be an implicit rider on this principle, that only those *in a similar situation* can reasonably be willed to act in the same way, and that this addition essentially destroys the coherence of the whole notion:

Kant's maxim Act in such a way that your conduct can become a norm for all men in similar conditions is less simple and obvious than it appears at first sight. What is meant by similar conditions ? The immediate conditions in which one is operating, or the complex and organic general conditions, knowledge of which requires long and critically elaborated research? ...

Kant's maxim can be considered as a truism, since it is hard to find anyone who does not act in the belief that in the conditions he is in everyone else would act in the same way. A man who steals for hunger maintains that hungry people steal; a man who kills his unfaithful wife maintains that all betrayed husbands should kill, etc. It is only madmen in the clinical sense who act without believing themselves to be in the right. This question is connected with others: 1. Everyone is indulgent towards himself, because when one acts in a non-conformist fashion one knows the mechanism of one's own sensations and judgments and of the chain of cause and effect which has led one to act as one did; but one is much more severe with others because one does not know their inner life. 2. Everyone acts according to his culture, that is the culture of his environment, and as far as one is concerned all men means one's environment, people who think like oneself. Kant's maxim presupposes a single culture, a single religion, a world-wide conformism.

People in very different circumstances are *bound* to have different ideas about what moral maxims (if any) should be upheld "by everybody, everywhere"; people in an exploited economic class for example versus people in the exploiting class.

Clearly Kant believed that this Categorical Imperative method would result not just in moral maxims that had validity only for one person in his or her immediate circumstances, but rather maxims with wide generality and which would apply to everybody everywhere. That is, maxims such as "Thou shalt not lie" and "Thou shalt not kill". That sounds fairly plausible, until you *think* about it for ten seconds! Consider lying. We all agree that generally lying is a wrong thing to do. But anybody with even a little common sense knows that there are times when lying is not wrong. (This is why we have expressions like "a little white lie".) And in fact, there are times when lying is not only *not wrong,* but in fact it would be wrong *not to lie!* (Consider an extreme case to prove the point: Suppose a berserk individual with an ax comes running into the room asking where some innocent child went and says "Tell me where the kid went or I'll kill *your.* Should you tell him the child ran into the closet, refuse to answer at all, or should you lie? Only a Kantian would have problems with a question like this!)

As hard as it is to believe, Kant did in fact claim that lying is *always* wrong! And the absurdity of this shows that the Categorical Imperative approach is completely erroneous. Virtually all the common practical moral maxims (against lying, stealing, killing, etc.) are generally valid, *but not always valid.* And moral maxims themselves must be judged for their appropriateness in particular situations by reference to more important or more abstract moral principles. (More on that point later in the book.)

However, it is not just that the Categorical Imperative leads to unreasonable absolutes when it comes to generating various moral maxims (which in a less absolute form are generally reasonable).

In addition to that severe problem, the Categorical Imperative principle—if taken seriously—leads to the generation of utterly absurd "moral maxims", and this shows that the Categorical Imperative is a completely foolish idea which is unusable as a means of deciding on the morality or immorality of anything. Suppose, for example, that someone decides to become a shoemaker. Can we "will" that *everyone* should become a shoemaker? Of course not! If everyone did, then no one would be a farmer, and we would all starve to death! Hence, becoming a shoemaker must be highly immoral! (Becoming a Kantian philosopher is also extremely immoral, by that same "logic"!)

There are other aspects of Kantian ethics which are just as untenable as the Categorical Imperative. We will discuss some of them later in this essay.

Ethical Relativism

And finally there is the view that *nothing* really makes anything right or wrong, good or bad, that these are merely arbitrary biases that people have, either in different cultures, or even individually. There seem to be three main motives for holding this view:

1) The argument from ignorance.
2) Extreme cynicism about humanity. (Everybody tries to justify what they say and do, but at bottom it is all just excuse making for doing whatever they selfishly want to do.)
3) Learning about other cultures which have different ideas about right and wrong.

This third reason is why cultural anthropologists have been particularly prone to ethical relativism, and why the theory was first put forward in a systematic way by philosophers such as Edward Westermarck who were strongly influenced by the rise of modern anthropology. A number of cultural anthropologists have at various times gone to live with native peoples in various parts of the world and have found (to their evident surprise) that these peoples have somewhat different conceptions of morality, conceptions which seem to serve them just as well as the differing moralities of other cultures serve those societies. Since these anthropologists had also not thought through the basis for morality in their own society, they tended to jump to the conclusion that no particular morality is really better or more valid than any other, but rather that all of them are merely somewhat arbitrary conveniences for particular cultures.

More recently, this same sort of thinking has been generalized and spread to other academic departments, especially to English faculties at universities, in the form of post-modernism, which goes so far as to claim that the world views of the scientific community are really no better than those of native peoples living in the Amazon, or those of religious communities such as Christian fundamentalists who believe the world was created in 4004 B.C.!

As with some of the specific traditional explanations of morality surveyed above, there are no doubt some small and secondary aspects of truth to the relativist viewpoint. Different societies, with different ways of living and different levels of social production, do require somewhat different social norms and moral codes in order to function smoothly. But what the central core of the relativist viewpoint fails to understand is that there is a deeper level of analysis which will explain why the moral systems of different societies still have so much in common, and also explain the differences between them in terms of the same underlying analytical concepts. Once we have that explanatory analytical framework in place we will be able to more rationally discuss the differences between moralities in different forms and stages of society.

Lenin's Summary of Ethics

The most popular ethical theories around today are simply untenable. But is there a Marxist-Leninist-Maoist alternative? And what is the general MLM approach to ethics? In his 1920 speech, The Tasks of the Youth Leagues, Lenin introduces the subject this way:

But is there such a thing as communist ethics? Is there such a thing as communist morality? Of course there is. It is often suggested that we have no ethics of our own; very often the bourgeoisie accuse us Communists of rejecting all morality. This is a method of confusing the issue, of throwing dust in the eyes of the workers and peasants.

In what sense do we reject ethics, reject morality? In the sense given to it by the bourgeoisie, who based ethics on God's commandments. On this point we, of course, say that we do not believe in God, and that we know perfectly well that the clergy, the landowners and the bourgeoisie invoked the name of God so as to further their own interests as exploiters. Or, instead of basing ethics on the commandments of morality, on the commandments of God, they based it on idealist or semi-idealist phrases, which always amounted to something very similar to God's commandments.

We reject any morality based on extra-human and extra-class concepts. We say that this is deception, dupery, stultification of the workers and peasants in the interests of the landowners and capitalists. There is, then, a communist theory of ethics which is based on human and class concepts. What are these concepts? Lenin continues:

We say that our morality is entirely subordinated to the interests of the proletariat's class struggle. Our morality stems from the interests of the class struggle of the proletariat.

And a couple of pages later: The class struggle is continuing and it is our task to subordinate all interests to that struggle. Our communist morality is also subordinated to that task. We say: morality is what serves to destroy the old exploiting society and to unite all the working people around the proletariat, which is building up a new, a communist society.

Communist morality is that which serves this struggle and unites the working people against all exploitation, against all petty private property...

And again: When people tell us about morality, we say: to a communist all morality lies in this united discipline and conscious mass struggle against the exploiters. We do not believe in an eternal morality, and we expose the falseness of all the fables about morality. Morality serves the purpose of helping human society rise to a higher level and rid itself of the exploitation of labour.

And finally: Communist morality is based on the struggle for the consolidation and completion of communism.

So, according to Lenin, whatever serves the class struggle of the proletariat, whatever helps bring about proletarian revolution and the overthrow of the bourgeoisie, and whatever advances the transformation of bourgeois society into communist society, is in accordance with communist morality.

This view of morality has been generally accepted within the communist movement since Lenin's day, but not universally so. There have been those—and especially the more or less unremolded intellectuals from petty-bourgeois backgrounds who tend to be most preoccupied with such questions—who have been unsatisfied with Lenin's formulations and who have sought something better, something less expedient, something more profound. And of course in the camp of the enemy there are endless attacks on, and snide put-downs of, this crude communist theory of morality, even more so than against the other aspects of Marxist-Leninist-Maoist theory.

The fact is, whether Lenin's theory of ethics has been accepted or rejected, it has seldom been taken truly seriously. Bourgeois writers tend to dismiss it out of hand, without really considering if there might be an ethical theory of substance beneath it to investigate. The same goes for the revisionists, the hidden bourgeoisie. While the followers of Lenin have accepted Lenin's view, they haven't thought about it much, or its deep significance. Nor have they adequately elaborated it and defended it.

It therefore seems to me that it is high-time that an extended defence of the MLM theory of ethics is put forward into the realm of the ideological class struggle. Lenin's views correct, but that they can be shown scientifically to be correct. Moreover, far from being a naïve, or superficial theory of mere political expediency, as its enemies claim, the profundity of MLM ethics is of an order undreamed of by its numerous detractors. And, after all, is anything ever more profound than the truth?

MLM Class Interest Theory of Ethics

The major purpose of this book is to demonstrate the validity of MLM ethics. It may therefore be appropriate to outline the central points of this theory before we begin the detailed discussion of its various aspects. This will give the reader the overall perspective to keep in mind as we proceed. The central concept in the ethical theory behind the principles of proletarian morality summarized by Lenin is that of *class interest*. But this "class interest" theory of ethics explicates not only proletarian morality but also the various moral systems of other classes: it explains all such moral systems in terms of the basic class interests of those who develop and propagate them. When a particular moral principle proclaims, say, that it is wrong to steal, it is expressing, in the final analysis, the viewpoint of a definite class about its interests, especially its material interests.

This is not always obvious however since different classes may use these identical words to mean completely different things. The bourgeoisie, for instance, does not consider it stealing to exploit labour (to steal a worker's labour through the expropriation of *surplus value*), while the class-conscious proletariat for its part does not consider it stealing to take back what was stolen from it through exploitation. To say that something is (morally) good or bad, right or wrong, is to say that it answers to, or satisfies, the interests of a particular class. It doesn't matter if a person understands this equivalence or not—objectively it is true. Generally people express the interests of their *own* class through their moral principles, but sometimes they do not correctly understand their own class interests. This is especially apt to be true of the lower classes which are always infected, to one degree or another, by the moral ideology of the ruling class. Proletarian morality is based on, and expresses, the class interests of the proletariat. Now of course the proletariat, like all classes, has various kinds of interests, some more basic than others, some just momentary, others long-term, etc. Naturally the most basic interests take precedence over the less important ones. For the most part the most basic class interests of the proletariat, like those of every class, are those concerned with the material well-being of its members. The proletariat has, in short, basic interests in food, housing, clothing, health, transportation, education, and so forth.

The satisfaction of material interests such as these, and other more abstract interests as well (such as freedom, friendship, security, etc.), depends upon the socioeconomic system which exists, the nature of the prevailing class relations, and so forth. It is an objective fact that capitalism, and class society in general, cannot satisfy the material and other interests of the proletariat, and therefore the basic interests of the proletariat—and hence proletarian morality— *require it to overthrow capitalism and abolish all class exploitation.*

The class struggle, proletarian revolution, and the advance of society to communism are all morally justified *because* they are the only way to satisfy the basic interests of the proletariat and the rest of the masses. All the principles of proletarian morality are subordinate to this one fundamental principle: whatever answers to the interests of the proletariat is right. On the other hand, the moral justification of proletarian revolution and the achievement of communist society follow immediately from this general principle since all the basic, long-term interests of the proletariat are encompassed and encapsulated in communist revolution.

Since the basic class interests of the proletariat require it to lead all society to the stage of communism, where all classes have ceased to exist, it also follows that in liberating itself from exploitation and oppression the proletariat necessarily liberates all humanity. In communist society all humanity will have the same basic collective interests and society will exist to satisfy those interests. Therefore proletarian morality is not just another class morality, no better nor worse than any of the others. On the contrary, proletarian morality is higher (better) than any other class morality because it is not only in the interests of the proletariat but also in the *ultimate interests* of humanity as a whole to advance to communist society.

That is the gist of the MLM theory of ethics. It remains now to elaborate on and back up all these assertions.

Methodology

The broad areas to be investigated and analysed with respect to ethics are mostly human relationships and human society. For example, it will obviously be relevant and useful to investigate the origin of morality in primitive human society insofar as this is possible, and so anthropology is one relevant science. But there are also other sciences with considerable relevance to ethics but which have only tangential connections to human society *per se.* One of these is neurology, where we will later investigate one small topic, namely the physical location in the brain of the seat of the conscience, and what is known so far about the neural connections to that area of the brain. But there is one treasure house of information right at our finger tips—perhaps we should say "right at the tips of our tongues"—which must not be overlooked: our language. The questions "What is morality?" and "What is good?" are obviously closely connected with the questions of scientific linguistics, "What does the word 'morality' mean?" and "What does the word 'good' mean?".

Sometimes it is said that philosophers who concern themselves with language are concerned only with ideas and ignore the real world. And yet language is part of the world. Human languages must necessarily reflect the realities of human existence and human society (though of course they also reflect, in part, human fantasies). Otherwise language would be of no use to us.

There are indeed pitfalls to watch out for here. In *The German Ideology* (1846) Marx and Engels wrote: One of the most difficult tasks confronting philosophers is to descend from the world of thought to the actual world. *Language* is the immediate actuality of thought. Just as philosophers have given thought an independent existence, so they were bound to make language into an independent realm. This is the secret of philosophical language, in which thoughts in the form of words have their own content. The problem of descending from the world of thoughts to the actual world is turned into the problem of descending from language to life.

We have shown that thoughts and ideas acquire an independent existence in consequence of the personal circumstances and relations of individuals acquiring independent existence. We have shown that exclusive, systematic occupation with these thoughts on the part of ideologists and philosophers, and hence the systematization of these thoughts, is a consequence of division of labour, and that, in particular, German philosophy is a consequence of German petty-bourgeois conditions. The philosophers have only to dissolve their language into the ordinary language, from which it is abstracted, in order to recognize it as the distorted language of the actual world, and to realize that neither thoughts nor language themselves form a realm of their own, that they are only *manifestations* of actual life.

In considering the use of moral terms in English, therefore, we must be sure that we are conducting an empirical investigation of the ordinary language and not an investigation of a distorted language incorporating ideological biases, and bearing a consequent distorted relationship to the real world. But what of the "ordinary language" itself? Is it free of all ideological distortion due to the domination of the ruling class in every sphere? No, it is not. Marx and Engels gave the following convincing example of this:

For the bourgeois it is all the easier to prove on the basis of his language the identity of commercial and individual, or even universal, human relations, as this language itself is a product of the bourgeoisie, and therefore both in actuality and in language the relations of buying and selling have been made the basis of all others. For example, *propriété*—property *[Eigentum]* and characteristic feature *[Eigenschaft]*; property—possession *[Eigentum]* and peculiarity *[Eigentümlichkeit]*; *"eigen"* ["one's own"]—in the commercial and in the individual sense; *valeur,* value, *Wert;* commerce, *Verkehr; échange,* exchange, *Austausch,* etc., all of which are used both for commercial relations and for characteristic features and mutual relations of individuals as such. In the other modern languages this is equally the case. If Saint Max [Max Stirner] seriously applies himself to exploit this ambiguity, he may easily succeed in making a brilliant series of new economic discoveries, without knowing anything about political economy; for, indeed, his new economic facts, which we shall take note of later, lie wholly within the sphere of synonymy.

Language does reflect the realities of society, and these social realities include the prevailing relations of production, the ruling position of one class, and so forth. *In addition to this* there are words and phrases in every language which embody the ideologies of the classes which exist in that society (e.g., 'free enterprise', 'dictatorship of the proletariat'). Most of these words and phrases are not the property of just one class but have different uses, different meanings, or at least different connotations when used by class conscious members of opposing classes (e.g., 'freedom', 'democracy').

However, as Stalin pointed out in *Marxism and Problems of Linguistics,* language as a whole is not the creation or property of any single class but of society as a whole. To say that there are "class languages" is to speak hyperbolically. Language is, furthermore, not part of the superstructure on any socioeconomic base; it is a historical phenomenon created by all classes through the course of various socioeconomic formations and is not replaced with the change of the economic system. Speaking on this point Stalin says: Yes, classes influence language, introduce into the language their own specific words and expressions and sometimes understand one and the same word or expression differently. There is no doubt about that.

However, it does not follow that specific words and expressions, as well as differences in semantics, can be of serious importance for the development of a single language common to the whole people, that they are capable of detracting from its significance or of changing its character. 4

Stalin goes on to say that the words and expressions which the various classes introduce, or understand each in their own way, are very few in number. The class influence on language is considerably greater than Stalin suggests. But what we really need to know here is if the *particular* moral words we are concerned with (such as 'good') are among these relatively few class-biased expressions. The answer to this, as with many such simplistically formulated questions, is "yes and no".

The means of showing the extent to which class viewpoints modify the meanings of various moral expressions is, however, the same sort of procedure as is used to show the root meanings of these words and phrases. In other words, in so far as different classes have modified the meanings of words (in general or in specific contexts) this will become evident in any complete and truly scientific investigation of the meaning of those terms. But there is a more basic question here. No one can seriously defend the view that the way to scientifically investigate political economy is to study *language!* This is so even though a scientific study of linguistic terms related to economics would indeed tell us something about the bourgeois relations of production which presently exist in the real world and which are reflected in language, as Marx and Engels noted in the quotation above.

So if the investigation of political economy, or physics, or biology by the method of analysing the "relevant" linguistic terms in these various sciences is such an obviously absurd procedure, why should philosophy be any different—even if we do restrict ourselves to ordinary language? This question arises only because of a very basic confusion about what philosophy is.

To help straighten this out let's consider for the moment not philosophy, but the science of linguistics itself. Part of linguistics is the investigation into the meanings of words—lexical semantics. Thus, even though linguistics is just as much a science as is physics, it inquires into ordinary language concepts while physics doesn't *because* the meaning of words is (part of) what the science of linguistics is *all about*.

Every science, including physics and linguistics, has a stock of technical terms, that is, words which are defined in terms of the theories of that particular science. Words like 'force' or 'mass' in physics, for example, are defined within the body of current physical theory and have meaning only in light of that theory *despite* their concurrent but *irrelevant* use in ordinary language. (Of course the use of ordinary language expressions such as 'force' and 'mass' tends to follow their technical uses in physics—and this is a good thing. To the greatest extent possible ordinary language should change to reflect current scientific theory.) When physical theory advances, the meanings of such technical expressions may well be changed. In linguistics there are many technical terms such as 'phoneme', 'morpheme', 'allomorph', etc., which should not be confused with ordinary language words which linguistics (semantics) inquires into the meaning of. Despite the fact that linguistics investigates the meanings of ordinary words in natural languages by scientific procedures, it does not determine the meaning of its own technical expressions in the same manner. As in any science, these technical terms are simply assigned meanings by fiat in the course of propounding scientific theory. The entire theory is then compared to the real world to test its correctness.

Philosophy, properly speaking, may well consist only of the laws of logic and dialectics (as Engels remarked in *Anti-Dühring*) together with a materialist conception of the world. But the separate sciences we have today all started out as areas of philosophical speculation (in the conventional sense) and only split off when they started to become something more than mere speculation. Furthermore, over the centuries numerous linguistic confusions and errors of semantics have become entrenched in traditional philosophy. The multitude of idealistic and metaphysical philosophical views embody all kinds of misconceptions about the world and about language. The history of philosophy is replete with such nonsense as "The concept of perfection includes the concept of existence; therefore God exists." Although the real sources of such error and confusion are primarily the various reactionary class ideologies, and not language, to a significant extent philosophical confusion and error is fostered by the simple failure to understand the meaning of various key words. The motive is reactionary class outlook; the means is abuse of language.

It is true that what is called linguistic analysis or ordinary language philosophy is actually linguistics (semantics) and not philosophy at all. But why quibble about this? In order to expose (most) philosophical errors and confusions it is necessary (*among other things!*) to scientifically analyse the meanings of certain problematic words. Since this has yet to be adequately done (in most cases) by professional linguists there has grown up a tradition in the period after World War II—and especially in English speaking countries—of professional philosophers attempting to do it under the name philosophy. Many have even gone so far as to assert that this is *all* there is to philosophy, thus carrying the trend to the ridiculous extreme of defining traditional philosophy out of existence altogether, along with its rational core of materialist dialectics.

It is true that the results of this linguistic philosophy have been limited and spotty, that this is largely to be explained by the bourgeois or petty-bourgeois class stand of these philosophers; the fact that they are hobbled by the same old reactionary motives in philosophy even while questioning the means by which it has been conducted in the past. Among other things this has resulted in linguistic, ordinary language, or analytic philosophy (as it is variously called) focusing mostly on very trivial questions. The following ditty to make fun of this tendency:

ANALYTIC PHILOSOPHY

To analyse is to figure out What the world is all about But to do it safely and not offend Analytic philosophy came in the end To work on trivial concepts which In no way could upset the rich.

On the whole, analytic or linguistic philosophy has been either trivial, reactionary, or both! Nevertheless, it is a good thing to add the techniques of scientific linguistics, and especially lexical semantics, to the philosophical toolbox. It can be a powerful tool in the battle against reactionary philosophical views which have managed to survive (and be continually reborn) partly because of semantic confusion.

There is a point to linguistic analysis in philosophy (unlike economics or physics) in so far as it is a task of philosophy to knock down the fantastic philosophical language of reactionary philosophers, and to put such traditional branches of philosophy as ethics on a completely scientific basis. Repeating once more the comment of Marx and Engels: The philosophers have only to dissolve their language into the ordinary language, from which it is abstracted, in order to recognize it as the distorted language of the actual world, and to realize that neither thoughts nor language in themselves form a realm of their own, that they are only *manifestations* of actual life.

Therefore, that a semantic investigation of the meaning of key terms in people's talk about morality is highly appropriate in ethics. Moreover—and this is why this is *most* important—this semantic investigation will demonstrate that there is indeed something rather fishy about moralizing and moral terminology; it exists more to *hide* the essential nature of morality, rather than to bring it out! And this, we will see, explains Marx's antipathy to using moral language.

"DIMENSION WORD" IN ETHICS

The investigation of the semantics of moral terms on the word 'good'. Why 'good' rather than 'right', 'justice', 'duty', 'ought', or some other moral term? Moral terms are obviously closely related.

That is, their *meanings* are similar; so similar in fact that in many contexts one moral term can replace another without much, if any, change in the meaning of the utterance as a whole. Because the meanings of moral terms are so interrelated it is possible to paraphrase the meaning of any one of them in terms of another. Thus it is possible to give at least a rough, more or less adequate, definition of 'ought' in terms of *right* and *wrong* or conversely a more or less adequate definition of 'right' in terms of *ought*. The statement that "one ought to do what is right", is thus very nearly a tautology. Similarly, the question which is sometimes debated by bourgeois moral philosophers, "Why should I be moral?", is really quite nonsensical.

The fact that moral words can be given rough definitions in terms of each other has led to a great deal of superficial "analysis" in ethics. The game is played thus: one moral word is defined in terms of a second, the second in terms of a third, and so on until we come to the last moral word on the list which is declared to be so "fundamental", so "obvious", so "unanalyzable", that nothing more can possibly be said. The listing of related moral words is passed off as real analysis.

Crane Brinton provides us with an illustration of this in his book *A History of Western Morals 8* where he defines 'good' (in morals) as meaning 'morally desirable' and 'bad' as 'morally undesirable'. 'Ethics' and 'ethical' he defines in terms of 'ought', and the ethical "component" of 'morality' is basically defined in terms of 'ought' as well. But 'ought', which he has made into his keyword, he doesn't define. "Only the very self-conscious semanticist," he says, "will try to pursue that word 'ought' further; it is surely one of the clearest of words..." Actually 'ought' too can be defined in terms of other moral words and phrases, such as in terms of "moral obligation" or "duty", etc. Thus other writers have thought 'duty' was the "clearest" or most fundamental moral word which itself needed no further comment. Still others have settled on 'right', or 'good', or 'justice'. At one time or another probably every single moral term has been picked out as *the key* with which to explicate all the rest. But what then is to explicate the key? In point of fact *any* moral term *could* serve as our starting place, as our keyword or focus for analysis. But the thing to be emphasized here is that the selection of the "key" does not mark the conclusion of a proper analysis but its beginning.

It is completely arbitrary which moral word we focus our analysis on, that it makes no difference at all? No. We *could* select any moral term, but there are good reasons to select 'good'. The various words in moral discourse do not mean *precisely* the same thing-even those which can often be substituted for each other. In other words, in addition to the elements of meaning which they have in common there are other elements of meaning which they do not share. These other elements are more complicated or less complicated, more specific or more general, in different instances. So some moral words are a little simpler to analyse than others—though none are intractable.

In English the most general, most abstract, and hence most straight-forward word in moral language is the word 'good'. This has been recognized by a number of people including the British philosopher of "ordinary language" John Austin who described 'good' as a "dimension-word", that is, as "the most general and comprehensive term in a whole group of terms of the same kind, terms that fulfill the same function." Unfortunately Austin somewhat spoiled this fine insight by going on to state that the function of all the words in good's dimension is that of expressing commendation, which is not correct. One could also dispute certain other aspects of Austin's formulation, such as the implicit claim that all moral words have the same function. But the most important point here is that among a group of semantically related words there is often a keyword, a dimension word, more general and abstract, and hence more basic, in a sense, than the rest.

The word good' is the most general and most basic moral term (though it is not *exclusively* a *moral* term). It is therefore the easiest and most convenient term to focus on for the semantic analysis of moral language. To the state again that good' is not an all-important or indispensable term. The bourgeois philosopher Paul Ziff, from whom we have learned much about the semantics of the word good' and lexical semantics in general, put it this way:

The word good' is not important. It is useful, not indispensable. One can say whatever one wants to say without using it. This would entail only loss of brevity: what can be said and what can be said briefly are not the same.

The word good' *is* rather important, and so evidently does Ziff, despite his comment here, since he wrote a whole book whose culmination was the statement of what the word good' means. But his point about good' not being indispensable is very well taken. The same thing goes, incidentally, for all other moral terms. They are all dispensable, either individually, or as a group. This is a point we will come back to.

Definitions of the Word 'Good'

What does the word good' mean? A familiar method of determining what a word means is to look it up in a dictionary. If you look up the word good' in a good dictionary you will find a long list of definitions of the most diverse character. *Webster's Third New International Dictionary (Unabridged),* for instance, has a whole page of fine print devoted to good' and its various combined forms (goodness', good morning', etc.). Leaving the combined forms aside, this dictionary divides the definitions into three broad groups corresponding to the three parts of speech—adjective, noun and adverb—and assigns each a separate entry. It lists several senses, sub-senses and even sub-sub-senses for its three entries. The adjective, for example, is assigned two main senses, the first of which is assigned six sub-senses, each of which is in turn assigned from three to nine sub-sub-senses. A total of 71 different definitions is given under the three entries (again not counting combined forms), with one or more example contexts for each. This dictionary thus tells us what the word good' means in each of 71 different contexts, and in each of these no doubt carefully chosen contexts it means something different from what it means in all the others. What then does the word good' mean in general ? It doesn't say! Moreover, the common relationships among the various meanings of the word which allow them to be grouped together as sub-senses (or sub-sub-senses) of a distinct sense are not stated either. These are remarkable omissions, and are none the less remarkable for the fact that it is standard procedure for dictionaries whenever an entry is given more than a single sense (definition).

In other words, this dictionary, like most others, fails to give an *overall,* or *central,* or *standard,* or *core,* or *root* definition of the word good', and fails even to give root definitions of the main senses and sub-senses of the word. It simply (of course this is really no simple matter) gives a large number of definitions of the word 'good' as it appears in various contexts without specifying anything which these various uses may have in common (either all of them or a subset of them). It arbitrarily lists 71 definitions of the word as it appears in the given sample contexts, but it could just as well have listed 100 or 700 definitions together with sample contexts if it had the space and perseverance, and the determination to make more and more subtle distinctions and to locate more and more exceptional uses of the word.

Why do dictionaries tend to define words in particular contexts, but shy away from defining them in general? It is clearly because it is much easier to do the former than the latter, and because it is very easy to go wrong in trying to give the "core" or "root" or "general" meaning of a word that has diverse specific meanings in many different contexts. We see this in fact with the word 'good'. Some of the few large dictionaries that have attempted to give the root or overall meaning of the word 'good' are British dictionaries (e.g., the *Oxford English Dictionary)* which have been unduly influenced by the erroneous theory of the British philosophers John Austin and R. M. Hare that 'good' means "commending". It is actually better not to try to say what the overall meaning of a word is than to give the wrong answer!

So we cannot determine what the word 'good' means simply by looking it up in even the best of the currently available dictionaries since the dictionary makers have either not completed their job, or else have not completely correctly stated what the root or overall meaning of the word is.

As the *Encyclopaedia Britannica* put it, Good dictionaries offer a variety of contexts for the items listed, but, obviously, this is not enough. For one thing, no dictionary can list all the co-occurrences [of the word in question with all the other words it can occur with -JSH]. There must be devices to sum up, as it were, the information revealed by the contexts. This is the role of dictionary definitions.

The bigger and (in general) better dictionaries currently do a fairly good job of giving definitions covering each of the specific contexts they list, but either shrink from the attempt to give definitions covering groups of related contexts (let alone *all* contexts), or else do a rather inept job of it in many cases. Oddly enough, this sometimes means that you can get a better *overall* (root) definition of a word from a smaller, even "inferior" dictionary than you can from a "good" large dictionary! Thus *Webster's Basic*

English Dictionary gives just 9 definitions for the adjective 'good', the first of which is "suitable for a use: SATISFACTORY". This is quite close to the actual overall, general meaning of the word.

Even when a dictionary *does* provide us with an overall or core definition of 'good' the question still remains whether or not that definition is fully correct. Most people do not realize how many errors there are in dictionaries—even "good" dictionaries. Alfred North Whitehead put it this way: "Learning preserves the errors of the past, as well as its wisdom. For this reason dictionaries are public dangers, although they are necessities." Thus when it comes to problematic words, especially words which figure prominently in philosophical disputes, dictionaries can be of only limited use and reliability until the day when they are prepared by more consistently scientific methods.

Various Moral Terms

What then *does* the word 'good' mean? This is something about which there are many ideas and much disagreement. There are those, indeed, who claim that 'good' doesn't mean *anything* "in general"—that there is nothing which this word, or any other word possibly, has in common in all its uses or contexts. (We will look into this idea later on.) But most writers have thought that such a general or root meaning does exist and have merely differed as to what that meaning is.

Here are a few examples of such definitions of good' showing just how wildly diverse they can be. It is, at the same time, a somewhat wider survey of various ethical theories, since the meaning of the word good' is so central to ethics. (In a few of these examples we have quoted what various people have said about other moral terms, and ask the reader to adapt it to the word good'. For example, William Paley's views below about the word right' can easily be adapted to the word good'. Also, strictly speaking, many of the following are comments on what the good is, rather than on what good' means; we take these to be closely related things, though the phrase the good sounds peculiar to me, in the same way that the purple or the small sound peculiar.)

God's dictates or whims—the view that what is good is whatever God says is good: Melvin Rader remarks that In the Old Testament… we have the stories of God's command to Adam, his covenant with Abraham, and his dictation to Moses of the Ten

Commandments. The Book of Manu (*circa* 250 B.C.), an authoritative source of moral law for Hindus, is declared to be an emanation from the Supreme God. The moral teachings of Islam are likewise represented as a direct revelation from God, communicated word for word to Mohammed by the Angel Gabriel. Another example: ... right therefore signifies consistency with the will of God... (William Paley)

Teleological definition: It is thought that every activity, artistic or scientific, in fact every deliberate action or pursuit, has for its object the attainment of some good. We may therefore assent to the view which has been expressed that the good' is that at which all things aim'. (Aristotle)

Soul fulfillment: The good is the full realization of the faculties of the human soul... (T. H. Green, 1836-82)

Reverence for life: Good means the universal protection of life. (Albert Schweitzer)

Hedonism: The view that good equals pleasure. (Spinoza, Locke, Hume, Bentham)

Satisfaction: What is good is that which fulfills those impulses or strivings of which human nature essentially consists, and in fulfilling them brings satisfaction... *The* good is nothing short of what would fulfill and satisfy wholly. (Brand Blanshard) What is moral is what you feel good after. (Ernest Hemingway)

Desires: A person calls a thing good whenever it is the object of his or her desire. (Hobbes) We deem a thing to be good because we strive for it, wish for it, long for it, or desire it. (Spinoza)

Desire, approval, contentment and worth: We may speak of the good, generally, as that which satisfies desire. It is that which we approve of, and in which we can rest with a feeling of contentment. Or we may describe it again, if we please, as being the same as worth. (F. H. Bradley)

That which is pleasing to the senses: That which is not good is not delicious. (John Milton)

Majority likes and dislikes: What is morality in any given time or place? It is what the majority then and there happen to like and immorality is what they dislike. (Alfred North Whitehead) Morality is the custom of one's country and the current feeling of one's peers. Cannibalism is moral in a cannibal country. (Samuel Butler)

Emotivism: This is good' is synonymous with I approve of this; do so as well.' (Charles L. Stevenson)

Commending: Good' is a word used for commending. (R. M. Hare)

Wisdom or rationality: A is a good X if and only if A has the properties (to a higher degree than the average or standard X) which it is rational to want in an X, given what X's are used for, or expected to do, and the like (whichever rider is appropriate...) (John Rawls)

Survival benefits: ... at the basis of all moral ideas is the people's conception of the Good'. In whatsoever variety of ways it may be codified, the conception of the Good' which all peoples have arrived at may be phrased in the following way: The Good' is that, and that is Good', which confers survival benefits upon the group. (Ashley Montagu)

Power: What is good?—Whatever augments the feeling of power, the will to power, power itself, in man. (Friedrich Nietzsche)

Many meanings: The word *good* has many meanings. For example, if a man were to shoot his grandmother at a range of five hundred yards, I should call him a good shot, but not *necessarily* a good man. (G. K. Chesterton)

Indefinable: Good' is a simple indefinable property like yellow, only non-natural, i.e., unascertainable by empirical investigation. If I am asked, What is good?' my answer is that good is good, and that is the end of the matter. Or if I am asked, How is good to be defined?' my answer is that it cannot be defined, and that is all I have to say about it. (G. E. Moore)

This list could easily be expanded, but we think the point is clear enough: there are a great many conflicting ideas about what the word good' (and other moral terms) mean. As Pascal remarked, Philosophers count about two hundred and eighty-eight views of the sovereign good. Since Pascal's day, perhaps another 288 have been added.

Some of the theories listed above are ridiculous, some banal, some incoherent, some more sensible than others, and so forth. But as they stand all are incorrect. The first could be knocked down simply by pointing out that there is no God. There were a God it could not be correct (as even the cleverer theologians like

Aquinas realized), since for one thing it would no longer make any sense to even *claim* that God is good. We will not launch into a refutation here of each of the above theories of the meaning of good', though through the course of this book some of them will come under critical scrutiny. The point for now is just that we cannot hope to discover what the word good' means simply by searching through the writings of the wise men of the ages since they are hopelessly in disagreement on this issue. Dictionaries and wise men are of little help; in both cases they offer plenty of *opinions*, but little or no *evidence* to support those opinions. So let us turn next to science. In order to discover what the word good' means we must take a side excursion and inquire into the general question: How do you determine what a word means?

Defining 'Good' in Terms of "Interests"

If you look to see how the word 'good' is actually used you will find that it has a great variety of uses. The most common everyday uses of the word 'good' are in connection with everyday objects, activities, desires, needs and interests. "These are good apples!" "He has a good job." These are not moral evaluations (at least in their standard contexts). The word 'good' is also used in aesthetics, in evaluating artists and works of art. "That is not a very good painting despite the artist's reputation." And again, despite certain similarities, aesthetics is not ethics, and aesthetic evaluations are not moral evaluations (though we may wish to evaluate a work of art or an artist from *both* aesthetic and ethical points of view). And of course we use the word good' in ethics, in moral evaluations of people, groups of people, human institutions (e.g., governments), and their actions. A good deed. A good person.

Ludwig Wittgenstein, one of the most famous and influential bourgeois philosophers of the 20 century, put forward the family resemblance theory of meaning. He asserted, for example, that the word good' must have a family of meanings —that is, numerous different meanings depending on its different uses, any two of which may have some similarity or common semantic elements, but having no common semantic elements through *all* its different uses. This theory has been accepted by many and has generated an enormous amount of discussion. The prime motivation behind this theory is once again the commonplace observation that words seem to have somewhat different meanings in different contexts.

But something that is often overlooked about the family resemblance theory is that it is subject to empirical test. Wittgenstein himself, in the worst tradition of armchair philosophy, evidently never thought of making such an empirical test of the theory. Instead he says that thinking about the many diverse uses of words such as good' will enable you to see that they must have a family of meanings. But what is wanted here is not a conjecture or assertion about what an investigation must disclose, but the actual investigation itself. When Paul Ziff made such an investigation he found that there were common elements of meaning throughout virtually all the occurrences of the word good' after all!

Perhaps, in passing, we should also briefly say something about another dogma from Wittgenstein, that *meaning is use*: For a *large* class of cases—though not for all—in which we employ the word meaning' it can be defined thus: the meaning of a word is its use in the language. While this is perhaps sniffing down the right trail, it is far from correct as it stands. For one thing, as Ziff points out, words can be *misused*. If a word's meaning *is* its use, how are we then to identify its misuse? Similarly, Ziff points out that the actual use of any word depends on additional factors besides its meaning. Wittgenstein would have been much closer to the mark if he had focused on how the precise meaning of a word derives from its *context,* rather from its *use.*

Returning to the main theme, we can at least say that no theory to the effect that words like 'good' *do not have* an overall or core meaning have been proven. What then, if anything, is the common root meaning of the word 'good' in virtually all its uses, whether in everyday affairs, morals, aesthetics, or otherwise?

An actual investigation of the sort required—careful, thorough and convincing. He showed that except for a small number of highly idiomatic, derivative uses the word 'good' does have a single, common root meaning. In its standard use in practical affairs, in aesthetics and in moral discourse, the word 'good' means "answering to certain interests".

It is by following the analytical procedure outlined above that the root definition of 'good' as "answering to certain interests" has been determined. You may check the 71 diverse definitions given in *Webster's Third New International Dictionary* to see that this root meaning does in fact occur in most of them. The first definition given for the adjective, la(l), for instance: "having a favourable or auspicious character" is obviously compatible with the hypothesis since if something has a favourable or auspicious character it does indeed answer to certain interests in the thing's character. A few of the definitions given do not accord well with the hypothesis, such as 1d(3), "FULL—used as a qualifier to indicated a quantity not less than and generally greater than the stated figure" as in "a good inch long" It is these cases however which are declared to be highly idiomatic, derivative, or non-standard uses. In these cases it is not too difficult to see how the derivation may have arisen; in this particular case a complete or full thing generally answers to our interests better than a partial, incomplete, short,... thing. (A board that is too long can be sawed down; a board that is too short is... "no good".)

It is interesting to note that one of the 71 definitions given by this dictionary is pretty much the same as what has been determined to be the root meaning of the word in its standard uses: la(4), "favorably affecting one's interests...". No special prominence is given to this definition, however, and actually it is construed very narrowly as in usages like "wished him good luck".

Perhaps the most instructive aspect of the whole page in this dictionary devoted to the word 'good' is the etymological note that in its origin the English word 'good' is akin to that of words in Old Frisian, Old High German and Sanskrit which mean "uniting" or "fitting" or "to fit together". It is easy to see how "fitting" something is which answers to our interests. Indeed, it would not be such a bad gloss to say that what is good is that which *fits* our purposes.

All of these kinds of definitions of the word good' are on the right track, there have been thinkers down through the ages who have put forward one or another of these definitions. An apology for being so facetious in lumping them together with such wise men as religious prophets, Ernest Hemingway, and G. K. Chesterton! The only thing wrong with such alternative definitions of the word good' is that they are not quite as good as answering to certain interests, i.e., they do not cover quite as many occurrences of the word in as wide a range of contexts. But at least they are not completely off the wall like some of the traditional definitions!

There are variations on the theme, but this is what good' means: answering to certain interests.

DETERMINING WHAT A WORD MEANS

How does everyone learn the meanings of most of the words they know? Well, sometimes, we look up words in a dictionary, but most of the time we do not. In fact, when we are very young and have not yet learned to read, we obviously cannot yet look up words in a dictionary at all. So, clearly we learn the meanings of at least our initial stock of words in some other way. And, actually, as we all realize, people learn the meanings of most of the words they know *from the contexts* in which they hear (or see) the words, both the linguistic contexts (the other words around the new word) and the real-world (extra-linguistic) contexts. This is also how dictionary makers themselves learn what words mean. So our question comes down to this: *How is it that we can determine what a word means from the various contexts that it occurs in?*

A comment first about the real-world contexts: It may well be that most of us learned the meaning of the word dog' by first having our parents say something like Look at the dog! (or Doggie!) in the presence of a dog. However, when you look up the word dog' (or something less common, say dugong') in a dictionary the animal will normally not be present. In other words, real-world contexts can virtually always be replaced by linguistic contexts (in this case the dictionary definition) in order to learn the meaning of a new word. Or, as one linguist puts it, any aspect of an extra-linguistic context can in principle be mirrored linguistically. For this reason, in discussing the meaning of any word (and moral terms specifically) we will focus mostly on linguistic contexts.

For most linguists, it is now almost a truism that meaning is determined by the context. For example D. A. Cruse, in his book *Lexical Semantics*, states that It is taken as axiomatic in this book that every aspect of the meaning of a word is reflected in a characteristic pattern normally (and abnormally) in grammatically appropriate contexts. Who was the first to put forward this doctrine of contextual meaning but one of the first proponents seems to have been the early Soviet writer Valentin Nikolaevich Voloshinov. The meaning of a word is determined entirely by its context. In fact there are as many meanings of a word as there are contexts of its usage. At the same time, however, the word does not cease to be a single entity; it does not, so to speak, break apart into as many separate words as there are contexts of its usage. The word's unity is assured, of course, not only by the unity of its phonetic composition but also by the factor of unity which is common to all its meanings. How can the fundamental polysemanticity of the word be reconciled with its unity? To pose this question is to formulate, in a rough and elementary way, the cardinal problem of semantics. It is a problem that can only be solved dialectically.

Of course we have to understand that in saying that The meaning of a word is determined entirely by its context Voloshinov cannot be claiming that the word itself contributes no meaning to that context. If no individual word brings any meaning to the context, then the entire context becomes the unit of meaning, an unanalyzable morpheme, a meaningless string of symbols (words) which somehow as a whole has meaning, and that meaning is then apportioned out to those individual words in an entirely inexplicable way. If the linguistic context is assumed to be *only the other words* in the utterance, then each word is somehow supposed to derive its entire meaning from all the others without making any contribution itself—which makes absolutely no sense. Consequently we have to say *both* that the context determines the meaning of the word and that each word also contributes some meaning to the context. As Voloshinov said, we have to look at the situation dialectically.

The meaning of a word is in fact an abstraction from all its various specific meanings in all its various contexts. When such a coherent overall abstraction is impossible, we say the word has two (or more) completely different *senses* or even that there are two or more *different* words which are homonyms, that is, words that sound alike and are perhaps spelled the same but which have *completely* unrelated meanings (such as the noun 'bear' and the verb 'bear').

We learn the meaning of words from their contexts. But sometimes we get the wrong idea about what a word means; we can be mistaken. And we also get that *wrong* idea from the contexts in which we hear the word. So what is going on here? Often it is a matter of not having heard the word used in a sufficiently broad range of contexts, or in other words, of jumping to a conclusion based on too little contextual evidence.

What usually happens is that when we hear a new word, perhaps once or perhaps a number of times, we seem to almost unconsciously form something of an idea about what that word means. Suppose you never heard the word 'dugong' before, but a friend says to you "Guess what I saw at the zoo today—a dugong!" You might very well tentatively jump to the conclusion that a dugong is some sort of exotic animal. In this case you would be right. But the evidence is still fairly weak; perhaps a dugong was instead some new Chinese automobile your friend saw in the zoo parking lot. If your friend had gone on to say, "These dugongs look well-built and get great gas mileage!" you might well have abandoned the "exotic animal" notion, and—on the basis of the additional contextual evidence—jumped to the new idea that a "dugong" is a car.

However, in some other cases, the problem of coming to understand the meaning of a word is quite different. It is not due to any lack of familiarity with the word, or any shortage of contexts in which you've heard the word used and even used it frequently yourself, but rather the difficulty of deriving a correct definition *out of* all that extensive contextual evidence. This problem especially arises for words expressing very abstract or abstruse concepts of the sort that often give rise to philosophical confusion or disputes. Words like 'true', 'beautiful', 'time', 'space', 'spirit', 'mind', 'consciousness', 'good', and so forth.

In these cases, it is often difficult for someone to initially even come up with any guess as to how the word in question should be *defined* (even if they do know very well how to *use* it). But over time, some few people at least give the matter various amounts of thought, and come up with different ideas about what the word supposedly means. Some of the rest of us then latch onto one or another of these conflicting ideas, usually without giving it a whole lot of thought ourselves. But what we should really say here is that we now have a bunch of diverse *hypotheses* about what the word in question actually means.

What is needed to scientifically determine what such a problematic word means is mostly *a systematic method of testing different hypotheses.* And lo, and behold, there is such a method! It is actually very close to the method we more or less unconsciously and less systematically use with less problematic words, namely, to test each hypothesis against the many contexts where the word is properly used as well as against those contexts where its use would be linguistically deviant (i.e., something that sounds weird). This basic idea has been considerably refined, however, and one of those who made a contribution in this area was the philosopher/ linguist, Paul Ziff. The *Encyclopaedia Britannica,* after first mentioning the limited value of pictorial dictionaries and the importance in a dictionary of an abundance of good example contexts for a word, goes on to say this about Ziff's theory and method:

> These intuitions are behind the U.S. philosopher Paul Ziff's semantic theory. According to Ziff, the meaning of a word is a function, first, of its complementary set, which consists of all the acceptable sentences in which the word can occur, and, second, of its contrastive set, which consists of all the words that can replace that word in all of these sentences without rendering the sentences deviant. Clearly, the elaboration of the contrastive set will produce words more and more similar in meaning to the word in question, the limiting case being synonyms that can occur wherever the word in question can occur.

In further defence of taking the contrastive set into consideration, Ziff himself wrote that the significance of what is said depends on what is not said but which *could* have been said in that context.

One of the basic things that linguists do in studying a language is to make a morphemic analysis. A morpheme was originally defined as one of the minimum meaningful elements in a language, consisting of a string of phonemes (the discrete sounds used in the language) which go to make up words or parts of words. These days many linguists prefer to define morpheme' as the minimal syntactic unit or as one of the set of primary elements resulting from a special kind of distributional analysis of phoneme clusters in the language (since that is how morphemes are identified). But either way, it is true that morphemes do correspond closely with the basic units of meaning in a language.

This is a remarkable fact, and one of the strongest arguments which Ziff adduces in support of his approach to semantics. *Why* should a morphological analysis of English, for example, which does *not* employ any appeals to questions of *meaning,* nevertheless manage to pick out just those basic *units of meaning* in English?

Such a result proves that there is *some connection* between the techniques employed in a morphological analysis and meaning. Those techniques are based almost exclusively on distribution and contrast, and specifically on the consideration of partial contrasts between pairs of utterances as the context (linguistic or otherwise) varies. Such a remarkable result, says Ziff is not an accident; neither is it a miracle. Any theory of meaning that fails to account for and explain the fact is *ipso facto* an inadequate and unilluminating theory.

Thus the meaning of a word is in some sense a function of the distribution of the word in the corpus of the language (i.e., in the set of possible, non-deviant utterances in the language). Or, in Ziff's more precise terms, meaning is a function of features of the distributive set (or complementary set), and the contrastive set for the word in question. Consequently to determine the meaning of a word, the first step is to determine as precisely as possible the membership of its distributive and contrastive sets. That is, one must determine as best as one can all the contexts in which the word could be used, and all the alternative words that could be used in place of the word in those contexts. That is obviously a huge task! However, in practice it is not actually necessary to try to list all such contexts (which are, after all, virtually infinite in number), nor to itemize every single item in the contrastive set for each of these virtually infinite number of contexts. What is necessary is to gather as wide a *range* of such contexts as you can, so that (for example) you include contexts for all the senses of the word you can find in the important large dictionaries, and hopefully quite a few beyond that. It is not so much the *number* of example contexts and contrastive words in those contexts which is important, as the *diversity* of those contexts and contrasts.

However, determining as best you can the diverse contexts in which the word is used, and the contrastive set of words which could also be used in those various contexts, is by itself not enough. Ziff notes that it is possible to determine the membership of these distributive and contrastive sets with great precision and detail and still have no idea what the meaning of the word in question is. This is in fact the explanation for why dictionaries tend to be better at giving a large variety of sample contexts and the definitions (meanings) appropriate to those contexts, than they are at give root or overall definitions for words.

There are additional steps which can be taken at this stage, however. One fairly obvious one is to figure out the part of speech of the word in question (if that was not already obvious) and to examine its grammar and precise syntax.

The *Britannica* article goes on to say, for example, that the grammatical restrictions on a word represent, as it were, the skeleton' of its meaning before the flesh' is put on by the co-occurrences [contextual evidence]. The very first step in giving the meaning of a word is to specify its grammatical category—noun, verb, adjective, adverb, connective, and so forth.... A refined grammar yields much more: the fact that the adjective good,' for example, unlike adjectives like yellow' or fat,' can occur in the frames (He is) good at (playing chess)'; (The root is) good to (eat)'; It is good that (it is raining)'; It was good of (him) to (come)' says a great deal about the meaning of that word. The co-occurrences then complete the picture.

However, the most basic thing to do at this point is to start gathering *hypotheses* as to what the meaning of the word in question might be, and to test each of these hypotheses against the range of sample contexts of the word, and in light of the contrastive set of words which could have been used instead in those contexts. This is the way that any hypothesis about the specific meaning of some particular word is *tested against the evidence* in lexical semantics.

While there is no doubt that Ziff's general approach to lexical semantics is correct, we need not necessarily accept his entire theory as he outlined it in his 1960 book. Indeed, Ziff by no means claimed to have presented a complete and polished theory, and various criticisms of some of the details have been made of it. There may also be better ways of formulating this sort of semantic theory. The *Encyclopaedia Britannica,* for example, notes that the essence of Ziff's insight can be reinterpreted in terms of the notions developed by [the linguist] Zellig S. Harris: co-occurrence (instead of complementary set) and co-occurrence difference (instead of contrastive set)... It is not Ziff's precise theoretical arguments, terminology, or exact overall theory that we are concerned with, but only the basic approach that he developed *and* the example exposition he gave of that approach with the very word that we are now concerned with, the word good'.

The Word 'Good' in Morals

At this point we have determined that the central or root meaning of the word good' is answering to certain interests. But this abstract formulation covers (virtually) all its uses in everyday affairs and art appreciation as well as in moral discourse. If we restrict our view to just morals alone is there anything more we can say about what the word good' means? Yes, there is! Once we take the word good' to mean answering to certain interests, we immediately confront the questions What interests? and Whose interests?. On this Ziff remarks:

On the hypothesis under consideration, good' has associated with it the condition of answering to certain interests, which interests are in question being indicated either by the element modifying or the element modified by good' or by certain features of the context of utterance. The interests in question are the interests one has. The answer to the question Whose interests?' is this: whichever one has the interests in question. Thus the question is essentially irrelevant. The relevant question is whether what is in question does or does not answer to the indicated interests.

Consider the sentence That's a good apple. You and I could have a genuine disagreement about whether or not a particular apple is good depending upon our various interests. We might be interested in just eating an apple; you might be interested in making an apple pie (a good pie apple is not necessarily a good eating apple), or painting a still life (in which case all you would be interested in is the apple's appearance, not its taste), etc. It may seem that this is a matter of *my* interests versus *your* interests. But Ziff s point is that *in determining whether or not the apple is good* it is really not a matter of *whose* interests, but *of which* interests are in question. In this case the diverse interests might be:

- One's interest in eating an apple.
- One's interest in making an apple pie.
- One's interest in painting a picture of an apple.

It is easy to see that Ziff is correct here, for at one time or other *either you or I* might have any of these interests in an apple. It is not *which* of us that has the particular interest which is important, but which *of the various possible interests* which is important in determining whether or not the apple is good.

But suppose that you are a painter who specializes in still lifes, and furthermore that you do not eat apples because of your dentures or some peculiar allergy. Suppose that I am not a painter, and not a cook, and that my only ordinary interest in apples is in eating them. Then when we dispute about whether or not this is a good apple, there may be a point in distinguishing *whose* interests are in question. The reason is obvious; in this contrived case, *which interests* is a function of *whose interests.* Thus if we specify *whose* interests are at issue, we are indirectly specifying *which* interests are at issue.

In morals we find this same situation, but it is no longer a matter of contrived differences in the interests of individuals. Different groups of people, and specifically *different social classes,* do in fact have different sets of interests, especially economic or material interests. The capitalist has an interest in paying his workers less, and getting more work out of them. The workers have an interest in getting better pay, and limiting (and ultimately ending) this exploitation. These interests are at odds, and therefore many things which the capitalist will call good, the workers will call bad, and vice versa. Clearly, for example, a pay cut for the workers will be seen as good by the boss (if he can get away with it) and bad by the workers.

Of course it is true that the real difference which leads the capitalist and his workers to disagree about whether the pay cut is good or bad is their differing economic interests. But because these interests are generally opposed, and opposed in regular, predictable ways, for the two classes in question, it is natural and appropriate to identify these opposed interests with the classes that have them. For the same reason, we are correct in saying that these two classes have moralities which are in major respects opposed.

But in mentioning class moralities here I am jumping ahead in the argument. After all, there were moralities before classes came into being, and there will be morality after classes cease to exist. We must take this one step at a time. Before discussing the modifications which must be made to our definition of good' in morals *in class society* we must first consider the case in non-class society. So, for now, the point of raising this has just been to demonstrate that in the sphere of morality we must be concerned *both* with *which* interests are at issue and also with *whose* interests are at issue, and often it is enough just to specify *whose* interests. Recall, now, all the more specific meanings that the word 'good' has in very specific contexts, as we discussed in the last section. 'Good' means "answering to certain interests", but in a specific context just *whose* interests are at issue, and just *which* interests are at issue, become clear. Consequently, in those specific contexts, to say something is "good" gives us a lot more information. In a standard context, for example, saying "That's a good knife." tells us not just abstractly that the knife in question "answers to certain interests", but that it is sharp, keeps it edge well, won't rust, and so forth, *because those are our usual interests in knives.* (Of course we might also say, "That's a good knife, but it needs sharpening." In that case we are admitting that the knife in question does not meet, in one important way, our normal interests in knives, but also affirming that this can be corrected by sharpening it.)

In general, the more we restrict the context, the more the matter of just *whose* and just *which* interests are at issue also become more definite. When we restrict our attention to just morality and moral discourse, we have restricted both these conditions in very important ways, which we must now start to bring out and make explicit.

In general, as we have been saying, 'good' means "answering to certain interests". In general it is "one's" interests which are relevant; the "one" (or group) whose interests are at issue as determined by the context of the utterance. But in morals the interests in question are nearly always (or at least are nearly always *represented to be)* those of the people considered as a whole. (Even where this is actually impossible, as is usually the case in class society, the moral terminology still *pretends* that it is so. More on this later.)

Thus in *morals* the word 'good' means "answering to the interests of the people as a whole". Which of their interests? That is narrowed down, too. It is their common, collective interests which are at least *mostly* at issue. So here is our full, more concrete definition: In morality, or moral discussion, 'good' means (for the most part) "answering to the common, collective interests of the people as a whole."

How do we know this? It is simply a matter of looking at numerous typical cases of moral terminology in use. We must remember that morality is a matter of inter-human relationships. My interest in having toast for breakfast instead of cereal is hardly a moral issue (except for contrived situations). For the most part, and as an initial approximation, only actions which affect others fall into the province of morality, and not even all of them. If my choice of toast negatively impacts the shareholders of General Mills Corporation (in some tiny way!) because less cereal is sold, it can be said to affect other people. But eating toast for breakfast is still not immoral. Only actions which affect the common, collective interests of the people as a whole are relevant in morals; this is what a general examination of clearly moral or clearly immoral actions shows.

It should be noted, of course, that often what affects us as an individual can nevertheless reflect a common, collective interest. If Tom shoots Dick, that obviously negatively affects Dick's individual interests. But if you think about it for a moment you can see that it also affects *everyone's* common interest in not being shot.

Moral terminology thus *presupposes* that the people as a whole *have* common, collective interests. As we shall see, this is true in only a very limited sense in class society. This makes moral language *inherently deceptive* in class society. (And this, in turn, often explains why it is being used in the first place!)

It is not surprising that 'good' has a somewhat modified, i.e., less abstract, definition in morals than it does in general. After all, the general definition of 'good' was arrived at by abstracting its core meaning from all its possible socio-linguistic contexts. If the range of contexts is limited to a specific type, then of course the abstraction of the common elements of meaning in that limited range of discourse can be expected to include elements which would otherwise have to have been abstracted out. The narrower the range of contexts considered, the less abstract the common elements of meaning need to be.

The definition of 'good' in morals is less abstract than its definition in general because we can now say something more definite about *which* and *whose* interests are at issue.

Terms in Moral Discourse

Any moral term (any word used specifically in moral discourse, such as 'good', 'bad', 'right', 'duty', etc.) can be roughly defined in terms of any other moral term. Since we have now determined what the word 'good' means in morals we could simply proceed to define all the rest in terms of 'good'.

However, we have determined that 'good' means (in morals) "answering to the common, collective interests of the people as a whole." So it is not only "just as easy" (in fact easier) to define other moral words *in terms of this definition of 'good'*, namely in terms of the people's interests, than it is to define them in terms of 'good' itself. This will also allow us more flexibility and precision; that is, our definitions of the other moral terms will not be as rough as they would necessarily have to be if we used 'good' as our starting point.

Where John Austin's "dimension-word" concept was introduced, all moral words, that is *in morals* all words in 'good's dimension, are definable in terms of "answering to the common, collective interests of the people". Austin said that the dimension-word was the keyword in a group of words all with the same "function". While it is not clear to me that this concept of a group of words having the same "function" is always helpful, in this particular case. Moreover, it seems pretty clear that *the function* of not only 'good', but of all words in its moral dimension, is to allow discussion on the subject of "answering to people's interests", but to do so *without explicitly referring to those interests.* Why would people want to do that? We'll get into this more later on, but the brief answer is that this is extremely useful when those who are really concerned only about their own individual or group interests desire to put social pressure on others to act in a way that goes against *those other people's* own individual or group interests!

It might be objected that really we should use the same contextual method of defining each additional moral term as Ziff used in determining what 'good' means, instead of trying to define other moral terms in variations of the same words that happen to best define 'good'.

Of course the meaning of all words (other than technical terms defined by fiat) should be determined by the same sort of contextual procedure as was used to discover the meaning of the word 'good'. The present effort is in relation to the question of how one goes about formulating hypotheses for what a word means, which one should then proceed to test against example utterances of the word. You see, the major difficulty in attempting to apply Ziff s method is that it does not provide us with much of a guideline for formulating such hypotheses. Ziff suggests using paradigms where appropriate, such as in defining the meaning of tiger' or lion'. But with more abstract words, such as good' another technique is required:

The second procedure, and one that I shall employ in connection with the word good', is essentially indirect in character. It is the most powerful method of analysis. One proceeds first by considering and examining deviant uses of the words in question. Secondly, one must formulate some sort of hypothesis to account for the fact that the utterances in question are or seem to be deviant. Thirdly, one determines whether or not it is possible to generate deviant utterances on the basis of the hypothesis. Thus the concerned to define the word ought', the first step would be to formulate some hypothesis that would serve to account for the fact that I ought to do it if I were you.' is somewhat odd.

While this is an important and useful suggestion, it's only a partial solution. Formulating the hypothesis that good' means answering to certain interests from this initial suggestion might well take a lot of work, and considerable imagination. It would be nice if we had some more suggestions or clues.

One such suggestion is that you might consider the definitions in existing dictionaries as possible hypotheses for the core meaning of the word. This is at least something to try if you can't *think* of any hypotheses yourself. If you tried this with the word good', using *Webster's Third New International Dictionary,* you would have 71 candidate hypotheses. That's quite a few to sort through, but in fact one of them is actually very close to the mark (favorably affecting one's interests...).

An even better suggestion is to make use of any known meanings of other words which are related to the one you are investigating.

The starting from scratch in attempting to define an abstract word, there might be nothing much else to do but follow Ziff s suggestion, to concentrate first on deviant uses of the word, and perhaps browse through existing dictionaries looking for a clue. But if you know that a group of words are related in meaning, and if you have already determined the meaning of one, then you already have a tremendous head start in determining the meaning of the others. You have some ready-made clues to help you in formulating a hypothesis, namely, the words or concepts in the definition you already have, together with words whose meaning is close to them.

This is our present situation. We know that good' means (in morals) answering to the common, collective interests of the people as a whole. And we know that words such as right', just', moral', etc. are closely related to good' (in that rough definitions of each of these words can be given in terms of any of the others). Therefore we have every reason to believe that we might be able to form hypotheses about the meaning of these other related words in much the same language.

The meta-hypothesis that *all* moral terms can be defined, and can only be satisfactorily defined, in terms similar to answering to the common, collective interests of the people as a whole.

But similar is not the same as identical. There is work not only to be done to come up with these various hypotheses for the meaning of other moral terms, but much more work to be done in actually carefully and systematically checking out these hypotheses by comparing them to the evidence of the distributive and contrastive sets of contextual data. We readily admit that what we have mostly done here is just to generate the hypotheses, not to prove them correct via careful reviews of the evidence. My investigations here are by no means as thorough, nor my conclusions by any means as certain, as Ziff s corresponding work on the word 'good'. My justification for this lack of diligence is simply the feeling that for my purposes providing the precise definitions of these other terms is not essential. Some of these definitions slightly wrong it should not affect the conclusions in the rest of the book.

'BAD' (Adj.) - In most cases when the word 'bad' is used, if the word 'good' were used in its place the utterance would mean the opposite of what it does. However, there are various kinds of opposites. "Short" is the opposite of "tall", and so is "not tall". But since some people are neither short nor tall it cannot follow that 'short' means the same as 'not tall'. Similarly some actions or behavior are neither good nor bad, right nor wrong, such as (in most situations) drinking a glass of water. Drinking a glass of water is not a (morally) bad thing to do, but neither is it a (morally) "good thing" to do.

My suggested hypothesis for the meaning of the word 'bad' (in morals) which we believe gets around this difficulty is "failing to answer to the sought-for common, collective interests of the people". If in the case of some innocuous action, such as drinking a glass of water (in ordinary circumstances), there *are no* such sought-for common, collective interests at issue, then the action is not morally bad.

'RIGHT' (Adj.) - First note that 'right' and 'wrong', as moral adjectives, seem to refer just to *actions* or *activities*. Whereas we can characterize a man, from a moral point of view, by saying "He's a good man." we cannot properly say "He's a right man." And presumably this is because the adjective 'right' (in moral discourse) is reserved for characterizing actions and not those who engage in those actions (or their traits, motives, or intentions).

One other important thing to note about 'right' and 'wrong' is that the use of the comparative and superlative forms of each adjective seems to be quite strained. Most single syllable adjectives generate their comparative and superlative forms by adding -er and -est to the root. 'Righter', 'lightest', 'wronger', and 'wrongest' all sound somewhat peculiar, though they are occasionally used. The other common method of forming the comparative and superlative forms is to use 'more' or 'most' together with the root word. This is generally done with multisyllabic words (e.g., 'more beautiful' rather than 'beautifuller'). But these forms of the comparatives and superlatives of 'right' and 'wrong' are also not very common.

It is true that we sometimes say of two people in a dispute "Well, they're both right, but Ed is *more* right than Bill is." I find it significant, however, that in cases like this, there is special emphasis given to 'more', indicating that something out of the ordinary is going on.

The comparative and superlative forms of 'good' (i.e., 'better' and 'best') are of course very widely used. My theory to account for this difference between 'right' and 'good' is that with 'right' there is less of a question of *degree* at issue. It is more of a question of either meeting some moral standard or not meeting it. In moral contexts, my hypothesis is that the adjective 'right' is normally used to characterize actions, and means "conforming to the standards we have for answering to the common, collective interests of the people as a whole for that sort of activity."

Note that this close similarity in meaning between 'good' and 'right' in morals explains why the two words can often (but not always) be substituted for each other (even though this does usually change the meaning slightly. Thus we can say with equal validity:

1) "It is good to support the masses in their struggles against oppression."

2) "It is right to support the masses in their struggles against oppression."

But statement 2) is a bit stronger here, since in addition to saying what 1) says, it also says that this means meeting the *standards* for moral conduct that we uphold in these circumstances.

'WRONG' (Adj.) - My corresponding hypothesis for the core meaning of 'wrong' in morals is then "failing to meet the expected standards (assuming such to be relevant) for answering to the common, collective interests of the people as a whole for that sort of activity."

'JUST' (Adj.) - The adjective 'just' in morals has a meaning very close to that of 'right', including the element of "meeting a moral standard". The biggest difference that we have found so far is that 'just', as compared with 'right', can more readily refer to people, collective agents, human traits, intentions, motives, and the like, which 'right' usually cannot. Thus we can say "Her motives are just." though it would be odd to say "Her motives are right." (We would normally say instead that her motives are *good)*

In moral contexts, my hypothesis is that the adjective 'just' means "conforming to the standards we have for answering to the common, collective interests of the people as a whole."

Consider the following three statements:

1) "Her (moral) decisions are good."

2) "Her (moral) decisions are just."

3) "Her (moral) decisions are right."

On my theory, all three are very close in meaning, but there are some subtle differences. Statement 1) means "Her decisions answer to the common, collective interests of the people as a whole." 2) means "Her decisions meet the standards which answer to the common, collective interests of the people as a whole." And 3) means "Her decisions meet the standards which answer to the common, collective interests of the people as a whole in decision making." Of the three, therefore, the strongest seems to be 2), which not only means that her decisions answer to the interests of the people, and that they go beyond that by meeting the set of standards we have for answering to the interests of the people, but—beyond that—there is not as much of an implication that we are concerned merely with the one specific sort of action being discussed here, namely her decision making. On the other hand, talk about what is "just" also carries a connotation of what is *legal,* and of course what is legal is not necessarily what is moral (especially in bourgeois society)! Furthermore, 'just' carries a connotation *of fairness,* which also relates in part to legal contexts. These are the kinds of connotations and subtleties that abound in moralistic language.

'JUSTICE' (Noun) - Even more so than the moral adjective 'just', and even within moral discourse, the word 'justice' has legal connotations. The local courts in San Francisco, as well as the police, are headquartered in what is officially known as the "Hall of Justice"—though many of us (and not just revolutionaries) prefer to refer to it as the "Hall of Injustice", since injustice is at least as common there as justice! The 1960s radical H. Rap Brown (later known as Jamil Abdullah al-Amin) once said that because of the rampant racism in America "Justice means 'just us white folks'." So for many of us, the term 'justice' when used in this society frequently has a bitter irony to it. But leaving aside the connotations that the word has acquired in bourgeois society, and because of its association with the very unjust capitalist legal system, what is the core meaning of the word 'justice' in morals?

Because of the association of the word 'justice' with legal matters, dictionaries often give as one definition of the word "the quality of conforming to law". But if we are concerned not with law but with morals, and in light of the definition of 'good' which we arrived at in morals, the hypothesis which we shall put forward is that 'justice' means "the quality of conforming to the standards which answer to the common, collective interests of the people as a whole". In other words, we are simply transforming the adjective 'just' into a noun.

'MORAL' (Adj.) - The word 'moral' is often a slightly more formal near synonym for either 'good' or 'right', depending on the context (though sometimes the syntax needs to be slightly changed). Thus "He's a moral person." means something very nearly the same as "He's a good person."

However, the core meaning of 'moral' seems to be somewhat more general and abstract than for the words 'good' or 'right'. My hypothesis is that 'moral' means "concerned with, or pertaining to, questions of right or wrong and the standards which govern this". This covers statements such as "Moral discourse annoyed Marx." But it also covers the statement "He's a moral person." since someone who is "concerned with right and wrong" is also generally presumed to *act* rightly.

'MORALITY' (Noun) - Codes or doctrines concerning what is moral conduct. Thus, in the positive sense, "codes or doctrines concerning which conduct or behavior answers to the common, collective interests of the people as a whole."

'MORAL OBLIGATION' (Noun phrase) - The last three moral terms we will briefly consider here are a departure from those previously discussed in that they incorporate the concept of *obligation* into the meanings. To be obligated is to be "bound", or "constrained", or "required", or "forced", either legally or morally (or possibly in some other regard), to act in a certain way.

In the case of legal obligation we are bound, or constrained, or required to obey the law because of the penalties that will ensue if we do not (such as fines or jail). But in what way is anyone *bound,* or *constrained,* or *required* to be moral?! There seems to be something funny going on here! This "moral obligation" has seemed to many to be some sort of cosmic compulsion, some demand or threat from God, or something that seems almost mystical! But what will really happen if we flout our moral "obligations"? The universe and God will have nothing to say; we will then just be immoral.

Aren't there *any* real penalties when we ignore our "moral obligations"? Well, actually there are, and they are of two different kinds. (We are ignoring the legal penalties for flouting moral obligations which are *also* legal obligations.) First, there is the penalty that will likely ensue because of the different (and more negative) way that other people will relate toward you, assuming they learn of your immoral behavior. This comes about because most people are basically moral, and really hold it against those who flout what they consider to be appropriate moral norms. And, second, there is the penalty that will likely ensue from your own *conscience.* If you flout what you yourself believe to be a moral obligation, and—if you are a normal person with a normal conscience (not everyone is!)—then you will also suffer an internal penalty for your immoral act. In some cases, this can be a genuine torment and agony.

So, despite the claims of the religious and the Kantians, moral obligation is by no means a cosmic imperative. It is simply a matter of there being negative consequences, both socially and personally, when we act against what we (and the society around us) believe to be moral. To dismiss the concept of moral obligation, but rather merely to demystify it (something that sorely needs to be done!).

'Moral obligation' then means "the constraints on us to act in a way which answers to the common, collective interests of the people as a whole, constraints which are imposed on us both by the attitudes of society (other people) and by our own consciences."

'DUTY' (Noun) - In moral discourse 'duty' is simply the common word for moral obligation. However, 'duty' carries connotations that the more formal term 'moral obligation' does not, because of other actual or imagined "duties" we have, such as family duties, religious duties, or patriotic duties, where an extreme sense of shame is conditioned to arise in most people who fail to properly perform such duties.

'OUGHT' (Verbal aux.) - The word 'ought' is a "verbal auxiliary", which is used to add the element *of obligation* to the meaning of the verbal phrase (and hence the utterance as a whole). In moral discourse, it is the additional meaning of *moral obligation* which is added. Thus, in morals, 'ought' means "was (were) or am (is, are) under moral obligation (to do, be, have... something)."

There are many other words which have, in some contexts, a moral import, such as 'should', 'must', 'ethical' (often used as meaning the same as 'moral'), and so forth. There is no particular need to try to present an exhaustive list here.

Finally, we must not fail to mention that the meaning of *all* moral terms, including 'good' and those mentioned in this section, need to be further modified in a systematic way in class society.

Social philosophy 'Interest'

The most fundamental of all concepts in social philosophy is that of *interests.* In political philosophy the concept of interests stands behind, and explicates, its basic categories, such as that of social classes and ideology. The concept of interests enters aesthetics not only because of social (class) considerations, but also because of "purely aesthetic" considerations. But it is in ethics that the situation is most pronounced: one cannot really understand ethics *at all* except in terms of interests. For ethics, 'interest' is the key word, the key concept; it is *the key.*

A. Which Sense of the Word 'Interest' Are We Interested In? We have determined (following Ziff) that the word 'good' means (in general) "answering to certain interests", and that it means in morals "answering to the common, collective interests of the people as a whole". It is therefore apparent that the word 'interest' is a crucial one for ethics. But what exactly does *it* mean?

On this point Ziff himself says: Something must be said about my use of the word 'interest'. we mean to be using that word in an ordinary way. We shall assume that you know what that is, that you are familiar with the word.

Since the word has been used in extraordinary ways by philosophers it is, we suppose, necessary for me to disassociate myself from that tradition. That interests, motives, wants, wishes, hopes, cravings, longings, likings, hankerings, and so on are all different, cannot be identified.

Ziff goes on to say that he is not using the word 'interest' in some special way, as for example, the element of meaning common to all these other words ('motives', 'wants', etc.). He rejects the idea that 'good' might be better defined in terms of "ends" or "goals", or in terms of "wants", "needs" or "desires", any one of which might be taken to mean "more or less" the same thing as 'interests'. By 'interest' he means 'interest', he says, not something else. And he evidently does not believe it is necessary to define the word 'interest' beyond this.

It is of course true that one cannot be expected to go on defining one's terms indefinitely. Sooner or later you have to assume that people understand your definitions and do not require that the words in those definitions be defined themselves. Providing a correct definition of 'good' in terms of 'interest' is a tremendous advance. Unlike definitions of 'good' in terms of "rights" or "duties" or "justice", we have escaped from the realm of what is normally considered moral terminology. (We will return to this issue.) This is important because it allows us to understand moral terminology in terms which are less subject to endless and irresolvable passions and disputes. It puts the discussion on a more objective and scientific plane, less prone to interference by confused and mistaken theories.

Nevertheless the word 'interest' is not without some difficulties of its own due to the fact that there is more than one *ordinary* sense of the word 'interest'. If we are really to adequately define 'good' we must say a few words in explication of 'interest' as well.

'Interest' comes from the Latin word *'interesse'* which meant "to concern" or "to be of importance". But its more immediate etymological roots are the Medieval Latin and French words which meant "a compensation for loss", "ownership share" and "interest on money". In his book *Keywords* Raymond Williams notes that:

> Most uses *of interest* before the Seventeenth Century referred to an objective or legal share of something, and the extended use, to refer to a natural share or common concern, was at first usually a conscious metaphor:
>
> "Ah so much interest have (I) in thy sorrow
>
> As I had Title in thy Noble Husband. *(Richard III)*"

An example of this "extended" use is "He has an interest in mathematics", meaning that he *likes* mathematics, is curious about it, or some such thing. Sometimes this sense is called a "psychological" sense of the word since it has to do with someone's psychology, specifically their "likes" or "desires" or "concerns". Among the "non-psychological" senses of the word 'interest' are:

1) *Money interest*—the price paid for borrowing money, as in "They had to pay 19% interest on their loan";
2) *Ownership share—a* right or legal share of something of value, as in "The Rockefellers have a 30% interest in this company";
3) *Beneficial interest*— something which benefits, or is to the advantage of a person or group of people, as in "Flood control projects are in the interest of the people who live along the river."

It is this last sense of the word which concerns us here. Someone's "interests", in this sense, are what benefits them or is to their advantage. This is the sense of the word 'interest' which matters in the analysis of the word good' both in general and also specifically in ethics; and this is the sense assumed throughout this book (unless otherwise indicated).

Note carefully that in this beneficial, or objective, sense of interest', the individual's (or group's) psychology is completely irrelevant. The people who live along the river may *want* the flood control plan to be implemented, or may oppose it for some reason, or may be completely unaware of it. It is irrelevant if they are interested in the project (in the psychological sense), or not. And something may be in your interest even if you are not interested in it. (Two different senses of the word here.)

It is amazing to me that the very existence of this beneficial or objective sense of the word interest' has evidently not been noticed or separated out from the psychological sense by many people. Even Ziff, usually very alert to such nuances, does not seem to be aware of this, or of its importance.

A great many philosophers have gotten themselves into deep trouble because of the confusion of the psychological and objective senses of the word interest'. We find the confusion in Hume, Bentham, John Stuart Mill and many others. The whole ethical theory of utilitarianism has been essentially vitiated by this confusion.

Since this is such an important point, we would like to illustrate the kind of mess you can get into with an example from the recently developed trend of analytical Marxism. This school of higher criticism of Marxism seems to be characterized by an almost pedantic attention to detail, on the one hand, and a glaring obliviousness to the obvious, on the other hand.

In his book *Classes*, Eric Olin Wright has the following discussion about what he earlier calls the knotty philosophical problems with the concept of objective interests'. It should soon be apparent that these knotty problems are due entirely to the use of terms as objective interests' or true interests' in a psychological sense:

When Marxists talk about objective interests they are, in effect, saying that there are cases when choices can be made in which the actor has correct information and correct theories, but distorted subjective understanding of their *interests,* that is of the preferences they attach to different possible courses of action.

The problem of specifying true interests (undistorted preferences) is a difficult and contentious one... There are two basic senses in which we can say that a person has a distorted understanding of their true interests. The first, and simplest, is when what a person really wants is blocked psychologically through some kind of mechanism. The preferences that are subjectively accessible—that are part of the individual's consciousness —are therefore different from the preferences the individual would consciously hold in the absence of this block. The block in question is a real mechanism, obstructing awareness of preferences/wants that actually exist in the person's subjectivity. If we understand the operation of such psychological obstructions, then we can say something about the character of the resulting distortions.

The second way in which we can talk about distorted preferences does not imply that the undistorted preferences are actually present in the individual's subjectivity, only buried deep in the unconscious waiting to be uncovered. The second sense allows for the possibility that the distortion-mechanism operates at the level of the very formation of preferences in the first place. The obstruction, in a sense, is biographically historical; and the counterfactual is, therefore, a claim about what preferences the individual would have developed in the absence of such distortion-mechanisms during the process of preference formation. The usual form of such an argument is to say that true interests are the interests actors would hold if their subjectivities were formed under conditions of maximum possible autonomy and self-direction.

There are advantages and disadvantages with each of these approaches. The first has the advantage of being much more tractable and potentially open to empirical investigation. It is limited, however, in its ability to contend with the deepest kinds of effects cultural practices may have on the subjectivities of actors. The second alternative, however, suffers from an almost inevitable speculative quality that may have a crucial critical function but which renders the concept very problematic within scientific explanations.

... To the extent that the conscious preferences of people lead them to make choices which reduce that capacity [to make choices] or block its expansion, then, we would say, they are acting against their true or objective class interests.

It is of course true that people sometimes have confused or conflicting preferences, and perhaps also blocked or subconscious desires. But this is all very secondary to the main point, that what are in people's true interests are simply those things which truly benefit them, whether or not they are conscious of the fact *at any level.* There is no difficulty at all in distinguishing *true interests* (objective interests, in my sense) from *perceived interests.* It is a simple fact of life that we are not always aware of what really benefits us (of what really is in our own interest).

Once you identify interests with preferences (or desires, or wants, or any similar psychological states) you inevitably get into the predicament of trying to explain how our true interests (undistorted preferences) could possibly be unknown to us. Somehow we must have preferences which we do not prefer; or wants that we do not consciously want. All the psychological mumbo-jumbo in the world about blocked preferences and the like is not going to satisfactorily clear up such a quandary. How would you deal with newborn infants living by our hypothetical river, for example? It is also in *their* interests that the flood control project be built, but obviously they are completely incapable of forming any preferences or desires on the issue, blocked, subconscious, or otherwise.

The ambiguity between the objective and psychological senses of the word interest' is also one of the main factors behind the problem of altruism. The argument here is that nobody is really altruistic since everyone inevitably acts on their own interests, preferences or desires, which occasionally happen to also benefit others. Thus if Sue does a favor for Betty it is really done, perhaps, because Sue enjoys the warm feeling she gets when helping others; i.e., it is really done for her *own* benefit (to induce internal warm feelings !).

Of course Sue helps Betty because she *desires* to, and if her interests were the same as what she desires, she would be acting in her own interests. But the point is, by doing that favor for Betty, Sue is consciously setting aside her own *objective interests* for the moment, and that is what altruism really is. People do often act against their own interests—against what benefits them—for one reason or another.

It is not difficult to see that any psychological sense of the word interest' will not do in the explication of good'. If interests were identified with likes or desires, for example, then a good butcher knife would simply be one that someone likes or desires. Instead a good butcher knife has certain objective characteristics, regardless of any individual's likes and desires, such as that it must retain its sharpness well, be properly shaped and balanced, not rust, etc. These are *objective* features of a good butcher knife that answer to our (standard) objective, beneficial interests in butcher knives; i.e., it (normally) benefits us when butcher knives have these characteristics.

Of course it is also true that we are *generally* aware of our objective interests in butcher knives or anything else. And thus we generally come to have conscious, psychological interests which parallel our objective interests. But it is objective interests, and not the possibly accompanying psychological interests, which are the fundamental thing here, and that is especially true in morality.

There is a different point that must also be discussed here. It might be objected that we are approaching some circularity in our definitions, since 'benefit' seems to sneak back in the word 'good' in a Latin form. And certainly it seems most straightforward to define words like 'benefit' and 'advantage', if not in terms of each other, then at least in terms of "good". But the circularity here tends to *confirm* our analysis and is by no means vicious. Consider, for example, a German-English/English-German dictionary which lists under 'Blume': "flower", and under 'flower': "Blume". This is circular and of no help to you if you don't understand one of the words. But if you do know one, either one, it helps you understand the other by relating the two. (It would be very disconcerting to find that while 'Blume' means "flower", 'flower' does not mean "Blume"!) Similarly our definitions of 'good', 'interest' 'benefit', etc., relate these words to each other and are helpful precisely because of that.

There is a point in carrying this game of further definition this far only to make clear which sense of the word 'interest' we are concerned with when we say that 'good' means "answering to certain interests", ruling out for example any psychological interpretation in terms of "desires". But it should be quite clear that in doing this we are *not* abandoning our definition of 'good' in terms of interests nor substituting for it a definition of 'good' in terms of "benefit" or "advantage". We have not made the definition of 'good' in terms of interests superfluous; we have merely made it less prone to misinterpretation.

Common, Collective Interests. In the previous sub-section it was pointed out that both individuals and groups of people can be said to have interests. At least we certainly speak that way all the time. But there is a quite common dogma that only individuals can really have interests, not groups. Melvin Rader, for example, states:

> Nothing can literally have an interest except an individual. Within the family, each member has interests, and these interests are affected by the family *esprit de corps* and by the relations between the members of the family. But the interests of the family are nevertheless the interests of the father, the mother, and each of the children—these and nothing more. There are no family interests over and above these individual interests. And what is true of a group of a few members is also true of a group of many members, even a vast nation. It too has no interests that are not the interests of its members, because it has no mind apart from the minds of its members.

The only real argument that Rader provides here is in the last sentence, where it is apparent that he must be using the term interest' in a psychological sense.

> The term *interest* is here used in an inclusive sense to mean any attitude of liking or disliking, of prizing or disprizing, of preference, selection, appreciation, or appraisal. It involves feeling, emotion, desire, will, or some similar attitude.

These are all mentalistic or psychological terms. Rader's argument thus depends for its plausibility on the use of the word interest' in a psychological sense—which we are not concerned with—and is only relevant to beneficial or objective interest insofar as one blurs the two senses. Unfortunately, it has been all too common to do this in philosophy. And in fact this is what Rader is doing as well: ... I shall maintain that intrinsic value resides in interest, primarily in the fulfillment of interest. It follows that the locus of intrinsic value is the individual because the individual, after all, is the seat of interest. The group exists for the sake of the individual, and not the individual for the sake of the group. The welfare of human beings, therefore, is what counts, and not the good of the state, the nation, the race, or the working class.

The above argument is sneaky, though perhaps only unconsciously so. First of all, Rader correctly states that intrinsic value can only be analysed in terms of interests. But this is only valid if the *interests* are objective, beneficial interests—not if they are psychological interests (what people want, desire, appreciate, etc.). Rader has the words right; but either he is incorrect in his understanding of what these words have to mean here, or else he is confusing and switching two senses of the term as his argument requires.

Second of all, Rader pulls a sneaky trick in contrasting the welfare of human beings with the good of *various subsets* of humanity as a whole, in particular three subsets (state, nation, race) *which almost everyone knows* must be subordinate to the welfare of humanity as a whole. One ironic thing here is that even in speaking of the welfare of human beings he is inadvertently speaking in terms of *collective beneficial interests* (not of the separate individual psychological interests he pretends to be), and is really contrasting the collective interests of humanity as a whole against those of subsections of humanity. If Rader had contrasted the individual welfare of human beings taken as a whole against the collective welfare of human beings, his whole argument would have collapsed into incoherence—because the two are in essence the same!

The fourth subset he mentions—and obviously it is the Marxist point of view that he is really out to attack—is the working class. And here we have the biggest irony in the passage. In fact, his sentence is literally correct, *but what he means by it, what he thinks he is saying,* is totally wrong! It is actually the case that the welfare of humanity as a whole does come before the welfare of the working class. Contrary to what Rader believes, *this is the Marxist-Leninist-Maoist viewpoint!* What bourgeois ideologists can never understand or accept is that the only path toward securing the welfare of the people as a whole lies through proletarian revolution, which is to say, focusing on the real interests of the working class first and foremost.

Well, let us set aside the more ridiculous assertion of the individualists and accept the common sense point of view that groups of people can in fact have collective interests, at least in our sense, where such interests are things which benefit these groups. Some things benefit the people as a whole—such as the continued capability of the earth to support human life. And some things benefit subgroups—such as the continued existence of capitalism benefiting those who wish to exploit other people.

But there is a lesser, somewhat more plausible claim that can be made. Recognizing that of course groups of people can have collective interests, the claim is that these collective interests amount to no more than shared individual interests. That is, if a group can be correctly said to have a collective interest in something, then every individual member of that group (it is supposed) must have that same interest.

This is something which is often true, but not always. Sometimes there are even things which are in the common interest of a group which are not (at least precisely in the same form) in the individual interest of *any* member of the group! Consider the bourgeoisie. In fact, most members of the bourgeoisie attempt to put this maxim into practice, with only slight modifications. However, while it is in the interest of any bourgeois individual to do anything and everything that benefits himself, whether or not it is at the expense of others, this type of behavior can actually be destructive to bourgeois society if it is not considerably restrained. Thus the more farsighted members of the bourgeoisie set up rules for what is fair (legal) and what is not, in the dog-eat-dog fray. It is not in the individual interest of any bourgeois to be restrained in his or her own pursuit of wealth; but it is in the interests of the bourgeoisie as a whole that at least some restraints be put in place, and some effort be made to stop those (such as the Mafia, and most other businessmen when they think they can get away with it) who ignore such restraints.

Rousseau, incidentally, was quite aware of this point, and in fact it figured prominently in his social theory:

> There is often a great difference between the will of all [what all individuals want] and the general will; the general will studies only the common interest while the will of all studies private interest, and is indeed no more than the sum of individual desires.

But if we take away from these same wills, the pluses and minuses which cancel each other out, the sum of the difference is the general will. ...If there were no different interests, we should hardly be conscious of a common interest, as there would be no resistance to it; everything would run easily of its own accord, and politics would cease to be an art.

Ignoring Rousseau's psychological focus, what is being said here is that the common interests of members of a group must be abstracted from their individual interests, and are by no means always identical to their shared individual interests. Quite a sophisticated observation for 1762!

Thus, groups, classes, etc., do sometimes have interests above and beyond those of their individual members. Before closing this subsection, we would like to return to one more comment made by Melvin Rader in the passage quoted earlier, which superficially sounds rather sensible: The group exists for the sake of the individual, and not the individual for the sake of the group. Do I really object to this? Yes, I do! Humans are social creatures by nature; we cannot live alone apart from society. We depend on society and therefore have an obligation to society. In actual fact the group does exist for the individual, but just as truly the individual also exists for the group. The human motto is All for one, and one for all. Rader, like every bourgeois individualist, wants to drop the one for all part.

Is 'Interest' a Moral Term? If moral expressions are to be explicated in terms of people's interests the question arises: Is interest' itself a moral term? In talking about interests are we engaged in discussion of morality? It seems to me that the answer is no for a couple of reasons.

First, because a concept A helps explicate a concept B, is not a sufficient reason for saying that concept A is in the same category as concept B. Consider for example the category *colors* which includes red, blue, green and so forth. We can explicate red', to a degree, by pointing out that red light is light which has a wavelength between (approximately) 6220 and 7700 angstroms. However, this last phrase is not itself a colour nor is it, nor any part of it, in the same category with red, blue and green.

Second, discussion of people's interests has rarely been considered moral discussion in the past. Indeed, very often the two have been completely opposed in such discussions, the standard theme (in Kant for example) being morality *versus* interests and expediency. It is true that many philosophers have brought up the concept of people's interests in discussing the nature of morality—few of them viewing the concept as being of central importance, however. Even those few philosophers who have considered interest' to be a key concept in ethics have not generally viewed the word interest' itself as a moral term.

Jeremy Bentham did say, however, that the interest of the community is one of the most general expressions that can occur in the phraseology of morals... but unfortunately Bentham was unable to appreciate the importance of his own remark since he rejected the idea of common or collective interests as being anything more than the sum total of individual selfish interests (a quintessential bourgeois viewpoint), and because his view of interests' was a psychological one, itself explicated in terms of pleasure.

But it could be objected that past practice should be abandoned here: given that the concept of people's interests does correctly explicate traditional moral terms, we should *from now on* view the phrase people's interests' as a moral expression. Possibly such a change may happen in the future, to one degree or another. But despite this there will still be an important distinction between discussion of what is good and right and what you ought to do, on the one hand, and what is in the people's interests to do, on the other hand.

Talk of interests gets to the heart of the matter; it is less indirect, less obscure, much less prone to idealist obfuscation, and therefore to be preferred whether or not it is considered to be moral terminology *per se*. It seems to me that we should follow the example of the great Marxist leaders and teachers in this regard and strive to *replace*, wherever possible, what has always been considered moral expressions with a discussion of people's interests and those of social classes. In other words, instead of worrying about *extending* moral terminology to include expressions like people's interests' and class interests', it seems simpler and more straightforward to ignore the old obscure expressions to the extent possible and speak directly of the essence, people's interests, which lie behind all that moral palaver —though not always very obviously.

MYSTIFYING MORAL LANGUAGE

If 'interest' were just another moral term, just as obscure in meaning and therefore just as mystifying as the rest, then there would be no real point in dwelling on it. There would be no more value in defining 'good' and the other words commonly associated with moral language in terms of "interests" than there would be in defining 'good' in terms of "right", or "justice", or "duty". There would be no real clarification involved.

Part of the trouble is that all these common moral terms, 'good', 'right', 'moral', 'just', 'moral obligation', 'ought', 'duty', etc., are fairly close synonyms. True, some of them strongly include the idea of "obligation" which is more implicit in the others. And some of them are slightly more general than others (with 'good' being the most general). Some, like 'right' focus mostly on characterizing actions or activities, while others can also be used to characterize humans, groups, and other agents. And of course one whole other group ('bad', 'wrong', 'unjust', etc.) is used to characterize agents or actions in the opposite, negative way. So, yes, there definitely are *some* semantic differences between any two moral terms. Nevertheless, as a whole, they are quite close in meaning *and abstractness,* and one moral term can quite often be substituted for another in some particular context with very little change in meaning.

In order to bring real clarification into our definitions of moral terms we have to define them not in terms of each other, but rather in terms of *what really lies behind them all.* And what actually does lie behind them all are the *interests* of individuals and groups of people. When we define moral words and phrases in terms of interests we bring in *something new,* a *new concept* which serves to explicate all the old terminology.

There are many analogies here; we could for example point to the clarification and explication of the concept of 'colour' that came about when it was determined that different colors are (basically) the result of different wavelengths of light impinging on our retinas. Or the clarification of biological inheritance that came about when the basic principles of genetics were discovered. Sometimes in order to more deeply understand something at one level we have to develop at least a beginning understanding of it at a deeper level.

Another important reason why discussion in terms of people's interests provides more clarification, than does a parallel discussion in moral terminology, is that much more *subjectivity* is involved in moral discourse. I should immediately say that I do not think that moral statements are themselves always or necessarily subjective! In one sense, at least, there is actually nothing at all subjective about statements such as Imperialism is wrong! or The capitalist system is evil. Those are simple objective facts. However, comments like these certainly *appear to be very subjective* to some people!

Statements couched in moral terminology can themselves be as true and objective as statements about the arrangement of the furniture in your apartment. But the difference is that when two people are standing in your living room they are not normally going to disagree about where the furniture is. There will not be big disputes about whether or not the sofa is really by the window, or whether the TV is really against the opposite wall. But people do disagree about moral evaluations all the time. One will argue that abortion is (morally) wrong, while another will vociferously deny it. One will say that capital punishment is wrong, while another will say that it is a good and necessary thing. If a capitalist and his workers could ever be brought together for a free and open discussion about whether the latest cut in real wages or health benefits for workers at the company was good or not, there would be two very opposed views on the matter. But *why* is it so clear to everyone what the objective situation is when we are talking about the furniture arrangement and so contentious when we are talking about what is good or bad, right or wrong?

The answer to this is that while the moral statements themselves are true or false, it is very easy to have totally subjective ideas *about the truth* of those moral statements. And the reason that this is easy is that there is nothing obvious to point to in order to back up your position. When it comes to moral language people are able to argue over what is actually good or right with the impunity that comes from knowing that they can't be seen to be obviously wrong no matter what they say! On the other hand, whether something is actually in someone's interests or not is far more obvious and less disputable.

In other words, moral language appears to be more subjective, and is so much easier to be subjective *about*, simply because it is more abstract language, language in which the underlying interests of people is no longer explicit, and *has apparently been abstracted out*.

In the case of the capitalist and his workers discussing the latest cut in health benefits, for example, it would be hard for even the capitalist to deny that this harms the *interests* of the workers. (He would be reduced to arguing that somehow it would at least be in the workers' long-term interests, since—he might claim—the company would go bankrupt otherwise, or some such thing. Of course then the workers—if they are class conscious—might reply that the inability of the capitalist system to provide decent healthcare for everyone only provides further proof that it is in their long-term class interests to get rid of the whole capitalist system entirely!)

In many cases there will still be disputes even when the question of interests is brought to the fore. In the abortion case, for example, there can still be a dispute over the correctness of allowing abortion. But at least now the dispute will be much clearer. Instead of arguing over abstract moral maxims and their applicability (Is abortion murder?) we are now talking about the interests of the pregnant woman versus the possible interests of the fetus. In the case of the debate about capital punishment, the discussion would be shifted to weighing the interests of human beings who are about to be put to death, versus the presumed interests of society in punishing and (possibly) preventing some crimes.

When we frame such disputes in terms of interests we can be more explicit, more concrete and more objective. Much of the time we can all even be calmer and more rational! And that is a very welcome development considering the notorious heat, and emotion-based irrationality typical of abstract moral arguments.

This is *why* we revolutionaries should—as much as is possible—talk in terms of the conflicting interests of different groups (and especially classes) of people, *rather than* simply joining all the frantic yelling about what is right or wrong. It is not that many things are *not* correctly categorized as right or wrong; it is simply that behind that, in any case, are the interests of different groups of people, and it is much more *to the point* to get right down to discussing those interests. All moral language can be translated into the clarifying language of the common, collective interests of the people; all subjective moral arguments can be reframed in the more objective language of people's interests. And as a general rule of thumb, this is exactly what we should try to do. Yes, this may not always be completely feasible, since in our present culture moral language is so central to people's thinking. (More on this point later.) But at least when talking about what is good or bad, right or wrong, we should generally also go on to bring out and emphasize the matter of just whose interests are involved and what those interests are. We should always strive to clarify abstract moralistic language by explaining the beneficial interests (for some group or other) which stand behind it.

Morality of Marx

Marx often laughed at moralistic language. That's a fact! But what does this actually mean? That Marx was immoral? That he was amoral? Or what?!

The first thing to consider here is that it is utterly ridiculous to suppose that Marx's views on ethics were absolutely constant from his early youth until his death. Marx was, if anything, a deep thinker, and that means that he changed many of his views over time. This book is about the MLM interest-based theory of ethics, and not about Marx's views specifically, let alone the development of his views. But we will note that in his very early writings Marx did use moralistic language; in the period of *The German Ideology* (1845-6) and the *Communist Manifesto* (1848) Marx and Engels very much avoided moralistic language and even seemed to be hostile to the whole idea of morality; and in their most mature later period they still usually carefully avoided moralistic language while developing a more sophisticated view of morality and moral systems (as presented, for example, by Engels in *Anti-Dühring*). Thus the hostility by Marx (and Engels) toward the very idea of morality is mostly from that middle period (of the mid and late 1840s primarily).

However, even in *The Holy Family* (1845) Marx and Engels began to explain the underpinnings of morality in terms of group interests. In the course of discussing the great French materialist philosophers of the Enlightenment, they wrote:

There is no need for any great penetration to see from the teaching of materialism on the original goodness and equal intellectual endowment of men, the omnipotence of experience, habit and education, and the influence of the environment on man, the great significance of industry, the justification of enjoyment, etc., how necessary materialism is connected with communism and socialism. If man draws all his knowledge, sensation, etc., from the world of the senses and the experience gained in it, then what has to be done is to arrange the empirical world in such a way that man experiences and becomes accustomed to what is truly human in it and that he becomes aware of himself as man. If correctly understood interest is the principle of all morality, man's private interest must be made to coincide with the interest of humanity. If man is unfree in the materialistic sense, i.e., is free not through the negative power to avoid this or that, but through the positive power to assert his true individuality, crime must not be punished in the individual, but the anti-social sources of crime must be destroyed, and each man must be given social scope for the vital manifestation of his being. If man is shaped by environment, his environment must be made human. If man is social by nature, he will develop his true nature only in society, and the power of his nature must be measured not by the power of the separate individual but by the power of society.

One sentence in the above quotation in bold type to give it extra emphasis. Marx and Engels seem very clearly here to be agreeing with the premise that correctly understood interest is the principle of all morality and then go on to draw what they appropriately view as an obvious conclusion from that fact, that man's private interest must be made to coincide with the interest of humanity.

It is therefore quite certain that Marx's opposition to *moral language* cannot be construed as being the same thing as opposition to *being moral!* To be moral is to act in accordance with the common, collective interests of the people, and Marx and Engels certainly *never* opposed that! But they did oppose moral terminology precisely because it was so easily hijacked by those who were actually opposed to the interests of the people. Their comments against morality—even when at their most extreme —were actually against moralistic terminology, and not against being moral. In fact, it is totally obvious that both Marx and Engels devoted their entire lives to working to promote the interests of the working class and the masses, and in particular, their central interest in making social revolution, overthrowing capitalism, and creating a classless, communist society. So, for us Marxist-Leninist-Maoists, Marx's position here presents no problems at all. But it is sometimes rather humorous to read what various other people have had to say about this. Many bourgeois ideologists have been happy to jump to the conclusion that Marx opposed morality, and that he was immoral down to his very core. On the other hand, even some of those who are sympathetic to Marx and Marxism have been sorely troubled by Marx's comments and attitude. Let me give just one example, that of the social democrat Brian Morton who once wrote in *The Nation* that

> After his beautiful philosophical work of the 1840s, Marx turned away from the language of morality. He grew so disgusted with the hypocrisies of bourgeois morality that he began to style himself an antimoralist, delighting in reductive demonstrations that moral claims were nothing more than masks for economic interests. Bending to a Darwinist age, he began to write as if socialism were an inevitability rather than a future that men and women might choose. He began to write in a less human voice. If you want to spend a month or so in the library you can come up with a strong case that Marx remained a humanist, remained an advocate of freedom to the end. But I've often wished that his voice were so humane, so generous, that this would be obvious to anyone who glanced at his work.

People like Morton *object* to translating moral terminology into the clarified terminology of class interests! They think that talking about class interests rather than questions of right and wrong is to (at least on the face of it) abandon humanism, generosity, and a focus on human freedom. They long for a return to the sort of obscurantist moralistic language in which they themselves think about the world. One could even say that they generally remain at heart merely somewhat-radical, bourgeois liberals who still *think* in the internally confused way that bourgeois liberals do.

Nevertheless it could well be maintained that there is at least a difference, or different emphasis, between Marx and many other Marxists themselves (notably including Lenin) about morality and the use of moralistic language. We think there is less of a difference here between Marx and Lenin than many people suppose, especially if we are talking about Marx's mature position. Yet we would grant that Lenin, at least in his 1920 speech, *The Tasks of the Youth Leagues,* seemed more overtly willing to promote morality and moralistic language than Marx probably was. Even so, the central thrust of Lenin's speech (as we saw earlier) was to show that communist morality is that which promotes the revolutionary class interests of the proletariat and broad masses.

The mature Marx and Engels, as well as Lenin, realized that moralistic language cannot be completely dispensed with at this stage in history, and therefore that we cannot completely avoid all reference to good and bad, right and wrong, justice and injustice. And certainly many others, including many who are firmly on the side of the workers and masses, will continue to use moralistic language to talk about the contemporary situation even if those with a deeper understanding of morality avoid such terminology much of the time.

Consequently, given this situation, we must have a more complex attitude toward moralistic language. We should:

- Try to avoid using it ourselves, at least most of the time, and speak instead directly of class interests.
- When we do use it, try to simultaneously explicate it in terms of what actually lies behind it, namely, the common, collective interests of groups of people (and, in class society, the common, collective interests of different social classes).
- And, recognizing that moralistic language will still be a major part of the thinking of the masses and in widespread public political discourse in any case, conduct a serious, continuing campaign to educate people about not only the class interests that lie behind morality, but also the ease with which the enemy can often fool the people with their arguments framed in lying moral language.

In short, we must help the people come to understand both the real meaning of moral terminology, and also how their enemies frequently use such moralistic language to trick them. People must come to both properly understand moral language, and to seriously *distrust it!*

3

Maoist's Revolutionary Strategies

The Maoist's revolutionary strategies were very important in many insurgent movements, especially in the middle of the 20th century. However, currently their role is less important than it used to be and the changes described above significantly contributed to such a situation. In order to better understand what the role of Mao's views on insurgency has on contemporary insurgent movements it is necessary to analyse its basic assumptions and than compare them to the current situation and the insurgent movements of 1970-1990s.

First of all, it should be said that Maoist revolutionary strategies and his views on the insurgent movements were very important because they turned to be quite effective in China since due to them the Chinese Communist Party "defeated its enemy, ignited fears about a possible global triumph of communism, radically altered the balance of power in Asia, and placed American, South Korean, and other UN troops in their first direct shooting war with a major communist power" (Whitson 1988:305). The Chinese Communists quickly positioned themselves as the patrons of other insurgent movements. It is not surprising, therefore, that Mao's theory of revolution, including the ideas of the mobilization of mass, people's war, the people war, and others, became a blueprint for other insurgents.

Basically, Maoist theory for revolution includes three distinct phases that, of course, "mirror the history of the Chinese Civil War" (Whitson 1988:455). This strategy has the supreme virtue of making the incredible appear credible: the revolutionaries start as a weak, vulnerable and desperate group and, by the end of the conflict, they have become an unstoppable political and military force.

In the first phase the revolutionaries are "building what Lenin called the 'organisational weapon' the political, military, logistics, intelligence and command infrastructure" (Schram 1996:347). According to Mao, the insurgents should organise where the state is weakest. In China, as in many other countries where the strategy has been attempted, such weak place of the state was rural areas. At this respect it is necessary to emphasise that this point is quite weak being applied to the late 1980-1990s because the end of the 20th century was characterised by a high degree of urbanisation even in developing countries.

Anyway, the first phase should be viewed as a preparation for the insurgency while the real action occurs in phase two when Maoist theory recommends "a strategy of avoiding direct confrontation with government forces" (Schram 1996:382). Instead, the insurgents should strike where the enemy is weak, notably remote police or army outposts, towns and villages beyond the government's reach to occupy, rail and telephone lines, anything else that is military or politically significant, but incapable of being defended adequately. In such a way, the insurgent movements need to maintain the initiative at all times by turning weakness into strength.

However, the main point of the second phase is not military. Military action is "one prong of the attack on the regime; so, too, are efforts to organize an effective counter-government in liberated areas, maintain a flood of propaganda, subvert the government through infiltration, and take all other measures that erode the regime's political foundations" (Schram 1996:422). Defeating the enemy army is not the point, destroying the confidence of the population in the government, and the confidence of the government in itself, is the ultimate goal. Military and political actions, therefore, is simply a tool to win allies in the population, or to convince an even larger audience that history is on the side of insurgents.

In such a situation, during the third phase, the insurgent movements carry out a final assault against the government, which should be destroyed and the regime completely changed.

Obviously, Maoist theory, effective it seems to be, cannot always be fully applied in the end of the 20th century and its role gradually became less and less important. Consequently, what is really important for the insurgent movements according to Maoist theory is to gain confidence of the population and attract possibly larger masses on the side of the revolutionaries, making the war against regime the People's War.

On projecting Maoist theory and strategies on the insurgent movements of 1970-1990s, it is obvious that they turn to be less and less effective and eventually they have not been used as often as before. For instance, the traces of Maoist influence are obvious in the Vietnam War, when American and South Vietnamese units defeated North Vietnamese and Vietcong forces on the battlefield time after time, but a communist regime now rules Saigon. In such a way, the military success prove irrelevant because the war was lost politically.

Furthermore, the 1980s may be characterised as a transition period, when Maoist theory was still important. For instance, peaceful revolutions in Eastern described above were successful basically due to the effectiveness of the struggle for people's 'minds', confidence of population in righteousness of ideas developed by insurgent movements in the context of total lost of confidence in the official governments. On the other hand, these movements did not use army force or attacks as suggested Maoist theory the confrontation was purely political and socio-economic but not military.

However, 1990 revealed new trends in the insurgent movements, which made the Maoist theory less effective. In fact in the situation when there is only one superpower and the world undergoes the process of globalization the insurgent movements, which basically operate in developing countries, realised the ineffectiveness of both military or peaceful revolutions if they are not supported by the US, which actually could cope with any rebelling state since this country did not face any opposition from any other country in the whole world. In such a way the military conflict, even if it has a character of the People's War, is doomed to defeat if the US take a decision to intervene.

As a result, the insurgent movements basically use the strategy of terror attacks aiming not only at the official governments but also at Americans and their allies. There are a lot of examples, revealing this trend. For instance, PLO and other Palestinian organisations are probably the most experience in such kind of insurgency for they struggle clandestinely against Israel supported by the US and their main strategy is terror attacks which aim at the weakening of the opponents and agreeing with the demands of the insurgents. The same may be said about Al-Quaeda and activity of other insurgent movements that are active even nowadays, especially in Iraq and Afghanistan, when been unable to win the military conflict and lacking resources to gain population confidence not only within a definite country but in the world because in the epoch of globalization international public opinion is also important as well as domestic one, they had to use terrorism as the main means of struggle while the People's War, the mobilization of the mass and Maoist strategies seem to be less effective and doomed to failure.

TARGETS OF THE INDIAN REVOLUTION

The targets in the present people's democratic stage of the Indian Revolution: 1. Imperialism 2. Comprador bureaucrat capitalism, and 3.Feudalism. Imperialism plunders the country's land, labour, raw materials, and other natural resources. It earns super-profits through ruthless exploitation by various means. It subjugates the entire economy, polity, military and culture of India; destroys indigenous industry particularly the small and medium industries, throws out millions of workers into the streets and hinders the free and independent development of the national economy. Comprador bureaucrat capitalism collaborates with imperialism and allies itself with feudalism. It destroys the small and medium industries, oppresses not only the working class, peasantry and other toiling masses but also the national bourgeoisie.

Feudalism acts as fetter on the development of the productive forces by holding down the vast majority of the Indian people under backward relations of production. Economically, it keeps the overwhelming majority of the people in dire poverty and destitution, and depresses their purchasing power. It thereby, restricts the growth of the home market, retards industrial development and leads to massive unemployment and stagnation of the economy. Politically, it suppresses the democratic rights of the masses and in some places, even creates a 'state within a state' i.e. a parallel landlord raj in the rural areas with their own private armies or with the support of state-hired armed mercenaries. It keeps the peasantry in perpetual subjugation and bondage.

These three big mountains that are weighing down the backs of the Indian people should be smashed in order to build the new democratic society.

FORMS OF REVOLUTIONARY WARFARE

Commencing the war with guerilla warfare and then going through the forms of mobile and positional warfares will resolve the question of state power. Protracted people's war is in constant development. In accordance with the changing conditions and keeping the ultimate aim in mind decisions have to be made with swiftness, initiative, and mobility. By destroying the enemy forces by means of guerilla warfare and mobile warfare, we have to bring a change in the balance of forces between the enemy and ourselves and ultimately destroy, or render impotent, the enemy forces through positional warfare. In order to achieve this we have to first build the guerilla army from small guerilla units and then transform it into the PLA and solve the question of state power. The general principles of these three types of warfare will be as follows:

Guerilla Warfare

Guerilla warfare is a method of warfare by means of which the working class and the oppressed masses of the peasantry liberate themselves. As guerilla warfare is a phase in the protracted people's war, it will be waged in accordance with some specific scientific principles due to the special features it has. Whoever neglects the implementation of these principles will be defeated. In every country these general principles have to be creatively implemented depending on the political, economic, social and geographical conditions. Guerilla warfare is a war waged by the vast masses. It is a people's war. PLGA will be the focus of the fighting masses. It is a method of warfare that is waged when one is short of resources by basing on heroic revolutionary spirit. Not resorting to fighting when the enemy is strong but conducting attacks when the enemy is weak; dispersing the guerilla forces at one time and concentrating the forces at another time; retreating at times and destroying the enemy at other times; being ever prepared to confront the enemy anywhere-such are the methods of guerilla warfare. Guerilla warfare is a method of war through which the weaker side in terms of weapons, training of troops and army formations than its enemy, defends itself by delivering blows on its enemy through hit and run methods and wipes out smaller enemy troops. Alertness, swiftness, mobility and sudden attack in the shortest time i.e., short, swift and sudden-these are the strategic points of guerilla war. Having a grip on enemy's condition and terrain conditions, it will adopt the methods of delivering a lightning blow on the enemy and withdrawing in a moment. It adopts tactics like seeming to come from the east and attacking from the west, choosing and attacking vulnerable positions of the enemy, etc.

Divide our forces to arouse the masses, concentrate our forces to deal with the enemy. Since in a guerilla war, the lower level units have to operate independently, on their own, they will have relatively more independence in military operations. Especially in the fluid situation in enemy controlled areas, the lower units will be given initiative to some extent. As a result flexibility in changing tactics and operations, which is vital to a guerilla war will be obtained. In a guerilla war, the supply system will be totally decentalised and all the units should be self-reliant. For this, they will have to mainly depend on the people and on the enemy. In all matters, people's support is the lifeline of a guerilla war.

In the all-round offensives and the encirclement-suppression campaigns unleashed by the enemy we have to enhance the capacity of the masses to face difficulties and their heroic fighting spirit. In a guerilla war, do not go in for protracted battles. Operations of quick decisions should be taken up. The essence of guerilla war is-when the enemy advances, we retreat; when the enemy camps, we harass, when the enemy tires, we attack; when the enemy retreats, we pursue. Seen from a strategic perspective guerilla war creates many losses and difficulties for the enemy. His morale will be broken and will become tired. The sum total of victories in several small battles render impotent the manpower of the enemy. The dispersed battles will develop into a more centralized war. For destroying the enemy troops on a large scale and to establish the Base Areas the guerilla warfare has to transform itself into mobile warfare. Guerilla war by itself cannot win a revolutionary war as an all-independent form. The guerilla war will continue to develop until the guerilla army grows gradually and acquires the features of a regular army (PLA). After the development of the PLA, victory will only be possible when the enemy is destroyed by developing the guerilla warfare into mobile and positional warfare and is waged in co-ordination with them.

Mobile Warfare

The mobile warfare is a war, a regular army wages by concentrating its forces in a vast area with fluid battle-fronts and deployments and often changing from one place to another. It will have the mobility of attacking the enemy at his relatively vulnerable spots and withdrawing quickly and the potential for changing tactics when the conditions change. *"Fight when you can win, move away when you can't"*-this is the real essence of mobile warfare.

Mobile warfare will not aim at retaining or capturing territories, instead it aims at wiping out enemy troops. In a mobile war, the moment advantage slips out of the hands of our troops, that territory will be vacated immediately.

While the safety of troops in positional warfare is secured through defence positions and fortifications, in mobile warfare it is secured through quick fluidity, through rapid counter attacks and through the extensive utilization of concentration-dispersal.

In the mobile warfare too, primarily, battles of quick decisions should be waged. The important difference between a guerilla war and a mobile war is that, in mobile warfare, the troops will be concentrated in large numbers. The troops engaged in mobile warfare, will comprise of regular soldiers who have relatively higher political consciousness, greater discipline and military training. The guerilla forces engaged in guerilla war will be of a relatively lower level in the above matters. This mobile warfare which possesses the elementary features of regular warfare, will have the ability to annihilate the enemy forces in a big way. By thus wiping out the enemy forces on a big scale, this will serve as a key strategy to gain the upper-hand over the enemy and for transforming the war from the stage of strategic defensive to the stage of strategic stalemate or equilibrium and from the stage of strategic equilibrium to the stage of strategic counteroffensive.

Positional Warfare

Positional warfare is a war waged face to face with the enemy, from fixed positions either to capture or to retain a territory. The positional warfare primarily depends on the theory that retaining of a territory will ultimately lead to victory. Though the above three types of war have their separate distinct characteristics, there is no Chinese Wall demarcating the three in the period of transition. The guerilla operations undertaken by small guerilla squads, will have guerilla nature to a greater degree. However, as the people's guerilla army grows and as guerilla operations conducted by concentrating them increase, they will acquire some elementary features of a mobile warfare. Similarly, in the preliminary phase of mobile war, guerilla nature will be somewhat more, and the mobile war, which goes on with increased concentration of troops, the primary features of positional warfare appear.

When taken as a whole, in our revolutionary war, mobile warfare comes first and guerilla warfare will be secondary, and in the last stage of strategic offensive, we will capture state power through full-scale positional warfare.

Strategic-Tactical Principles of the PLGA

The following basic principle of the military line developed by Mao should be followed under all circumstances by our people's guerilla army: *"You fight your way and we'll fight ours: We fight when we can win and we retreat when we cannot."*

"The guiding principle of our strategy must be to prolong the war". The above general principle stated by Mao will be the strategy of our people's guerilla army. This is because time is required for preparing the masses for the war by mobilizing and consolidating them, for annihilating the enemy forces and render them impotent, to gradually bring a fundamental change in the balance of forces, to turn the domestic and international situation in favour of the people's war and to achieve an upper-hand over the enemy.

Our people's guerilla army should creatively apply the following tactical principle pointed out by Mao: *"In every individual campaign and from a tactical view point we must achieve rapid settlements."* The enemy must be annihilated in a methodical, sector-by-sector process, in which superior forces suddenly strike him when he is unprepared, weary, eating or sleeping. The guerrillas strike at the less mobile enemy's communication lines, harass him constantly, render his forces lame, lost, hungry, thirsty. As the enemy's strength and morale are sapped, guerrilla strength increases and morale improves. And as the war drags on, the guerrilla army will gain experience, will acquire recruits and arms. The PLGA should strive to implement the under-mentioned important tactical principles: Protracted people's war is arduous and torturous. The spirit of prolonged self-endurance should be upheld. In campaigns and battles it must oppose the use of the few to defeat the many and must adhere firmly to the use of the many to defeat the few. To confront a strong enemy it should rely on the masses and its own forces. PLGA should integrate with the masses. *"We must mobilise the people to support our armed forces enthusiastically and to fight the enemy together with them. The people are the eyes and ears of the army; they feed and keep our soldiers. It is they who help the army in sabotage and in battle. The people are the water and our army the fish."*

PLGA should rely on the battle front in order to enhance its fighting capacity; rely chiefly on the enemy for arms; be frugal in supplies; increase its patience; overcome difficulties; participate in production and increase production; establish arms factories for the production of weapons; and strive to carry on the people's war in the most trying circumstances.

THE CENTRAL TASK OF THE REVOLUTION

The above principle is equally applicable to the Indian Revolution too. The Central task of the Indian revolution also is the seizure of political power. To accomplish this Central task, the Indian people will have to be organized in the people's army and will have to wipe out the armed forces of the counterrevolutionary Indian state through war and will have to establish, in its place, their own state-the People's Democratic State and will have to establish their own political authority. The very act of establishment of the state machinery of the people by destroying, through war, the present autocratic state machinery-the army, the police, and the bureaucracy of the reactionary ruling classes-is the Central task of the People's Democratic Revolution of India.

It is absolutely indispensable for the Party of the proletariat in India to study the experiences of the world socialist revolution particularly the experiences of the two great proletarian revolutions of Russia and China. The application of the above principle of conducting the revolutionary war followed two different paths in the two countries depending on the special characteristics specific to their respective countries. The revolution in Russia took the form of a country-wide armed insurrection for the seizure of political power, while in China the path traversed by the revolutionary war was the path of protracted people's war. Whatever the forms assumed by the revolutionary wars in various countries, the content remains the same i.e., the seizure of power by armed force.

Protracted People's War is our Path

In order to guide the revolutionary war in India, it is necessary for us to grasp the experiences and the theoretical summing ups of these revolutionary wars made by comrade Lenin, Stalin and Mao. And particularly it is necessary for us to grasp the essence of Mao's contribution on military science. Generalising the experiences of the proletarian revolutions in the era of imperialism, we can broadly categorise the revolutionary wars in the various countries in the world into two types according to the character of their respective socio-economic-political systems. If it is a capitalist country where bourgeois democratic rights prevail, the Party of the proletariat prepares the working class and its allies through open, legal struggles-parliamentary, trade union, general strikes, political agitation and such other activities, in order to organise a country-wide armed insurrection at an hour of revolutionary crisis, seizing power first in key cities and then extending it throughout the country, at the same time strengthens appropriate secret party apparatus and combines secret, illegal and semi-legal activities with open and legal activities in accordance with concrete conditions.

Thus the Path followed by the Russian Revolution is: Inflict decisive smashing blow, at a hurricane speed, first, on the urban centre which is the well-fortified, consolidated and well-organized controlling centre of the state power of the enemy, crush the heart of the enemy's state machinery. Establish the Centre of power of the rèvolutionary state in the urban area. Then spread the revolution rapidly to the countryside-march forward by smashing the enemy's state machinery in the countryside. Capturing the urban area first, though war of strategically quick decision, establish revolutionary authority in the urban area, and thereafter, capturing the villages and establishing the revolutionary authority in the state power of the whole country through insurrection and establishing the revolutionary political authority of the people-such is the general Path followed by the Great October Revolution in Russia.

If, on the other hand, the country is ruled directly or indirectly by some foreign imperialist power or powers and is semi-feudal where there is no independence and democratic rights for the people, the Party of the proletariat from the very beginning arouses and mobilizes the people for armed struggle, relies on the peasantry-the main force of the revolution-makes backward rural areas its main centre of work, builds a people's army and people's militia; establishes dependable, strong and self-sufficient base areas or liberated areas in the vast countryside, constantly expands them in the course of protracted people's war, (in such a situation the cities under the control of the enemy will look like small islands in the ocean of the vast rural liberated areas); encircles and finally captures cities by way of decisively smashing the state power of the reactionaries and establishing the state system and political authority of the people throughout the country-such is the Path traversed by the Chinese Revolution to win world-shaking victory in 1949. And the history of the revolutions in colonial, semi-colonial, semi-feudal countries of Asia, Africa and Latin America have shown that this Path is applicable to all such countries also. In all these countries the main form of struggle is armed struggle and the main form of organisation is the army, but other forms of mass struggles and mass organisations are also indispensable.

Before the outbreak of a war all organisation and struggle are in preparation for the war and will serve it directly or indirectly after war breaks out. The path followed by the Chinese revolution is also applicable in semi-colonial, semi-feudal India due to basic similarities in the conditions between India and pre-revolutionary China. It is the principal characteristics of the objective conditions of India that determine the Path of the Indian Revolution as the path of protracted people's war.

The Principal Characteristics of India's Revolutionary War

1. India is a vast semi-colonial and semi-feudal country with uneven political, economic and social development, with favourable terrain for guerrilla warfare, that has witnessed a long period of armed struggle by the peasantry and also now witnessing the ongoing agrarian revolutionary guerilla struggle in which the peasantry is playing a heroic role.
2. Our enemy is big and powerful having centralized state machinery and a well-equipped modern army.

3. The Communist Party, the guerilla army and the agrarian revolutionary movement in India are still weak.
4. Our country is a prison-house of nationalities where some nationalities are engaged in bitter struggles against the Indian state to achieve their right to self-determination.

Since it is the above principal characteristics that determine the line for guiding India's revolutionary war as well as many of its strategic and tactical principles, let us analyse these characteristics more deeply. Uneven economic and political development and the semi-colonial, semi-feudal character of Indian Society is the most important characteristic that basically determines our political strategy and tactics as well as our military strategy and tactics.

The unevenness in the economic and political development of India is quite glaring. On the one hand, there is a distorted capitalist economy that is being increasingly integrated into the imperialist world economy. The capitalist economy has given birth to a huge industrial proletariat and other wage earners in non-industrial establishments running to around seven crores. This ensures that the proletariat of India is strong enough both in numbers and organization to lead the Indian revolution if it is imbued with the ideology of Marxism-Leninism-Maoism.

On the one hand, the capitalist economy coexists with, and stands on, a preponderant semi-feudal base. Although capitalist relations are penetrating the feudal setup in the Indian countryside and are partially remoulding it to suit the needs of imperialism, it is impossible (given the collusion between feudalism, comprador bureaucrat capitalism and imperialism) to bring a radical structural change in the semi-feudal base and its super structure. Consequently, the vast majority of India's population still lives in the countryside and the vast majority of them languish under semi-feudal conditions of existence.

The vast majority of the peasantry is in urgent need of the agrarian revolution to change the miserable, wretched semi-feudal conditions of existence. This circumstance derives from the fact that the democratic revolution in India remains unfinished and that the land question remains unresolved. Hence the content of the new democratic revolution remains the peasant war for land and political power-a factor that can be effectively utilized by the Party to rouse and organize the vast peasant masses into the

People's Army. Hence the proletariat finds its principal ally in the peasantry and can lead them to victory in the agrarian revolutionary war if proper Strategy and Tactics are pursued. It is possible to establish strong mass base among the peasantry and mobilise them into class struggles in the form of armed struggle for the seizure of land and establishment of people's authority in place of feudal authority. Several areas in the country have seen an upsurge of the peasantry against the semi-feudal exploitation and semi-feudal production relations, particularly since the great Naxalbari struggle. In the past decades the agrarian revolutionary war has spread to several strategic regions in our country and has created the condition for an unending flow of armed peasant militants and cadres into the revolutionary movement.

The unevenness of development in India indicates that it is not possible to stage a simultaneous revolution (i.e., an armed insurrection) throughout the country and that the line of area wise seizure of power through the strategy of protracted people's war has to be adopted basing on the relatively backward and strategic areas of the countryside. This means revolutionary war has to begin in those regions that are relatively more backward and where the social contradictions are sharp. The strength of the armed forces of the reactionaries is quite inadequate in the vast countryside of India and the inadequacy of the transport and communication system and other infrastructure makes it inconvenient for the quick movement of the enemy forces. The people's armed forces-the people's army and the people's militia, on the other hand, can advance and retreat easily, according to the needs of the struggle, in the vast countryside, that is, there is enough room for their manoeuvre in face of a big military offensive by the enemy's armed forces.

Thus the vastness of the countryside, the inadequacy of the transport and communication system and the isolation of the remote countryside from the military centres, and above all, the inadequacy of the reactionary armed forces in comparison to the vastness of the country and the population, if all these are taken into consideration, the military strength of the reactionaries is relatively weak in the countryside compared to that in the cities, and hence, from the military point of view, the vast countryside is the most advantageous for the revolutionary people's army to strike at the enemy. Hence, we can transform the vast tracts of the countryside into red resistance areas, guerilla zones, guerrilla bases and liberated areas by making use of the favourable terrain which is abundant in some regions of the Indian countryside. Liberated areas can also be established in the plains when the domestic and international situation becomes more favourable and the people's army becomes powerful i.e., when the revolutionary war is at a high peak.

The semi-colonial nature of Indian society also breeds conflicts and rivalries among the various imperialist powers for their domination and control over India. This is bound to generate acute conflicts and rivalries among the Indian ruling classes. Such an unstable political situation can be utilised by the Party of the proletariat to hasten the pace of building guerrilla zones and liberated areas and thereby advance towards completing the New Democratic Revolution. Thus while the first characteristic incontrovertibly proves that protracted people's war, and not armed insurrection, is the path to be followed by the revolutionary war in India, we must analyse the other characteristics to understand how protracted people's war in India could be waged.

The second principal characteristic-the enemy is big and powerful with a centralized state machinery and a well-equipped, well-trained modern army, Paramilitary and other forces-makes it imperative for the Party of the proletariat to take extreme caution from the very beginning in conducting the revolutionary war. This factor underscores the need to wage our revolutionary war from the weakest links of enemy rule-the vast tracts of the backward Indian countryside. It also warns us against engaging in strategically decisive battles with the enemy's armed forces for a long time, and to use the tactics of guerrilla warfare and preservation of our foıces while destroying the enemy's forces bit by bit through guerrilla methods of warfare, to accumulate strength by extending and deepening the armed struggle over ever-wider areas and to make the best use of the favourable terrain in the strategic regions in the countryside.

It should, however, be noted that the enemy is superior only from the tactical point of view. In the strategic sense, enemy's armed forces are only paper-tigers. Their interests are diametrically opposed to the interests of the broad masses and hence cannot get any cooperation from the people. Their morale and combat capacity are quite low primarily because of their mercenary nature; and the contradiction between officers and soldiers also contributes to it considerably. Moreover, since the vast majority of them are peasants in uniform, the influence of the agrarian revolutionary war will have a deep impact on them.

The third principal characteristic-the weakness of the Communist Party, the people's guerilla army, and the revolutionary movement in the country at the present juncture-has a profound influence on the nature of the revolutionary war in India. It shows that the people's guerrilla army that is built in the course of anti-feudal struggles and advancing the agrarian revolutionary guerilla struggles, has to accumulate strength over a period of time before being transformed into the PLA and prior to the transformation of guerrilla zones into liberated areas. It also warns us that we should not expose our forces to the enemy; should accumulate our forces considerably before entering into decisive engagements with the enemy's forces and should build a strong, stable, underground party mechanism from the very beginning. Thus from the sharp contrast of the weakness of the Party, the guerilla army and the revolutionary movement as a whole with the strength of the enemy's armed forces, arises the strategy and tactics of our people's armed forces and the Party.

However, this weakness relates to the present situation only. The conditions for overcoming this weakness are relatively developing. Already people are getting mobilised in various parts of the country into armed agrarian revolutionary struggles under the leadership of the Communist Party, which is growing in strength day by day. People's guerilla army is getting expanded and people's war is spreading to new areas. Since our agrarian revolution is a just one, and since it defends the interests of the majority of the people, the support of the people is increasing day by day.

The inferiority in arms and other things can be made up by relying on the mobilization of the vast masses as correctly observed by Mao:

"The mobilization of the common people throughout the country will create a vast sea in which to drown the enemy, create the conditions that will make up for our inferiority in arms and other things, and create the prerequisites for overcoming every difficulty in the war.........To wish for victory and yet neglect political mobilization is like wishing to "go south by driving the chariot north", and the result would inevitably be to forfeit victory."

Hence, by adopting appropriate and correct strategy and tactics, as the war is drawn out, the enemy's disadvantages and our advantages will both grow, and inevitably, the degree of the strength and weaknesses of ours and that of the enemy will continue to change, and changes will continue to occur in the position of relative superiority and inferiority too of both the sides, And, in this way, the military power of the people will continuously and definitely attain supremacy over the military power of the enemy and will finally decisive defeat on the military power of the enemy.

To sum up, at the initial stage, that is, up to a certain stage of development of the people's war, the military strength of ours is liable to remain weaker than that of the enemy. But this strength of the enemy and the weakness of the people are never absolute, they are relative, they are temporary. By way of relying on the vast rural areas and on the poor peasantry, by way of strictly pursuing the class line and mass line and the principles of guerrilla struggle and the protracted people's war, in words and in deeds, as shown by Com. Mao, the military strength of the people can gradually and definitely overwhelm that of the enemy as the revolutionary war draws out and can finally inflict decisive defeat on the armed forces of the enemy. However strong the forces of the enemy may be and however weak the people's forces may be at the beginning of the revolutionary war, through the realization and creative application of the total teachings of the flexible strategy and tactics of the guerrilla war and the Protracted People's War, it is possible to build up a new type of army, that is the red army, and to establish one after another-advanced base areas in the backward rural areas, and it is entirely possible to carry forward the revolution towards its final victory by gradually consolidating and expanding the people's army and the base areas through struggles. Beginning with the great Chinese Revolution, the very historical experiences of the revolutionary wars of countries like Vietnam, Laos, Cambodia, etc., bear testimony to the above truth.

The fourth principal characteristic-the irreconcilable contradiction between the various nationalities and the Indian ruling classes leading to incessant armed confrontation-contributes greatly to weaken the enemy and helps the advance of the revolutionary movement. This circumstance arises from the fact that the unfinished democratic revolution in India has left the national question unresolved and it is the Party of the proletariat that should take up the historic task of solving this problem from a class perspective. A large part of the remote countryside, most advantageous for the establishment of red liberated areas form the geographical and military point of view, are being inhabited mainly by the discontented and agitated nationalities and tribes, who are engaged in a bitter armed confrontation with the Indian state. Hence, it becomes imperative for the enemy's armed forces to be deployed in large numbers in ever-wider areas to contain the armed struggles waged by the various nationalities.

Lakhs of enemy's armed troops have been deployed since long in Kashmir and the North Eastern states alone. More and more nationalities may come into armed confrontation with the reactionary Indian state that is keeping them in a state of subjugation and oppression and denying them their right to self-determination. As a considerable part of the enemy's armed forces will inevitably be engaged against the growing tide of struggles by the various nationalities, it will be difficult for the Indian ruling classes to mobilise all their armed forces against our revolutionary war. If our Party can lay down the correct basis to win over the nationalities and tribes through our policy of guaranteeing self-determination for the nationalities and political autonomy for the tribes and forge a powerful united front against the common enemy (i.e. imperialism, CBB and feudalism) with these forces we can spread the flames of armed struggle to almost all the strategic regions in the country.

Needless to say, this will be a great positive factor for the rapid advance of the people's war by developing the people's guerrilla army into the PLA, establishing several base areas and then advancing towards countrywide victory. The above four principal characteristics determine the line for guiding India's revolutionary war as well as many of its strategic and tactical principles. It follows from the first and fourth characteristics that it is possible for our Party and People's army to grow and defeat the enemy. However, it also follows from the second and third characteristics that it is impossible for our Party and our People's army to grow very rapidly or defeat our enemy quickly. Hence the revolutionary war in India will be of protracted nature.

However, the revolutionary situation can become even more favourable for the rapid advance of the people's war due to several factors such as: further intensification of the imperialist crisis; a war with the neighbouring countries or on a world scale; intensification of the internal contradictions among the Indian ruling classes that may lead to an even more severe political crisis and instability and thereby forcing the enemy to divert his armed forces and economic resources to deal with the growing mass revolts; possibilities for the emergence of revolts among the police, Paramilitary forces as well as the army, and so on.

Some people argue that in India it is impossible to establish liberated areas, to build the red army and to carry out protracted people's war because there is relatively more industrial development, capitalist relations in agriculture and better transport and communication facilities, and because the Indian government has a strong centralised administrative system with a very big modern army when compared to pre-revolutionary China. These arguments are wrong. However strong the enemy's military power may be and however weak the people's military power, by basing ourselves on the vast backward countryside-the weakest position of the enemy-and relying on the vast masses of the peasantry, eager for agrarian revolution, and creatively following the flexible strategy and tactics of guerrilla struggle and the protracted people's war,-as a full meal is eaten up mouthful by mouthful, exactly in the same way,-by applying the best part of our army (a force few times stronger than that of the enemy) against different single parts of the enemy forces and following the policy and tactics of sudden attack and annihilation, it is absolutely possible to defeat the enemy forces and achieve victory for the people in single battles. It is thus possible to increase the people's armed forces, attain supremacy over the enemy's forces and defeat the enemy decisively.

While taking into account factors favourable to the enemy, we must, in the course of carrying out the protracted people's war, take many more precautions and we should establish liberated areas by developing guerrilla zones keeping in mind that it is not possible to build liberated areas in quick succession. We will have to mobilise people into class struggle more skilfully and cautiously based on class line and mass line. We must remember that the only positive factor that the enemy has (even that is temporary) is the superior strength of the state machinery, particularly the mercenary armed forces. On the other hand, all other factors are on the side of the revolutionary Party and the people's guerilla army-the principal among these being the just cause of our war, our historic responsibility of solving the land question and the nationality question that are the aspiration of the overwhelming proportion of the country's population, the ever-increasing crisis and contradictions within the ruling classes, and the fact that we are waging not the old type of conventional war but a people's war by mobilizing the people on a massive scale both militarily and politically.

Thus the factors favourable to the enemy cannot change the protracted nature of the Indian revolutionary war which ensues from the principal characteristics of our country, as well as from the lessons drawn from the Chinese and Russian revolutions, ans mainly from the Chinese Revolution.

Not only India, but every country has, in addition to the general characteristics, its own specific characteristics and its own peculiarities. We must also remember that the revolution will suffer losses if we fail to take into account the specific characteristics and peculiarities while formulating the guiding principles of our revolutionary path. However, we have to keep in mind that these specific characteristics and peculiarities cannot alter the general characteristics of revolutionary war or the revolutionary path determined by those characteristics.

INDIAN REVOLUTION IS A PART OF WORLD REVOLUTION

Our document on strategy and tactics clearly asserted that, " *The history of social development throughout the world since the emergence of class divided society is the history of class struggles itself. In the process of social development the revolutionary struggles of the peoples of different countries proceed through different stages and these struggles will have their peculiar characteristics too; but they are always subordinate to the general laws of development of the history. The motion of development of world history through class struggle is towards the very establishment of a society without class and without exploitation, towards socialism and communism. The revolutionary movement of the Indian people is also advancing through different stages; it has got its own peculiarities too. But it remains within the general laws of development towards socialism and communism.*

The world-historic objective of the international proletariat and its vanguard, the Communist Parties of the whole world, is in full conformity with the laws of development of history. The historic goal of the working class of India, as well as of the whole world, is to establish socialism and communism in the world as a whole.

The Great October revolution was nothing but an inevitable outcome of the revolutionary struggles of the international proletariat and the people and the Great Chinese Revolution was the continuation of that process. The Indian Revolution too is an inseparable part of the revolutionary struggles of the international proletariat and the people."

The document further said that *"India, a vast country inhabited by 105 crores of people, rich and abundant in natural wealth, is one of the strongest bases of imperialism. And that is why the progress and success of the new democratic revolution of India, directed against imperialism, comprador big bourgeoisie and feudalism, will not only liberate the Indian people from the ruthless exploitation and oppression of imperialism but will also elevate to a new stage the struggle of the people of the whole world for independence, democracy, socialism and peace. The success of the new democratic revolution of India and the establishment of a people's democratic state in India will play an important role in accelerating the world proletarian revolution and will signify an important historical advancement towards the establishment of a new world free of imperialism, capitalism and the exploitation of man by man."*

In this background, here we have to see Anil's arguments. Anil Biswas wrote that the contradiction between socialist camp and imperialist camp still exists. Our documents says that, *"Another fundamental contradiction-the contradiction between the socialist camp and the imperialist camp-that had characterised the world for almost six decades from the Great October Revolution, went out of existence at present with the restoration of capitalism in the last Socialist Base of the world proletariat, People's Republic of China, after the demise of Com. Mao in 1976.*

However, the struggle between socialism and capitalism will continue to exist through out the era of imperialism and proletarian revolution. Today it is manifested chiefly in the ideological, political and cultural spheres and as a struggle between the two contending classes – the proletariat, representing the forces of socialism, and the bourgeoisie, representing capitalism. The victory of revolutions in one or a few countries and the re-emergence of a socialist camp will once again bring the fourth fundamental contradiction into existence."

The CPI(M) considers the present China, Cuba and North Korea as socialist countries. So, naturally the CPM will find socialism in the post-Mao China under so-called market-socialism. The CPM claims itself a genuine Marxist party, adopting Marxism in the concrete conditions of India. So certainly, it will claim, the contradiction between socialism and imperialism still exists.

If one analyses the class character of the CPM one finds easily that it never represents revolution. Let us see its tall claim. Recently when its ideologue and first ranking leader Sitaram Yechury led a multiparty delegation team to Nepal. *Peoples Democracy* the central official organ of the CPM, reports on Nepal visit in the first week of October 2005 claiming that "The solidarity visit was fruitful" and "as a gesture of reciprocation the Indian delegation invited a delegation of the seven party alliance in Nepal to visit India at their convenience." The leader of Indian delegation further assured that, *"There cannot be any question of India harbouring Nepali Maoists"*.

When the Nepali Maoists are fighting to overthrow the monarchy and have established base areas and a revolutionary army and are controlling more than 85% land of the Himalayan Kingdom and representing absolute majority of the masses the CPM extended all support to the state of Nepal, and Nepali bourgeois parties, and revisionists were welcomed and supported by the CPM. It only glaringly shows that counter revolutionary forces like the CPI(M) never support revolution and always represent the interests of oppressor classes politics. Actually the delegation represents the views of Indian expansionism using the name of Marxism and to serve better the Congress/UPA government the delegation went to Nepal with a big fanfare. One can remember the proverb: birds of the same feather flock together.

Our Stand On Elections

In European countries capitalism and its institutions came into existence through intense fight against feudalism. Whereas in our country feudalism and imperialism co-existed and the parliamentary institutions were formed with the blessings of the British Crown. Before it was Constituent assembly and after 1947 we had a parliament yet the laws and rules have not changed much. An independent and feudal India changed into colonial and semi-feudal India and then into a semi-colonial and semi-feudal

India. When the first General elections took place in 1952, the undivided CPI participated in it. However, participation in the electoral process started during the colonial period itself. At that time of the first general elections the Telangana armed revolution was withdrawn to participate in general elections. Within the Party it was a big debate whether to continue the Telangana struggle or to withdraw. The majority of the CC opted for elections. The Telangana cadres and masses opted for continuing the struggle. At this juncture a delegation went to Russia to meet Com. Stalin and after coming back, they falsely propagated that it was advised by the then international leadership to participate in elections.

It should be remembered that the leaders of the Congress considered that the British rule was necessary and a boon for India. The colonial government supported by the opportune-seekers portrayed a rosy picture of the British sense of justice and fair play'. Under the growing pressure of the freedom movement, in the year 1861, the 'British government decided to install a legislative body in India. The Indian Council Acts, 1861 came into being. Right in the following year emerged India's first legislature. In a state like Bengal, the Legislative Council of Bengal was born in 1862 and within 30 years its membership rose to 20, out of it 7 were elected. The colonial government introduced the process to derail the mounting militant outbursts and diffuse the tensions.

The significant steps that followed were (i) Morley-Minto Reforms (1909) enabling one Indian to be a nominated member of the Governor General's Executive Council, along with an increase in the representatives, to the central and state legislatives. (ii) The Montague Chelmsford Reforms of 1919-20 creating two central houses delivering some limited responsibilities to some Indians along with allowance of some responsibilities to the Indian ministers as regards states, an improved dual-rule system and (iii) the most important, the Government of India Act 1935 — ironically that also constitutes two-thirds of the so-called free Indian's Constitution — bringing about a change for greater participation of the natives in India. The 1935 Act, under the colonial system based on Lord Linlithgow proposals, was initially opposed by the CPI and the Congress but was soon accepted as a step forward, 'marking a non-violent path to freedom and democracy'. Indian business magnets and Gandhian leaders soon jumped to the prospect of ministry-making under this Act. with all its limitations, even "remaining silent about Dominion Status" On the very next day of the RIN revolt, on 18th February 1946, the British Prime Minister Attlee announced the formation of a Cabinet Mission comprising Lord Pethic Lawrence, Sir Strafford Cripps and Mr. A.V. Alexander. The Cabinet Mission declared a plan on the future Indian constitutional set-up prior to the transfer of power. On June 26, 1946, P.G.Griffiths, leader of the European Group in the Indian Central Legislative Assembly, said in a speech: " *India, in the opinion of many, was on the verge of a revolution before the British Cabinet Mission arrived. The Cabinet Mission has at least postponed, if not eliminated, the danger*". On 6th July 1946, the Congress Working Committee approved the Cabinet Mission Plan. Later, on 5th March, 1947, Stafford Cripps said in the British Parliament that there were two alternatives before the British Government either to maintain British direct power in India by a considerable reinforcement of forces or to make a political transfer of power on the 1947 settlement. Cripps was candid to declare that the second option was the best possible one. This alone could ensure British presence through the transfer of power to the Indian reactionary classes, making them junior partners in defending British interests and avoiding an anti-imperialist revolution.

British imperialism studied the gravity of the situation. The February Declaration of 1947 led to its expected end by dishing out the notorious Mountbatten Plan to grant Dominion Status with the partition of India. The February Declaration made it clear that no constitution for India drawn up by a Constituent Assembly be acceptable if not *"in accordance with the proposals"* contained in the Cabinet Mission Plan. Revealingly it further warned that if the Indian Constitution is not approved by Britain, the British government would have to " *consider to whom the powers of the Central Government in British India should be handed over* ".

This notorious Declaration of February 1947 was the significant policy statement for the peaceful transfer of power on 15 August 1947. This makes it abundantly clear what role the Constituent Assembly in India could play, lacking in any power of formulating a Constitution for India. The very Constituent Assembly was also not formed on the basis of universal suffrage of the Indian people in a condition free from imperialist pressures, conditions and manoeuvres. It was not the sovereign will of the people and the preliminary preparations for the formation of the Constituent

Assembly were carried out by the governors of provinces according to the directive of June 16, 1946 from the British Governor General. The legislatures formed under the Government of India Act 1935 had the so-called elected representatives based on property and qualifications along with membership of Princely states. What is notable is that the provincial governors, acting on the strength of the Government of India Act 1935 called the provincial legislatures into session to elect representatives to the Constituent Assembly. The more ridiculous side of this farcical democratic basis of "free India" is that the most important personalities like Jinnah, Nehru, Ambedkar, etc. were not even 'elected' members of such legislatures formed and dictated by the colonial rule

A few words are necessary to shed light on the CPI role vis a vis the above farcical process. Soon after the operation of the Government of India Act 1935 the CPI joined the anti-revolutionary process and could send, in 1937 itself, its leader Bankim Mukherjee to the united Bengal legislature. In 1945, Jyoti Basu, Rup Narayana Roy and Ratan Lal Brahman could become the members of the Bengal Legislative Assembly. And then the CPI had sent Soam Nath Lahiri to the Constituent Assembly. The training in the notorious colonial "democratic" process, in however small way, had ultimately helped in opening the floodgates of parliamentarism in the future. The CPI leadership did not show any interest nor did it make any concrete analysis and plan to rally the people under its leadership (the then undivided CPI) to overthrow the Raj. Due to this wrong understanding and liberal bourgeois outlook, economism and class collaborationist opportunistic outlook of the 2 nd International the party leadership left the path of struggle and shifted to Delhi, to build an open and legal party which continues to participate in elections without any preparations for armed struggle.

This right opportunism of the leadership further consolidated and took a full shape when the international communist movement got divided over two lines for capturing the state power. One was the path of peaceful transformation advocated by the Russian leadership and the other was for armed struggles, may be protracted or insurrection, depending on the concrete condition of a country. The path of peaceful transformation suited to our great leadership's world outlook. So the Danges, Nambudripads, Gopalans, Rajeshwars, Sundaraiahs etc. all jumped to the politics of elections and pledged not to go underground and not to build an underground party, the people's liberation army for ever. So the forces within the Party that always represented the revolutionary outlook revolted against the bourgeois headquarters of the party and the spring thunder over India started pealing from Naxalbari.

Marxism was made into a dogma not as a guide to practice by the revisionists. Marx and Engles fought with these dogmas and enriched the dynamic theory further. Then Lenin further fought the dogmatic understanding of the 2 nd Communist International (CI) and formed the 3rd Communist International to unite the workers of the world in order to win the world socialist revolution.

Way back in 1871 Marx made a devastating criticism of parliamentarism. The parliament as a body is formed once in three or six years to decide which member of the ruling class was to represent and repress the people. Lenin wrote that professional Cabinet Ministers and parliamentarians, the traitors to the proletariat and the *"practical"* socialists of his day had left all criticism of parliamentarism to the considered bourgeois anarchists, and, *"on this wonderfully reasonable ground, they denounce all criticism of parliamentarism as "anarchism"!!"*. Lenin added this in a mood of exposure: *"To decide once every few years which member of the ruling class is to repress and crush the people through parliament – this is the real essence of bourgeois parliamentarism, not only in parliamentary – constitutional monarchies, but also in most democratic republics."*.

Lenin bitterly criticized the revisionist cowards of Russia who opposed the steady revolutionary preparation for insurrection. He wrote: *"One of the most vicious and probably most widespread distortions of Marxism resorted to by the dominant "socialist" parties is the opportunist lie that preparation for insurrection, and generally the treatment of insurrection as an art, is "Blanquism".. Lenin adds that Bernstein also accused Marxism of Blanquism.* Blanquism means the seizure of power by a minority'. It is an utterly revisionist view preached by Indian revisionists that the actual preparation for the revolution will start when the majority of the people switch over to the revolutionary front. The situation for the revolution in Russia was created by the objective condition and mainly by the bold non-parliamentary preparations made by the Bolsheviks. Even in April 1917 Lenin anticipated two possibilities: *"Possibly the peasantry may seize all the land and all the power" and that "....*

It is possible that the peasants will take the advice of the petty-bourgeois party of the Socialist-Revolutionaries, which has yielded to the influence of the bourgeoisie, has adopted a defencist stand, and which advises waiting for a Constituent Assembly..." Comrade Lenin did not bother when the Socialist Revolutionaries charged the Bolsheviks with Blanquism for making the preparations for materialising the upsurge.

Lenin's Bolshevik Party participated in elections in the European context but such participation was not obviously for 'providing relief' from within the exploitative system but to root out the illusion of bourgeois parliaments. Indian social democrats like the CPI, CPI(M) etc. have had enough of experience in parliaments, legislative bodies in India but is there any voice heard to expose parliamentary democracy? Rather we find the reverse i.e. how to add to the dangerous illusion itself. They even dream a false dream of social change by using the Parliament in India. The CPI, the CPI(M), etc. have also joined the ministry in the crisis-ridden semi-feudal, semi-colonial set-up.

When the Socialist Revolutionary Party and the Mensheviks joined the bourgeois ministry Lenin made a devastating criticism. Lenin said "*...Revolutionary democratic phrases to lull the rural simple simons, and bureaucracy and red tape to 'gladden the hearts' of the capitalists this is the essence of the 'honest' coalition*". This is also the actual role of Indian social democratic parties. And if one ransacks the huge body of CPI or CPI(M) literature one hardly finds such Leninist critiques of parliamentary politics. Revisionists cannot change themselves. They only justify participation in the socalled democratic process of semi-colonial semi-feudal India, which actually needs agrarian revolution through protracted people's war.

Hitler attempted to capture power in Bavaria in the early 1920s by a coup when the communists enhanced their strength formidably in parliament and outside parliament. But he resorted to constitutional electoral means plus terror tactics with the full-throated backing and material support of racist sections of the bourgeoisie. Thus pushing aside and traumatizing the communists and other anti-Fascist forces, the Nationalist Socialist Party of the Nazis became the largest party in the Reichstag in 1931 and 1932, and Hitler was installed as chancellor by President Hindenburg in 1933. And then the edifice of the bourgeois parliamentary system exposed the skeletons in the cupboard when electoral competition was finally abolished. Obviously this was an extreme situation of acute crisis of the capitalist system. And it should be stated that Hitler had already Storm Troopers and Mussolini's party in Italy had set up fascist militia.

The present parliamentary system that emerged prominently in England and European countries during the anti-feudal struggles played some role during bourgeois democratic revolutions. Such parliaments at that stage reflected some democratic aspirations of various classes of people.

However, at present the most fundamental task of elections is legitimizing the right of some parties and individuals by any means to serve the existing system. An atmosphere is created by the state and all parliamentary parties in India including the CPI, CPI(M), that the upcoming election must bring in Himalayan responsibilities on the people to exercise their precious right and as if their failure shall push them towards the doom's day. The Indian people have grown habituated to such rhetorics during every election.

Elections, stability of the system, providing a semblance of democracy are all state matters. No class rule behind the state can afford to ignore the very crucial task of winning the support of the people. 'Participatory democracy', Parliamentary democracy', 'Greatest democracy' and all such rhetoric have come up to strengthen the stability of the existing class rule.

The great successful revolutions, the Russian and the Chinese – with socialism existing for decades was turned upside down by the revisionist camps and social fascist governments when capitalist roaders within the party captured party head quarters after the demise of Stalin and Mao. The Khruchves, Dengs who were in the party advocated capitalist ideology and captured the power and strengthened the hands of imperialism and the revisionist parties where genuine communist ideology taught by Marx to Mao took the back seat. In all the countries where capitalist roaders captured power with their revisionist rubbish destroyed the socialist base politically, economically, culturally and in every negative sense possible. In India the CPI(M), CPI, etc. have enjoyed the crumbs of power through electoral victories in not more than three states. The CPI(M) claims that in West Bengal its 29 years stint has been possible for people's struggle. Anil babu where is that people's struggle? Can you deny the actual reality that such a long stay in power in West Bengal has been possible only by his party's purging off even the threat of militant economic movement, let alone the actual movement and by providing the great safety value to the ruling classes as their agents to tide over all crisis the system is facing by misdirecting the people's wrath?

Revisionism in the garb of parliamentarism was also obvious in France and Italy after the rout of fascism in World War II. During the period of the anti-fascist war, the French Communist Party organized a 500 thousand (five lakh) people's armed force at one time liberated Paris. Thorez, the modern revisionist general secretary of France (CPF) returned to France in November 1944 after a period of self-exile abroad and handed the armed forces to the bourgeois classes in exchange for an official covetous post of vice-premiership and participated in the elections. It was the first National Assembly in November 1945 under the auspices of the de Gaulle government. France was, till then, seething with wrath against the new set-up. The CPF did not ask the people to boycott elections, it participated in it and formed the "Left majority" in the Assembly. But the fond hope of the revisionist leaders was shattered within years with the amendments to the electoral law by the ruling French bourgeoisie. The CPF saw a downturn in the elections of 1951 securing 103 seats but lost 79 seats. In the ensuing elections in 1958 with a further revision of the electoral law and the loss of the earlier militant role of the CPF, it secured only 10 seats. In 1968 when the youth movement spread to France the CPF lost its prestige and credibility further by its calculated indifference and evasive role. The CPF, which had a glorious role in the anti-fascist resistance struggle, is now a paralytic parliamentary force in the arena of electoral politics.

Like Thorez in France, Togliatti and his trusted coterie in the Italian Communist Party derailed a great prospect of advancing towards socialism after the fall of the fascist regime of Mussolini during the World War II and after. The Italian Communist Party boasted of a 256,000 strong armed guerrillas and insurgent workers. They liberated Milan, Venice and more than 200 other large and small cities and executed fascist chieftain Mussolini. Like Thorez, Palmiro Togliatti, the general secretary of the Italian Communist Party, returned from abroad after 18 years to Italy and began to preach the dangerous capitulationist line of bringing in socialism "*not by resorting to force and insurrections*" but by going through the process of reforming the social structure. His parliamentarism, like that of Thorez, later received the praise from Khrushchev and other revisionist parliamentary parties like the CPI in our country. Togliatti too destroyed the huge potential of advancing towards socialism after the heroic resistance by the party's armed force and militant workers against the fascist Mussolini regime.

The Chinese Khrushchev Liu Shao-Chi too advocated a similar line after the war of resistance against Japan ended in 1945. He too preached that "*armed struggle in general has come to a stop*" and that "*the main form of struggle in the Chinese revolution has now become peaceful and parliamentary, this is a legal struggle and parliamentary struggle*" and "*all political issues should be solved peacefully*". Had Mao Tsetung and the revolutionary leaders of China not bitterly fought and rejected such capitulationist parliamentary politics China would not be transformed into a People's Democratic Republic on 1 October 1949.

So also the revisionist leadership in the CPI readily accepted such a capitulationist theory in the 1950s and then the CPI(M) too theoretically and practically accepted such parliamentary revisionism adding some catchy left phrases. And now Indian parliamentary revisionism of the CPI or of the CPI(M), etc. has grown into a dangerous enemy of revolution in this country.

In Chile Com. Salvador Allende who came to power by peaceful means tired to change the law and rule of the country was brutally murdered in 1973, where 'our' CPM bosses transformed themselves into lawmakers using the mask of Marxist phraseology to misguide the people. The Indian big bourgeoisie understood the essence of the CPM's 'Marxism', so they put up Buddha as a role model Chief Minister of India. An uncompromising Allede of Chile or Aidit in Indonesia will be murdered and the Buddhas will be praised for taking the peaceful process to power by supporting the Congress without joining the ministry at the Centre or accepting the plum post of the speaker by the CPM's MP Somenath Chatterjee. Mr. Karat like people will try to 'guide' or to be guided by Sonia, the U.S. ambassador David Mullford, the World Bank President, etc.

Social democrats preaching revisionism cleverly try to make it a point that many people in India do still have expectations from the existing parliamentary system to deliver the goods. Well, we do accept that despite frequent elections and all their murky features many people still cast their votes. Several factors lie behind such false consciousness and it is a fact that the reactionary parliament will still continue.

Firstly, the state, the political parties in parliamentary politics and particularly the crude parliamentarism preached by the CPI, CPI(M) like parties are to be held responsible for such misplaced hope.

Secondly, the lack of a strong revolutionary alternative will take some sections of the masses to the polling booths or those sections are coaxed into voting by the leaders of the ruling class parties and even many are forcibly led to the polling booths by the goons of the parliamentary parties.

Thirdly, in the stage of protracted people's war with the existence of two state powers, one the highly powerful Indian state of the ruling classes and the other the burgeoning alternative revolutionary power centres in the villages, expected to gain strength through battles with the former, many people, except the conscious sections, shall not altogether reject the existing state along with its organs at one go, particularly the legal, administrative and parliamentary system.

Fourthly, and what is most important is, in the path of people's war in a country like India with extreme unevenness in the economic, cultural, social and political spheres, it does not lead to a simultaneous explosion of the crores of oppressed people throughout the country, or to a series of revolutionary upsurges within a short span of time in the early stage. In the long-drawn armed struggle, the parliamentary system of the bourgeois-feudal classes, particularly in a country like ours, will continue with all its perverted as well as increasingly refurbished features for many years like caste, communal and other varied factors. Here it is in order to state that even after the great October Revolution in 1917 capturing the main power centres in the cities, the revolution had taken a few more years to crush the remaining bourgeois power centres in the villages.

Here in India, the great worshipper of parliamentarism, the CPI(M), reiterates formulas senselessly learned by rote to kill Marxism by presenting a somewhat soft, state-friendly version of

Marxism in the name of these great Marxist founders. The CPI(M) leaders have got used to resorting to the cunning way of quoting from Lenin's book "Left-wing" Communism – An Infantile Disorder, written against the wrong tactics of some European parties working in a specific context, deciding to skip participation in the bourgeois parliament. Such revisionists never pointed to the wealth of Lenin's Writings concentrating on building a revolutionary party, making preparations for revolutions and also the need for boycotting elections during the revolutionary upsurge. Even in that valuable book meant for correcting the mistake of the West European Marxist parties (i.e. in the insurrection path), comrade Lenin stated the possibility for such participation in parliament *"to expose, dispel and overcome these prejudices..."* ['bourgeois-democratic and parliamentary prejudices" of the peasantry and workers This too was in the context where the seizure of power by armed force was the central task of the revolution and any occasional participation was linked to it. Besides, in the Russian experience the Bolsheviks sometimes participated, sometimes boycotted, utilizing whatever tactic served the central task best — i.e. preparations for the armed uprising. But here, the revisionists while utilizing Lenin's quotes, participate day-in and day-out in all parliamentary/legislative elections without any link to the armed struggle.

Imperialism will try to survive by using all the possible methods and will always try to smash communism because it bears diametrically opposite class ideology, which is engaged in a bitter class war. The two ideologies try to overthrow each other. For the bourgeoisie to stay in power and to strengthen the bourgeoisie dictatorship are the main aim. Imperialists adjusted with feudalism to continue in power and the native agents backstabbed the revolutionary fruits and those agents try to enjoy the fruits of power from inside. Even US imperialism assisted to dismember the USSR and now sanctioned ban on Russia trying to come out from its economic crisis. Here in India too Indian ruling classes absorbed the parliamentary left and put it in front of the people for their survival. This is the lesson for us to learn from the Indian parliamentary experience.

So boycott elections is the way to advance the agrarian revolution. There is no doubt that all forms of struggle come into the category of tactics. But some forms will be outdated in a given conditions. So the elections as a form of struggle are of no use in the Indian condition. The role of the CPM, the CPI and other parties like the RSP, the FB are helping imperialism and feudalism to get a breathing space to face from the outbursts and rebellions of the militant masses.

Simultaneously, it is to be made clear that boycott of elections does not mean abandoning myriad forms of people's struggles. Nor does it mean not intervening in the on-going electoral political process. It only means that instead of supporting this or that party, or putting up candidates, one widely propagates the politics of boycott. Practice has shown there is enormous response to this propaganda, even if people finally go and vote due to lack of a powerful alternative. The level of the campaign depends on our subjective strength in a particular area, and will assume various dimensions. In the areas of intense struggle, with popular support of the people, and its armed detachments, the boycott call would be an action slogan concretely resisting the farcical electoral process through a mass upsurge (like what is often seen in Kashmir). Here, the Old Power will be sought to be smashed and the New Power established. In areas where the movement for alternative people's power has developed and the enemy forces are actively locked in battles with the revolutionary forces, the boycott call will mainly assume the form of an agitation slogan. On the other hand, in other areas where revolutionary movements are at a low ebb or yet to take shape, the election boycott, for a period of time will be a mere propaganda slogan. But in all areas the political focus will be the same.

So, Anil Biswas and co. need elections as a line for their survival and to serve the semi-feudal and semi-colonial system as faithful servants. If the Maoists get engaged in a war to destroy the system itself they will be called anarchists and phrases from Marx to Mao can be put forward to confuse the masses. The CPI(M) will claim that its struggle with the Maoists is an ideological battle, but thousands of forces will be deployed to crush them in West Bengal. Even at the time of last elections to suppress the people 25 army helicopters roamed about West Bengal. Midanapore, Bankura and Purulia district, which carried the message of resistance to the people, witnessed the actual show of the CPM. The people who are living in the guerrilla zones generally boycott elections. The administration, police and the parties in power utilize force to see it that votes are cast. It is another thing whether they will cast votes or oppose.

The CPM and other parliamentary communists and socialists are losing day by day their electoral appeal. The trend of wining the seats has declined all over India except in Bengal for various reasons. Even those so called CPI(ML) parties which have been participating in elections never have recorded expected performance as they claim to use the parliaments as centres for revolutionary politics. Secondly they failed to develop any real tactics to advance the revolution.

Till the final victory the drama of elections will be continued. Without a strong red army and base areas total boycott and stopping the very process of election will not be possible, but the politics of boycott and the reasons for boycott and the debate on the forms of boycott, about the stand taken by Maoists etc. will continue.

Whatever it may be, our strategy and tactics document defined our approach towards elections in the following way, *"In the concrete conditions of semi-colonial, semi-feudal India where bourgeois democratic revolution too has not been completed and uneven social, economic and political conditions exist, the objective conditions permit the proletarian party to initiate and sustain armed struggle in the vast countryside. In the name of preparation for armed struggle, participation in election will only sabotage the revolutionary movement. No peaceful period of preparation for revolution is required in India, unlike in the capitalist countries where the bourgeois democratic revolutions were completed and armed insurrection is the path of revolution."*

CHALLENGES OF REVOLUTIONARY VIOLENCE: THE NAXALITE MOVEMENT IN PERSPECTIVE

In Revolutionary Violence: A Study of the Maoist Movement in India (1977), a book wherein we attempted to analyse the first decade since the outbreak of the Naxalbari uprising, we advanced three propositions on the nature of the movement and the political challenge it posed to the Indian state.

At present when the Naxalite movement has spread over some 165 districts in 13 states of India and the prime minister has described it as the "single biggest internal security challenge" it may be worthwhile to recall the propositions and assess where the movement stands today and whether the Indian state has now a better understanding of the nature of the challenge of the Naxalite movement.

The propositions were:

(i) The Naxalite movement was a pre-organisational movement;

(ii) it practised ideological parallelism to a large extent mechanically applying formulations of the Chinese revolution to contemporary India; and

(iii) the strategypursued by the Naxalites was a narrow construction of revolutionary strategy and was not always one of revolutionary violence.

At the end of the four decades it seems that there have been significant changes in all three respects, yet some elements of each dimension persist. The dispersed fragmented character of the early Naxalite movement has now evolved into three streams of fairly organised formations-CPI(ML)-Liberation, CPI(Maoist) and CPI(ML), each having their own distinct political programmes.

However, a large number of groups still remain outside these three streams in different parts of India and who are engaged in serious debates on policies and strategy of the Indian revolution. Hence the ideological challenge of the movement remains far greater than its organisational strength. The programme of agrarian revolution and anti-imperialist mobilisation has acquired a fresh appeal in the era of globalization and economic reforms seen in the past two decades and also since the US-led "war on terror" that began in 2001.

The neglect of the rural economy has been characterised by starvation conditions and farmer suicides in some parts of the country while farmers everywhere find agriculture less and less remunerative. Tribal people find themselves further distressed by their shrinking access to forest resources and large-scale displacement caused by mega-mining projects. The National Rural Employment Guarantee Act and the Forest People's Land Rights Bill, however welcome they may be, are only small measures that do not address the basic structural issue of peoples rights to land and other productive resources.

On the other hand, the US invasions on Afghanistan and Iraq, and its global counter-terrorism drive is a fine combination that involves a military strategy for world domination along with the economic drive for globalization under the aegis of western capitalism and the monopoly over communication and culture in world scale. The strategic shift in India's foreign and defence policy oriented towards forging a new bond with the US and symbolised by the Indo-US nuclear deal gives substance to the call for an anti-imperialist front.

Thus, the ideological appeal of the Naxalites has a material basis in the Indian environment and that explains their expanding social base. But the pre-organisational character is also evident in the fragmented existence of the movement with enormous hostility seen among the fragments.

Indian Naxalites have learnt many lessons from their experience of the first two decades and can be hardly accused of practising ideological parallelism with the Chinese revolution. None of the groups has any connection with the Communist Party of China whom they denounce as revisionist after it ushered in the reforms policies in 1978. But inspired by Mao Zedong Thought, they are all broadly committed to characterising the revolution as "peoples democratic revolution". On the question of the nature of the Indian bourgeoisie there is much more sophisticated understanding today than merely considering the leading section as a comprador bourgeoisie.

The CPI(Maoist) thinks that the recent phase of capitalist globalization has vindicated this understanding as the Indian bourgeoisie has accepted the role of a subordinate partner of the largely western bourgeoisie. The Liberation group also sees the Indian big bourgeoisie as an equal partner of the west in some cases and also a powerful force that has a global role in third countries. They use the term "dependent bourgeoisie". The emergence of a regional bourgeoisie in India which was reflected in the growth of regional movements is also a subject of much debate among the Naxalites. What is now agreed upon by many of the groups is the decline of the national bourgeoisie, which was once seen as the champion of Indian nationalism.

They point out that the talk of a rising India with an 8 per cent rate of growth, and its software success story, is mainly identified with India's monopoly houses whereas agriculture, small industries and much of the manufacturing sector lag behind miserably.

Similarly, developments in the Indian countryside have been analysed with special attention paid to the rise of the rich peasants in many parts of India though elements of landlordism persist in many areas.

The state-aided rural development programmes and panchayati raj have generated new processes, which have in most places strengthened the hold of the rich peasants.

Economic liberalisation has integrated the rural market with urban commerce, which has produced new structures of power based on land and capital. The most important social phenomenon of the 1990s was the mobilisation of "other backward classes" (OBCs) through the drive for reservation. Not all the Naxalite groups were forthright participants in the proreservation struggle.

In fact the classical Marxist discourse still considers caste focused analysis as a deviation from class analysis. The new differentiation of rural classes and castes has led to a fresh analysis in many quarters. Naxalites in Andhra and Bihar have upheld the rights of dalits and OBCs, but within their political framework of class-based political mobilisation. For example the social basis of Liberation in central Bihar was very much centred on the dalits' struggle for land, wages and dignity. The MCC had a large following among the yadavs as well as the dalits.

As for gender the Naxalite groups are perhaps only just beginning to absorb the significance of multi-pronged struggle against patriarchy. Each group has many women cadres and even soldiers in dalams and has a women's wing as well. However, patriarchal attitudes and practices persist within Naxal organisations and any programme for women's liberation is still not a prominent part of the people's democratic revolution. Thus it has to be stressed that the Naxalites' ideological formulation is still not adequately developed on the issue of class-caste-gender relationship.

On the issue of nationality, however, some of the groups have been very active. They have condemned state repression in the north-east and Jammu and Kashmir and have had solidarity action programmes with them. They aim at transformation of India into a multinational union of equal and participating nationalities by reversing the trend of unequal economic development pursued by a centralising polity backed by military, economic and cultural forces. However, the Maoists of Nepal have formulated a much wider understanding of their people's democratic revolution. One, that is not only anti-feudal, anti-imperialist and republican, but one that has addressed the contradictions of caste, tribe, gender, region and religion with a commitment to sustainable development and towards ensuring a democratic, decentralised and participatory political functioning of a polity that is secular, multilingual and multiethnic.

No wonder that in a short span of time they have achieved widespread support among Nepal's rural masses and have been able to steer the revolutionary process towards a realisation of their objectives. The new ideological understanding reached by the Naxalites of India has also meant a variety of changes in their strategy.

One of the main differences among the groups is over the issue of armed struggle. The CPI(Maoist) is the leading organisation committed to this line. With the successes accomplished by the CPN(Maoist) in Nepal this strategy has acquired a greater credibility among some sections of the movement. But the Liberation group argues that the Maoist line has invited strong repression by the armed forces of the Indian state and has weakened the movement in many areas such as Andhra Pradesh.

Groups such as Janashakti and CPI(ML) seek to combine legal and underground activities. That the liberal-democratic process does provide some political space for pursuing people's causes is a factor that yet to be fully resolved in the Naxalite political discourse.

However, there have been two distinct developments in the Naxalite political programmes over the last decade. One is the taking up of concrete local issues of livelihood in the tribal and other rural areas. Picking of tendu leaves now fetches a greater income for the tribals in central India than earlier. The contractors' exploitation of tribal labour in forest operations has reduced considerably in these areas. The issue of so-called minor forest produce and tribal control over these remains on the top of the Naxalite agenda in these areas both for the movement itself as well as for policy towards the state. Taking up programmes of irrigation in dry land farming, primary education and health programmes in remote areas are no longer considered as economisms, but constructive programmes of revolution. The second is the programme against globalization and the counter terrorism drive. The Naxalites have participated in many united activities such as the Mumbai Resistance in 2004 and the demonstrations organised as part of the visit of US president George W Bush in early 2006. They have opposed the harassment of Islamic youth and taken part in activities to combat Hindu communalism.

It had become clear during the first decade of the Naxalite movement that its preorganisational character was both a weakness and a strength for the movement.

The weakness lay in the fact that it could not be effective in implementing centrally formulated policies, as an organised party could. Units in different parts of the country did not support each another in the face of state repression. The movement could not expand systematically to different parts of the country. At the same time, the preorganisational character had an advantage.

The movement could not be destroyed by the state, which an organised party was vulnerable to. The Naxalite movement remained basically an ideological movement challenging the prevailing system and since the ideology had a certain objective basis in the social contradictions in India, it appealed to the oppressed sections of the society and those who sympathised with them. The many operations for suppressing them as also the counter-offensives launched by the state in the ideological sphere were unable to neutralise the

Naxalite ideology because the socio-political crisis of the country continued. So even without growing into a unified organised movement the Naxalite movement remained active and survived recurring onslaughts from the state.

Since the founding of the CPI(ML) in 1969 the movement has seen two phases of consolidation of the movement's groups. During the Emergency as many as 27 ML groups were banned and an estimated 40,000 persons were put behind bars in all parts of the country indicating the state of fragmentation and also the spread of the movement.

The post-Emergency period saw one phase of party-building among Naxalites whereas the post-reform years in the 1990s heralded another course of consolidation. This is not to suggest that the response to the Emergency and the economic reforms were the main reasons for the unification attempts. But the context may have accelerated the trend. Three streams of Naxalites emerged in the post-1977 years when many Naxalite prisoners were released either by the Janata government or acquitted by the courts. One was the CPI(ML)-Liberation led by S N Sinha with its stronghold in central Bihar. This group repudiated Charu Mazumdar's strategy of squad action and focused on mass organisation.

It expanded its support base in the 1980s and early 1990s under the leadership of Vinod Mishra. It floated the Indian People's Front for united political work but this was later dissolved and it started directly working under the party banner.

They decided to participate in electoral politics and slowly built up an all-India organisation of the party. Their mass organisations have an all-India character and have pockets of influence in different parts of the country: the trade unions, in the All India Central Council of Trade Unions (AICCTU), the All India Agriculture Labour Association (AIALA), the All India Kisan Sanghars Samiti (AIKSS), the All India Students Association (which has a strong base in JNU) as well as the All India Progressive Women's Association (AIPWA).

They have won seats in the Bihar legislative assembly and have played an important role in Bihar politics and later, even in Jharkhand politics as well. They have occasionally had a member elected to Parliament as well. Vinod Mishra's line of pursuing militant mass politics of both the parliamentary and extra-parliamentary kind with CPI(ML) Liberation as an open political party has been continued by his successors who include Dipankar Bhattacharya as the general secretary.

The second stream in the Naxalite movement that continued Charu Mazumdar's politics of rejecting parliamentary politics crystallised with the formation of the CPI(ML) People's War Group (widely referred to as PWG) in April 1980 in Andhra Pradesh. This formation is now known as the CPI(Maoist), which is the largest and the most powerful of the Naxalite groups in India. Starting as a movement based in Telangana, the PWG spread its operations in Bihar when the Party Unity group merged with it in 1996.

Even more significant was the merger of the Maoist Communist Centre (MCC) with it in September 2004. As an underground party pursuing the strategy of armed struggle, it has a wide support base among the peasants and tribals in many states, especially in several regions of Andhra Pradesh, Chhattisgarh, Bihar and Jharkhand. In fact when the union home ministry talks of 76 districts in nine states that are badly affected by Naxalism in its annual report of 2005-06 it mainly refers to the activities of the CPI(Maoist).

It has a set of regional and zonal committees with secretaries and members. In 2004, its armed wing merged with that of the MCC, leading to the formation of the People's Liberation Guerrilla Army (PLGA), which according to government sources has about 3,500 trained fighters.

In earlier years the Naxalites used local weapons to target landlords, now they use sophisticated guns such as AK-47, rocket launchers, grenades and land mines to wage a full-scale battles with armed police, and para-military forces such as the CRPF and the IRB. After the founder of PWG, Kondapalli Sitharamayya developed differences with his colleagues and was ousted, the party has functioned under a collective leadership with Ganapathy as general secretary.

The party responded to mediations by the Committee of Concerned Citizens and participated in peace talks with the Andhra Pradesh government in October 2004. But the police operations against the Maoists and the latter's counter-attacks thereafter have made a second round of peace talks difficult. The peace talks represented a historic moment with the government acknowledging the role of the PWG as a powerful revolutionary force working for the rights of the oppressed and the latter acknowledging the political spaces, which the Indian polity provided.

The Indian state for its part has now opted for an all-out coercive response. The party now seems to have shifted its focus of activities from north Telangana to Chhattisgarh and Jharkhand. It has survived many onslaughts from the state though several of its top leaders have been killed in police encounters in different states. The latest state to ban the CPI(Maoist) and its front organisations was Orissa on June 9.

Thus the PWG, Party Unity and MCC that formed into the CPI(Maoist) and their militant strategy represented a major organisational development of the Naxalite movement in India. The third stream which differs from both these formations and still has failed to get all the remaining groups united within it is currently symbolised by the new CPI(ML) with Kanu Sanyal, the legendary hero of Naxalabari, as its general secretary. Sanyal had a group with him under the name Communist Organisation of India (ML) with which the CPI(ML) Unity Initiative, the Unity Centre and some groups of Andhra Pradesh, Maharashtra and Kerala merged. With the coming into it of a section of the CPI(ML) Janashakti, the party based on the line of thinking developed by Nagi Reddy and Chandra Pulla Reddy, it further acquired a degree of strength.

The Andhra Pradesh mass organisations, Raitu Coolie Sangham (Peasant Labour Organisation; the CPI(Maoist) also has one with the same name which has been banned), AP Federation of Trade Unions, the once powerful student group People's Democratic Students' Union (PDSU) and the Sthree Vimukti Sanghatana (Women's Liberation Organisation) belong to this formation along with their news organ Class Struggle. This group takes part in elections. CPI(ML) Janashakti however remains as a separate organisation mostly active in Andhra Pradesh carrying out both open and underground activities.

Similarly the CPI(ML) New Democracy-known as such by the title of its journal-is one of the groups carrying forward the Chandra Pulla Reddy perspective. It has continued to combine underground mobilisation with open political programmes. Known as CPI(ML) Prajapantha in Andhra Pradesh, it has had an MLA in the Andhra Pradesh state assembly as well as one in the Bihar assembly. Its mass organisations, Indian Federation of Trade Unions (IFTU) and All India Kisan Mazdoor Sabha (AIKMS), have been constantly active on national and regional issues. Besides its main base in AP, it has maintained pockets of influence in Delhi, Punjab, Orissa and Jharkhand. In addition to these there are still many Naxalite groups under various names.

The organisational consolidation of the Naxalites into three major formations in the last decade represents a qualitative development in the character of the movement in the sense that it is approach to parliamentary politics and the pursuit of armed struggle that has divided them into three formations. They cannot be described as personality-based formations despite the presence of Kanu Sanyal.

The cult of Charu Mazumdar which sprang up parallel to the cult of Mao Zedong during the high tide of the Cultural Revolution has no bearings in the contemporary state of the Naxalite movement. Each formation has gone through tortuous struggles in their own areas, suffered setbacks and lost the lives of many of its activists and has come to the present stage.

It should also be noted that in Bihar, Chhattisgarh, Jharkhand and Andhra Pradesh, all three parties, the Maoists, Liberation and the ML, have a significant presence. The talk of the "red corridor" that the media talks, which stretches from the border of Nepal through Bihar, Jharkhand, Chhattisgarh, Orissa, Andhra Pradesh and all the way to Karnataka is not much of a reality.

There are many gaps and variations in the degree of influence even though building a "compact revolutionary zone" is an objective of the Naxalites. Yet some elements of pre-organisational character persist. First, there are serious difficulties in conducting organisational activity as an underground party that is banned by the government and one that is under constant attack by the paramilitary forces.

Therefore often we see some actions by local squads (dalams), which have later been regretted by the Maoist central leadership. The burning down of a railway coach full of passengers near Warrangal some years ago or the land-mining explosion in Chhattisgarh killing a busload of adivasis last April are some examples. Yet members of each group remain united solidly on the basis of their ideological commitment to the programme of the party. At the same time, the differences among the three streams of Naxalites often make them fight one another, which reflects the pre-organisational weakness of the movement.

Activists of Liberation and CPI(Maoist) have threatened and even killed the opponent party's cadres in Jharkhand and elsewhere. But there are occasional unity programmes as well.

For example, the Maoists and Janashakti together came forward for peace talks in 2004 in Hyderabad. Above all the support that the Naxalites enjoy in some areas is basically for their ideological programme on the ground rather than organisational mobilisation under the party banner.

Thus when the state policy treats the Naxalites as an organised movement it fails to take into account the specificity of each group.

Banning an organisation, arresting or killing some cadres and leaders or mobilising one group of people to fight a group of Naxalites or using propaganda to vilify the Naxalite as "terrorists" misses the history of the last 40 years.

The experience shows that these acts of the state have not succeeded in destroying the movement because it is essentially an ideological force rooted in the objective conditions in India.

In the present juncture a new proposition seems to stand out: While the state failed to recognise the character of revolutionary violence, the Naxalites failed to abide by the norms of revolutionary violence. In May 2004 the common minimum programme of the United Progressive Alliance while expressing concern over the growth of extremist violence had said that "this is not merely a law and order problem, but a deeper socio-economic issue which will be addressed more meaningfully than has been the case so far. Fake encounters will not be permitted".

Such expressions have been heard over and over again since 1969 when Y B Chavan as home minister took the same view. But not only fake encounters have continued under the UPA rule, there have been new elements of coercive counter-insurgency adopted from the US and Israeli outlook and also the experiences learnt from counter-terrorism operations in Punjab under K P S Gill. Emphasis on intelligence-based counterstrategy with superior weapons and operational initiatives constitute some of these imported ideas.

The coordination centre in the union home ministry, the joint task force and the meeting of the chief ministers of the affected states are now being conducted with enhanced funding and equipment to accommodate this perspective. It should be pointed out that the use of modern technology is not the monopoly of the rulers. They are also available to the rebels. An even more serious development in the state's strategy is its new reliance on mobilising a section of the local people to fight the Naxalites. The 'Salwa Judum' in Chhattisgarh is a vicious example of escalatory violence that carries the "greyhound" approach – the anti-Naxalite formation in Andhra Pradesh to new heights. Groups of adivasis are evicted from their villages, given training in arms and used to confront other adivasis in the name of fighting Naxalites. Such measures initiated by the state intensifies violence in society making killing a norm and with rewards for such killing routinely handed out by the state. A lesson should be learnt from the failure of the Ranvir Sena and many other landlord armies in Bihar to stem the rise of the Naxalites in the last two decades. All evidence points to the fact that the Indian state has failed to understand the nature of revolutionary violence. Why is it that hundreds of men and women have taken part in armed attacks on police stations, jails and even on paramilitary forces?

How is it that they have been able to move around in a large number of states, depending on the support of adivasis and peasants? To treat them only as forces of violence and to brand them as terrorists has not helped stem their growth. The violent confrontation between the Naxalites and the Indian state has affected the political fabric of the entire society. The state agencies have given up all procedures under the rule of law on the pretext that forces of violence do not deserve it. That is exactly the ideology of counter-terrorism that George W Bush propounds.

The leaders of state assume that they can eliminate the influence of this ideology by liquidating the leaders, cadres and sympathisers of the movement. The experience of the 40 years proves otherwise. Questions can be raised as to whether the Naxalites have abided by the norms of revolutionary violence. Revolutionary violence, by definition is a response to ruling class or state violence.

It is a part of a wider strategy of people's democratic revolution that has many political, economic and cultural programmes of action. It is resorted to when other action programmes fail to achieve their goals. It is practised by only those who uphold the value of the human being and are dedicated to liberating the human being from all bondages so that humans can live in material, political and cultural conditions of peace, freedom and equality.

In other words, it visualises the building of a society without violence because violence is violation of the human being, physically or mentally. But the Naxalites have sometimes resorted to acts of violence either deliberately or in course of a chain of action that do not fulfil these criteria.

REVOLUTION BETRAYED: THE BETRAYAL OF THE CPI AND CPIM

In course of world revolutionary movements two revolutionary paths emerged. One is insurgency waged by Com. Lenin in Russia and another the Protracted People's War led by com. Mao in China. Both the revolutionary movements fought with the enemy to overthrow the then existing systems and establish proletarian dictatorship or people's democratic rule. Both the Russian revolution and the Chinese revolution in the first and second quarter of the 20 century respectively and the later revolutions in Europe, Cuba, Vietnam, Cambodia and other unsuccessful armed struggles of Asia, Africa and Latin America and currently ongoing revolutionary struggles of various countries are all armed revolutions. In the protracted people's war the red army was built from the beginning whereas in case of insurgency in Russia and Europe in Russia and it was first the workers to be armed to form the red army and the revolution spread from the city to the village. To seize power, the party, army and the people (the United Front) were always a must. This was the history of revolution everywhere.

When the leadership of a party with communist signboard carries an outlook of liberal bourgeoisie since its birth how will it think over seizing the state power? At the time of the Russian Revolution Lenin fought with the right opportunistic line of the Mensheviks to advance the Russian revolution. Lenin established the path of the revolution, organized the party and led the movement. In the mid-July of 1917 after completing the February Revolution when preparations were going on to seize the power, Lenin categorically told in his article ' *on slogan*' regarding the question of the political power in this way: *"And the political substance is that power can no longer be taken peacefully. It can be obtained only by winning a decisive struggle against those actually in power at the moment, namely, the military gang, the Cavaignacs, who are relying for support on the reactionary troops brought to Petrograd and on the Cadets and monarchists."* Further he added, *"We said that the fundamental issue of revolution is the issue of power. We must add that it is revolutions that show us at every step how the question of where actual power lies is obscured, and reveal the divergence between formal and real power. That is one of the chief characteristics of every revolutionary period."*

In his brilliant investigation of peasant movement in Hunan, Mao categorically said, *"The most violent revolts and the most serious disorders have invariably occurred in places where the local tyrants, evil gentry and lawless landlords perpetrated the worst outrages. "* He further said that *"A revolution is an insurrection, an act of violence by which one class overthrows another. A rural revolution is a revolution by which the peasantry overthrows the power of the feudal landlord class. Without using the greatest force, the peasants cannot possibly overthrow the deep-rooted authority of the landlords which has lasted for thousands of years."* This outlook was not at all grasped and practiced by the undivided CPI then how come we imagine the CPI, the CPI(M) will accept the ongoing revolutionary war? But the history of revisionism took new turns when the CPSU(B) turned into a revisionist party and brought forth the theory of peaceful transformation of political power. This rubbish was condemned by various communist parties of the world particularly the CPC under Mao's leadership, which vigorously fought with the CPSU(B) and opposed the line brought forth by it. A worldwide polarization happened and a new camp, which was called a revisionist camp, emerged.

Those who followed the peaceful process to capture power were identified as revisionists and those who practiced and supported armed revolution were known as revolutionaries. Then onwards a bitter struggle between the paths of revolution vs. counter-revolution has been going on. It will continue in future also because revisionism in course of its development has been playing the direct role of counter-revolution.

In our country the undivided CPI's leadership (majority in the CC) never supported the armed revolution. Before 1947 the then CPI always supported the Congress and its leadership and tried to trace out progressive elements within the Congress. It led to avoid armed revolution, and the question of seizure of political power by overthrowing British imperialism was not on the agenda of the party. When the Telangana armed revolution continued against the Indian Army, the then majority CC leadership of the CPI opposed and then withdrew it. Later they never thought over revolution on this or that pretext.

Peaceful transformation theory of revisionist Khruschev came on the agenda in the 20 Congress of the CPSU(B). At the time of anti-imperialist struggle itself the CPI joined the constituent Assembly and tried its level best to basically confine itself to the peaceful process and Gandhian forms against the British. Many a form of struggles emerged and the workers, peasants, and petty bourgeoisie fought on partial issues under the leadership of the CPI. But the party leadership never put forward an agenda for the tearing apart the Union Jack under its direct leadership. Why? Anil Biswas is now arguing against guerilla war and talking much on the Indian conditions but he avoided to tell about the situation between 1925 and 37 between 1940 and 45 period and other periods when different rebellious mass movements emerged on the scene. The CPI lower level activists led even some and others were spontaneous movements due to the maturity of the conditions against the British Raj. So many movements started peacefully but turned violent, which were inevitable due to the situation of that particular period.

When we received letters of 3 fraternal parties an agenda was prepared for militant struggle but it was not carried out by the party because the leadership never showed such a consciousness to seize the power under the leadership of proletariat. When the party was banned, when the Telangana armed revolution was practically led by the Telengana comrades and on a number of occasions there emerged scope, possibility, and conditions to organize agrarian revolution and the people actively participated in all the struggles. But a revolutionary party a completely new party which can lead the revolution and the people for it was absent and the CPI was unwilling to play its proper role. The central committee of the CPI adopted the line of right opportunism, which never accepted armed revolution.

This was the understanding of the undivided communist party. According to the teaching of Com. Stalin, correct political line is necessary to advance the revolution in any country. After that cadres will be motivated to implement the line that will be advanced properly. But in our country cadres sacrificed every thing but the Central leadership failed to put proper line before the cadres and the people. As a whole the CC or the majority in the CC never prepared itself as a proletariat class leader to learn which Lenin advised to Russian Communists and how he transformed the party into a revolutionary party fighting economism practiced in the name of Marxism, wrong theories of the 2 International, the Mensheviks and the Narodniks. Lenin prepared the CPSU(B) as a true revolutionary party, which ultimately led the Russian revolution to success and for the first time a soviet power was built and it existed on the earth and influenced the entire people of the globe. We learn from the CPSU(B) history the following.

"As to the structure and composition of the Party itself, Lenin considered that it should consist of two parts: a) a close circle of regular cadres of leading Party workers, chiefly professional revolutionaries, that is, Party workers free from all occupation except Party work and possessing the necessary minimum of theoretical knowledge, political experience, organizational practice and the art of combating the tsarist police and of eluding them; and b) a broad network of local Party organizations and a large number of Party member enjoying the sympathy and support of hundreds of thousands of working people.

We did not prepare this type of Leninist party in India at the time of anti-feudal and anti British Raj struggle. Anil Biswas and his party never accept the negative role of the leadership who were never eager like true revolutionaries for the seizure of power through armed revolution. Now in his article Anil Biswas claims that Indian soil and the people will never opt for guerrilla war and armed struggle. To say this means he is totally negating the history witnessed during the colonial period. Anil actually echoes the pet anti-communist theory that India being a spiritual land can not endorse any violent communist revolution! So, we understand that a proletarian party should forget class struggle, the question of overthrowing feudalism and capitalism as such thought is itself a wrong concept. Well said! Anil Biswas Babu!!...Long live the CPM and its leadership to serve the oppressor class without preparing the mass for revolution and for the people's democracy and then proletarian dictatorship. Political swindlers like Anil, Jyoti, Sundaraya and their ilk, however, never forget to claim inheritance to the Telengana peasant revolt, the peasant upsurge in Punnapra Vyalar, etc. which the majority CPI leadership – many of whom later joined the CPI(M) – simply betrayed. Why then Mr. Anil Biswas simply rejects any possibility of implementing the Chinese Path of guerrilla war even during the colonial period and why his party leaders try to bask in the reflected glory of the Chinese path adopted by the Telengana heroes? This is most dirty type of modern revisionism.

After the right opportunist role of the CPI, Indian masses witnessed 'left' opportunism for a brief period. Left sectarianism of Ranadhive is well known to the Indian masses. Sundaraiah, Basvapunnaiah, Rajeshwar Rao who once spoke of armed revolution took a 'U' turn and later remained confined to the parliamentary pigsty for ever. The leaders like Jyoti Basu, Ranadive etc. speak of Telangana, Anil Biswas borrows a few sentences from Lenin and Mao but put iron heel on genuine Maoist movement. These leaders never play the vanguard role because they practice revisionism and now prove themselves as counter revolutionaries.

In our country the CPM is not at all developing even the trade union consciousness, not to speak of revolutionary consciousness. Rather it has developed mafia consciousness and dog fights in the party. Politics and ideology were never in command because they lost their credibility, as communist, then how is it possible for the CPM to practise any thing for the oppressed classes. But without writing all this, they cannot pose themselves as Marxists. They are practising social fascist ideology. Lenin said that who talks for socialism and practise revisionism will be social fascists.

The CPM accepted the Marxism of the 2 International and it preferred to act as followers and agents of the Congress in the guise of Communists. Its leaders have always (except some CCMs at the time of the Telangana struggle and later) followed right opportunist line and never showed proletariat class-consciousness before and after 1947 to achieve the task of the proletariat dictatorship. The Telangana resistance was praised by all revolutionaries and it symbolized as a movement which sustained and was strengthened against the Nizam and later against the 'Socialist' Nehru. It is an irony who had openly or covertly opposed the Telengana peasant revolt later after its infamous withdrawal became its verbal supporters.

Jyoti Basu wrote in his article titled, 'The Communists and the Indian Freedom Struggle' that, *"In 1946 the communists inspired Punnapra-Vayalar uprising in Travancore. Almost at the same time the peasantry in Telangana rallied under the red flag to rise up against feudal exploitation. This revolt, lasting for five years between 1946 and Oct. 1951, was the largest guerrilla peasant uprising in modern India. This revolt took away at least 4000 peasant lives. Such peasant uprisings for a better social order will continue to inspire us in building a society devoid of exploitation of man by man"*

Jyoti Basu who was the CM of the West Bengal state for more than two decades never could think over armed uprising. Not only this he was the person who was instrumental in suppressing the great Naxalbari uprising which once again showed the path of Telangana to the Indian masses who joined in the struggle as a part of world socialist revolution. Jyoti Basu will praise Telangana, suppress Naxalbari to serve comprador bourgeoisie and big landlords, what can be more perfidious than his double speak?

Ranadive wrote another article titled, 'The role played by communists in the freedom struggle of India" in which he wrote *"It is obvious that the C.P. did not play a decisive role in the freedom struggle, otherwise the Indian people would not have been facing the miserable conditions they are facing today, with poverty and unemployment increasing with the spectacle of a nation at discord, victims of every divisive force. The leadership of the freedom struggle remained firmly in the hands of the bourgeois leadership of the Indian national Congress. Even when mass struggles sometimes went beyond, the limits set by the congress, when people turned to armed resistance, the consciousness of the masses accepting the leadership did not change and therefore the struggle could not spread all over India."* (Stress is ours)

Here one can see the way of approach and the assessment of the 'proletariat' party's leadership. The party veteran leader expressed that

1) Leadership was in the hands of bourgeoisie
2) Sometime People turned to armed resistance
3) the consciousness of the masses was that they were accepting the leadership of the Congress,

But he never said that

- the CPI never thought of emerging as an alternative to the Congress as a genuine revolutionary party.
- The CPI itself was serving and accepting the Congress leadership,
- The Communist Party had no agenda nor any role to properly lead the people for armed resistance and develop the people's liberation army (PLA).

Even our eyes were not opened when conditions matured so beautifully that an armed uprising was inevitable. This was the pathetic condition, class collaboration of the then central committee. After '47 also the CC never thought over organizing, moulding and driving the party for underground work to seize the political power. The blame was thrown on the masses always but the so-called vanguard leadership never expressed apology nor did it offer any self-criticism for its mistakes and for the collaborationist theories and anti-revolutionary role. The CPI and the CPI(M) were blaming the people that mass consciousness did not develop to participate in the revolution. Revisionists have never felt it as their failure not to develop people's consciousness. Was it possible for us to overthrow the British Raj and to change the colonial and semi-feudal system without concrete programme guided by Marxist Leninist ideology? It is the great duty of the Communists always to play the leading role to mould the mass opinion towards struggle.

So, our party, CPI(Maoist) programme correctly said that "*The victory of Great October Revolution of 1917 in Russia, under the leadership of comrade Lenin, the Marxist-Leninist ideology was disseminated in our country. Under the influence of this ideology, and as a result of heroic and militant struggles waged against British imperialism by the proletariat, the CPI was born in 1925. But despite innumerable opportunities, the leadership of the proletariat and its party could not establish itself in the liberation movement.*

The leadership of the Communist Party continuously refused to recognise the real character of the Gandhian leadership. Thereby it failed to demarcate itself and fight against it along with taking the correct revolutionary path and revolutionary initiative. Rather, they continued to trail behind the Gandhian leadership and turned their back in linking the universal truth of Marxism-Leninism with the concrete practice of the Indian revolution. This leadership also failed to integrate itself with the brave Indian people, particularly the peasantry. T hey also refused to learn and follow the triumphantly advancing Chinese revolution under the leadership of comrade Mao Tse-Tung and the Chinese communist Party. They did not take the path of armed struggle for the seizure of political power in the national liberation movement. Even though the objective revolutionary situation was extremely favourable in India at the time, yet the opportunistic leadership of the communist party always turned their back to take the correct path of protracted people's war and the armed national liberation war. Actually the leadership of the Communist Party helped in derailing the anti-imperialist people's militant movement and dragged the revolutionary masses behind the Gandhian leadership through forming an opportunistic alliance with it. Most of all, this leadership betrayed the great Telangana armed revolt of the peasantry and entrenched itself in the mire of parliamentarism and revisionism in the deceptive name of using parliament " (*Party Programme,* CPI(Maoist) pp. 8-9)

Anil Biswas wrote in his article that, *we the Maoists are totally negating the history of Indian Communist movement*. Actually we are making both positive and negative assessments dialectically without having any bias or prejudice against history. We are also a part and parcel of the past history, and representing its positive aspects but never hesitate to never disown the negative ones.

So our first party congress was considered as a continuation of the VII Congress, after which we disassociated ourselves from the CPM. We uphold the positive aspects as contained in our Programme in the following words: "*...brave revolutionary ranks of the Communist Party stood by the side of the fighting people and led many revolutionary struggles. They laid down their valuable lives to achieve the lofty aim of completing the Indian revolution as a part of the world proletarian revolution.*"

Actually people were always involved in struggles and a number of armed revolts were witnessed against imperialism and feudalism from the Santhal rebellion of 1854-56 to the culmination of the First War of Independence of 1857, which were the beginnings of Indian Democratic Revolution. But the undivided CPI since 1920s had no clear revolutionary programme, strategy, tactics and practice to be placed before the Indian Masses.

So we have to understand that most Indian 'Communist' leaders were grown with liberal bourgeoisies outlook, not with a genuine Marxist-Leninist ideology, politics and work methods, style to advance the Indian revolution. This basic truth is not acceptable to Anil Biswas like people waving red flags to crush a red revolution in India. History shall not forgive them.

MOTIVE FORCES OF THE INDIAN REVOLUTION

Proletariat

The proletariat is a class that is dispossessed of all means of production and is compelled to sell its labour power to the capitalist owners of the means of production. It is the most concentrated class in present-day Indian society and has a heroic history of revolutionary class struggle including anti-imperialist struggle. The strength of the Indian proletariat in the organised sectors, both in public and private sectors, is about 2.6 crores. The number of wage earners working in small-scale industries, construction work and as contract and casual labour comes to about four crores. Together their number is roughly around seven crores. The industrial proletariat of India has all the main characteristics that the proletariat all over the world has, such as being associated with, and concentrated in the developed capitalist economic system, having organisational discipline, lacking means of production etc., Indian proletariat is being subjected to oppression by imperialists, comprador bureaucratic bourgeoisie and big landlord classes. As the majority of the Indian proletariat comes from poor peasant classes, they have natural bonds with the peasant population. The proletariat and peasant classes have strong mutual influences and relations.

Apart from the industrial proletariat, there is also a sizeable rural proletariat. These farm workers mainly work in large plantations and farms like coffee, tea, cocoa, coconut, mango, rubber, areca nut, sugar, fruit and vegetables. They have no means of production of their own and live by selling their labour power to the big pro-capitalist landlords, the comprador bourgeoisie and the imperialists who own plantations.

There is also a small section in the working class, comprising of trade union bureaucrats who get various bribes from the employers. This section is the labour lieutenants of capital and represents the bourgeois ideology within the working class. Though this section, in general opposes the working class struggles, in the period of crisis, some of them may change their role and take part in the working class movements. The basic motive force in the New Democratic Revolution is the proletariat. But it cannot win victory by solely depending on its own strength. For achieving victory, this class has to give its leadership to all classes, especially the peasantry, and other strata of people that can participate in the revolution. The proletariat plays the role of leadership in the revolution.

Landless and poor peasants

Generally the landless peasants, including the agricultural labourers (rural proletariat), do not have land and agricultural tools of their own. They live by either totally or mainly selling their labour power. Some among the poor peasants own lands nominally or rent in small plots of land. Similarly some have meager agricultural tools. In addition to paying land rent and interest, they sell their own labour power and hence they are exploited in all these forms. They constitute 65-70% of the rural population. Of all classes that are existing in Indian society, the poor and landless peasants are the basic motive forces and are the firmest ally of the proletariat.

The Semi-Proletariat

The major component of the semi-proletariat is the huge mass of poor peasants. Those who own some simple implements like the small handicraftsmen, carpenters, masons, mechanics and the like also form part of the semi-proletariat. There are also those who earn their living working as hawkers, hamalis, rickshaw pullers, autorickshaw drivers, temporary rural construction workers, house servants and engaged in many other similar jobs, earning daily wages. Fishermen also form part of semi-proletariat. They are continuously becoming part of the proletariat.

Those semi-proletarians are an important motive force of the New Democratic Revolution.

Middle Peasant

Most of the middle peasants have their own lands. Some others take land on lease in addition to theirs. Generally they own sufficient agricultural tools. The entire income of the middle peasant, or most of it, is derived from their own labour. Generally the middle peasant does not exploit others and also does not sell their labour power and is subjected to exploitation by feudalism, imperialism and comprador bureaucratic capitalism. Some middle peasants exploit to a small extent but it is not their main income. Some of them (well-to-do middle peasants) have surplus land and hire labour occasionally. Some even lend small sums of money at interest.

Oppressed by feudalism, imperialism and comprador bureaucrat capitalism, the middle peasant will take an active role in the anti-feudal as well as anti-imperialist struggles. Hence, the middle class peasantry as a whole is a reliable ally of the proletariat. The positive or negative attitude of the middle peasants is one of the factors determining victory or defeat in the revolution, and this is especially true after the agrarian revolution when they become the majority of the rural population. They are important motive forces in the revolution. The middle peasantry can be considered as rural petty-bourgeoisie. They constitute roughly 20-25% of the rural population.

Rich Peasant

Rich peasants constitute 10-15% of the rural population. They possess considerable amounts of land. Some own only part of their land and lease in the remainder. Some others have no land of their own and lease in all their lands. The holding operated by them is a surplus-producing one. They generally own better instruments of production. They generally engage in labour themselves and in this sense form part of the peasantry but at the same time they always rely on exploitation for the part or even the major of their income. In general if the income of a peasant through exploitation is more than 50%, they should be classified as rich peasants. Though they adopt more or less all the existing forms of semi-feudal exploitation, their main form of exploitation is by hiring agricultural labour. They may rent out their land, may lend money or engage in trade, commerce, small business, etc. The procapitalist rich peasants use modern technology, engage in intensive cultivation, lease in land to expand scale of production and produce for the market.

The growth of capitalist relations in agriculture in some pockets and the increasing reliance of the rich peasants on the market for purchasing agricultural inputs as well as for selling the produce, is bringing them into increasing conflict with imperialism and the comprador big bourgeoisie who control the market and hence they are being drawn more and more into the anti-imperialist struggles of the peasant masses. But, by virtue of their class status, they tend to compromise in face of mounting state repression. Generally they remain neutral in the agrarian revolutionary struggle. As a class, they can be considered as vacillating allies of the revolution. A section of rich peasantry comes with us, another section remains neutral and a small section joins the enemies.

Petty Bourgeoisie

The petty-bourgeoisie includes the handicraftsmen i.e., those engaged in small scale production, small traders, the lower levels of intellectuals such as students, primary and secondary school teachers, college lecturers, office clerks, non-gazetted officials, engineers, doctors, lawyers, and those employed in various other professions who have largely middle-class incomes that are derived mainly from their own manual or mental labour.

The petty-bourgeois class consists of three sections though they broadly belong to the same economic strata. The first section consists of the relatively better-off i.e., those whose yearly earnings allow them to have some surplus over and above their consumption needs; the second section consists of those who in the main are economically self-supporting; and third section consists of those whose standards of living are continually declining and who find it difficult to make both ends meet.

The first section always aspires to go up the social ladder, is closer to the national bourgeoisie, has a lot of faith on liberal bourgeois propaganda and is suspicious of the revolution. This section which is a minority among the petty bourgeoisie constitutes its right wing.

The second section which is very numerous and makes up more than one-half of the Indian petty-bourgeoisie, never opposes the revolution but only hesitates to join it as it harbours doubts regarding the ultimate victory of the revolution.

The third section, equally numerous, whose living standards are fast declining, come out openly in support of the revolution and play an active role. Although these three sections differ in their attitude to the revolution in normal times, in times of war and acute crisis when the revolutionary movement is advancing towards victory, the entire petty-bourgeoisie class including even the right wing, sails with the revolutionary tide. This is because of its very class position in society i.e., its position as a class oppressed by feudalism, imperialism and comprador bureaucrat capitalism with more and more of its members facing social insecurity and becoming pauperised and being driven to the ranks of the proletariat or the unemployed with the deepening of the economic crisis. Hence as a class, this section of the petty bourgeoisie constitutes one of the motive forces of revolution and is a reliable ally of the proletariat.

Various sections of the petty-Bourgeoisie

(i) Intellectuals and Students: These do not constitute as a separate class or stratum in the society. Seen from the point of view of their family, living conditions and their political outlook, the majority among them may be treated as petty-bourgeoisie. Their number in India has been considerably increasing in the past few decades. The majority among them are oppressed by imperialism, feudalism and comprador bureaucrat capitalism and live in a constant fear of unemployment and social insecurity that they might be forced to abandon their studies and such other fears. Hence they tend towards revolution. Having bourgeois education and scientific knowledge and keen political outlook to some extent, they frequently stand in the forefront in the present stage of the revolution or act as a bridge between the people. It was first of all among intellectuals, students and youth that Marxism-Leninism in India had extensively spread and found acceptance.

(ii) Petty Tradesmen: Generally the small business men who engage one or two workers or self-manage their small shops without engaging anyone. They live in constant fear that they will become bankrupt due to the exploitation by imperialism, big bourgeoisie and moneylenders.

(iii) Artisans: They are very numerous, possess their own means of production and are themselves engaged in production. Their condition is similar to that of middle class peasantry.

(iv) Professionals: These are doctors, lawyers and such other engaged in various professions who derive their income more through their own labour, whether manual or mental, than by exploiting others, Those professionals who derive their income more through exploiting others than through their own labour are considered as part of the national bourgeoisie.

These sections of petty bourgeoisie are reliable motive forces in the revolution. Their weakness is that some of them are easily influenced by the bourgeoisie and hence we must carry on revolutionary propaganda and constant organisational work among them.

National Bourgeoisie

The national bourgeoisie in India consists in general of the middle and small bourgeoisie. This is a class with dual character which arises out of its economic position. The national bourgeoisie is a class which is politically very weak and vacillating. On the one hand it is oppressed by imperialism and comprador bureaucrat capitalism and fettered by feudalism. Hence it has a contradiction with all these three enemies of the people's democratic revolution in India. It has neither a share in state power nor any control over the state funds. It has comparatively few ties, with imperialism. Its market is continuously being gobbled up by the imperialist-comprador bureaucrat bourgeoisie combine, its growth is being restricted and sections of it are even liquidated due to the ever-growing onslaught of imperialism. Hence it constitutes one of the revolutionary forces in the present stage of the Indian revolution.

But on the other hand, it is inconsistent and lacks the courage to oppose imperialism and feudalism thoroughly because it is economically and politically flabby, depends on the state for licenses, raw materials and finance, still has some economic ties with imperialism and feudalism, and is scared of the working class revolution. It also aspires for establishing a state under its control and to become the big bourgeoisie. It exploits labour and derives its income primarily from this exploitation. It follows from the dual character of the national bourgeoisie that, at certain times and to a certain extent, it can take part in the revolution against imperialism and the Indian ruling classes, but that at other times, there is the danger of its tailing behind the comprador bureaucrat bourgeoisie and taking part in counter-revolution.

The right wing of this class has reactionary political tendencies, spreads illusions about imperialism and opposes the people's democratic revolution. We must unmask these sections before the people and liberate the masses from their reactionary influences. But at the same time, the majority of the national bourgeoisie either remains neutral or participates in the revolution. The targets of the New Democratic Revolution are only the imperialism, the comprador bureaucrat bourgeoisie and landlord class. Even after country-wide victory of the revolution, it will be necessary to permit the existence for a period, a capitalist sector of the economy represented by the small and middle bourgeoisie without, of course, allowing them to control the economic lifeline of the country.

In general the party adopts the policy of protection to the small and middle bourgeoisie wherever the state power of New Democracy extends.

The Lumpen-proletariat

This stratum of the Indian society are those who are deprived of all opportunities to participate in social production. This is due to the existence of a vast army of rural and urban unemployed which numbers over ten crores in the country and which is ever-increasing on account of the semi-colonial and semi-feudal conditions prevailing in India. The increasing in unemployment is leading to the increase in the lumpen proletariat. Petty thieves, robbers, criminals, goondas, beggar, vagrants, pimps and prostitutes and all those who are forced to make illegitimate means to make a living constitute the lumpen proletariat. They are mainly found in the slums of cities and towns. Many of them migrate to cities from the villages in search of living, but deprived of jobs due to the ever-intensifying crisis in the Indian economy, they end up as criminals and antisocial gangs. The ruling classes often utilize them as strikebreakers, disrupters or as mercenaries. Some of them are recruited by the ruling classes into counter-revolutionary militias and into the reactionary armed forces. Due to their position in class society lumpen proletariat develops hatred towards it. Hence they respond to the slogan of smashing the existing socioeconomic structure. But these people lack constructive qualities and are given to destruction rather than construction.

Hence it has some potential to be remoulded and employed in the service of the revolution. But extreme caution is necessary recruiting them into the party as they often become the source of roving rebel and anarchist tendencies in the revolutionary movement and have an aversion for discipline.

4

The 'Maoist Problem' and Naxal Challenge

The report has specific recommendations for addressing the 'Naxal challenge'. Though it endorses the approach of Prime Minister Dr. Singh of 'walking on two legs" : taking up military and development aspects simultaneously, the primary response for the authors appears to be military strategy and tactics, which is worked out in some detail in the report. One of the continuous refrains here is lack of coordination amongst different states under Maoist influence and between states and the central government. The report repeatedly laments the fact that the states are divided in 'political boundaries' while Maoist influence is not determined by any such boundaries, that the government has to follow the Constitution and the primary responsibility for security is that of the state governments, while they lack resources and the sophistication to put adequate challenge to the Maoists, militarily as well as from the development point of view. Additionally the large federal parties have splintered in recent times and there is rise in the influence of local-'caste based' parties, leading to further weakening of the Indian state.

Thus the Maoists have been able to exploit such lack of coordination and the government response has been largely incoherent and ineffective. The report strongly recommends a *National Counter Terrorism Agency* with an all India jurisdiction and where "the executive authority shall devolve on the central Government". It also recommends a separate *Ministry of Internal Security* with an independent minister to deal exclusively with counter terrorism and Left Wing Extremism.

Such a centralised agency should "have at its disposal forces trained for carrying out special operations with adequate mobility, technology (aerial surveillance, electronic monitoring mechanism et al.), and fire power...." The task force even goes to the extent of recommending some kind of conscription – it "strongly recommends that all entry into Central and State Government employment (IAS, IFS, etc. as well as lower levels) including into PSUs be made contingent on two/three years of compulsory service in the Armed Forces."

The police and military aspect of the recommendations have been worked out in great detail in the report and even the role of a beat constable has been discussed as a separate point. As a strategy to counter the Maoists, it has good words to say about Salwa Judum as well, as "People's defence against the people who want change through violence is an internationally recognised War Zone policy" but admits that "allegations of human rights (violation) against the group (has) defeat(ed) the very purpose of (its) creation."

Though ten out of thirteen points in the recommendation chapter deal with military aspects, it further stresses that such a strategy for "Regain(ing) mass control through superior targeted force" has to be accompanied by what it terms as *"National Repair Works* to fill in the fault lines" by providing basic amenities like education, hospitals, etc. It also emphasises that such a process of wresting initiative from the Maoists is going to be slow – "block by block" and it ought to be done "without seasonal and cynic(al) political gimmicks (perhaps meaning that it should not be tried only at the time of elections, and for immediate political gains, emphasis added, 54)." The report states that "the tribal areas have to be developed on a crash basis" and the "local democratic institutions should be strengthened". It goes on to recommend that the government should attempt to bring Maoists to the mainstream electoral politics by identifying those who have "political ambition"; it even sates that after Charu Majumdar when Vinod Mishra "came in, he formed the Maoist Communist Centre and fought elections." The recommendation chapter has interesting concluding lines:

When one looks at Kerala today, the Left Wing Extremism situation is much less grim than in other states... Has it something to do with the actions taken particularly by the communist parties while in power in Kerala at various times over the last five decades, and possibly other parties as well, to cap land holdings and provide land to those who worked on it? It may be useful to draw on that experience.

ANALYSING THE REPORT

We have attempted to bring out various strands on Maoism in the report, the question remains as to how to make an overall sense of it. There are some aspects that have been repeatedly stressed, some facets where the details have been worked out, at least to some length, while some other issues find only a brief mention. In our overall reading of the report, we find the following aspects worthy of further comment:

1. It is the state which has to be squarely blamed for such 'criminal neglect' which has resulted in the rise of such grievances. The Maoists have a well oiled and significantly superior (to the state) propaganda and military machine to exploit the wrongs for their own ends of building up a 'counter state' and seizing power in the long run.
2. In order to address the problem the state has to primarily better the Maoist military machine by setting up a sophisticated, unified and dedicated command which is effective across the country and take up some development works as well along with it to wean away masses from the Maoists.
3. According to the report, the Indian economy is going through an unprecedented 'boom' led by the big business and Maoists are a threat to this ongoing 'party'. Basically this growth is overall for the good of everyone but Maoists are exploiting some 'genuine grievances' which are arising in remote-rural areas.

Growth of Business and Economy

The underlying assumption here is that in contemporary India there is a party, an economic boom (right in the preface the report claims that India is "shak(ing) away the socialist lethargy") going on and as national-international corporate players join in, some people-the Maoists, are out there to spoil it by exploiting the grievances of those who have not been invited. The task force concedes that though some people have not been made part of the 'growth party', in its opinion it is only because of their remoteness and inaccessibility.

There is also an essential belief that it is the big business which is the engine of this economic growth, the real hand behind this party-the Mittals, the Rio Tintos, the Caterpillars... In fact the task force believes that the best contribution that business can make against terrorism is by continuing its business activities. That the very fact and nature of this economic growth could be a cause of serious problems did not even seem to have crossed the minds of the members of the task force. It does not appear that the strong correlation between the recent years of sharpest economic growth and the most rapid rise in the influence of Maoists in terms of area and population under their influence bothered the task force and motivated them to find its underlying causes. The report seems to be completely innocent of severe structural limits of the Indian economic growth – the epidemic scales of malnutrition, the significant majority much below any reasonable notion of living wage, the farm suicides, chronic unemployment and under-employment, lack of access to drinking water, health, education, etc., and the growing unrest of various kinds amongst the populace across the length and breadth of the country.

State is Primarily Liable

Since the report sees the primary problem as lack of access to development goods for some in remote areas due to which some 'genuine grievances' are arising, the problem is squarely put in the state's court-a state which is a distinct entity from business, especially big business. Thus nowhere in the report is there any hint of a relationship between a third world state like India and global capital – the 'inputs' it provides in making and influencing the policies, the contributions of the more material kind that big business makes in aligning the policies and practices to its own ends and/or building a nexus between government, polity and business.

The report stresses that if it is found that the politicians and officials are in league with the terrorists, then "this should be made public", but has nothing to say about the financial deals that business apparently strikes with the Maoists to continue with their operations. Even when the report mentions repeatedly about the crunch of resources for providing appropriate military and development response to the Maoists, there is no hint that such constraints can have anything to do with the zero taxes that big corporate houses aspire for, or for that matter any link with the massive subsidies that they wrench from the governments for their business deals-project after project and year after year. Interestingly even here, business finds an opportunity and recommends 'tax relief' for investing in its own security measures!

As per the report, if at all the state is weakened it is due to local factors-'caste based' parties-and not due to any constraint being imposed by national and international capital. It is the state and only state as distinct from business which is supposed to provide such development goods to the people – there is no mention here of any role for the private players or for the 'public private partnerships' which otherwise seem to be big favourites even for providing public goods and utilities in 'profitable' urban sectors. If the locals are not being compensated reasonably for the land acquired for big projects, it is the government which is not providing them adequate compensation and it has nothing to do with business! If at all there are some vested interests between business and politics it is at the local level between contractors, money lenders and politicians-no such thing finds any mention at the national level where big business operates. It even has something as strong as an accusation of 'scorched earth policy' to make against the government, meaning thereby that actually the government is destroying the farms and rural infrastructure to get back at the Maoists! But again, the corporations, as per the report, have nothing to do with it – the corporate farming and business interests in new technologies like GM foods, entry of big business into food retail, the burgeoning mining industry, the environmental costs of industrialisation, the buying spree of real estate for SEZs and massive investments of the corporate sector can be nothing else but good for 'everyone' if only various arms of the government were doing their job properly.

Dedicated Military Command

The report believes that the core of the strategy to counter Maoism lies in addressing the problem militarily and overwhelming them by force. The prognosis here is that the Maoists appear to be larger than life due to military failure of the state on various counts: lack of coordination between centre and states as well as amongst states, poor intelligence and lack of technological sophistication in weaponry as well as surveillance systems. Hence the recommendation of the task force is a centralised command exclusively for dealing with contingencies like Maoism with all the resources and technology at its command which can cut across the length and breadth of the country. Thus the task force has little patience for the plural and federal character of the Indian polity and they consider this as one of the biggest hurdles for containing the Maoists. It further recommends Salwa Judum kind of strategy of arming civilians to fight Maoists, though it does concede that Salwa Judum itself has got into 'human rights problems'. Additionally, the report also recommends short commission in the armed forces as a compulsory requirement for all those aspiring to get government jobs, though interestingly no such thing is recommended for private sector jobs. The second leg of the strategy, i.e., 'development', to counter Maoism does find some mention in the report but is very clearly supposed to play second fiddle-as the report itself suggests-to fill up, what it considers, 'fault lines' as a complimentary tactic to the basic military thrust.

Further, it recommends that the government should act in such places in its pristine form and counsels it to not being 'cynical' and get into short term calculations, and would like to see local institutions functioning at their best. All the same it has nothing to say how this will happen in real life? After all, if business interests have become the primary influence on the Indian polity from the central down to local levels, and if the only purpose of business is to earn quick profits, how can the government take care of the long term and discount the short term? It has nothing to say of an institution like FICCI that can possibly play any role here in chastising its member companies and/or advising them to help government consider longer term interests of the poor local population. It even goes on to recommend to the government to find ways of inducing the 'more ambitious' ones amongst the Maoists to join the mainstream electoral politics, of course the assumption being that ambition has only one trajectory-that of rising up the present political order by fighting elections.

Revive their Moribund Economies

The current form of economic growth is good for all and that the corporate houses are the ones who ought to get the real credit for it. When states want to "revive their moribund economies", they give mineral and other resources to the corporations, so that they can revive them. Thus the one significant assumption in the report is that business basically works for the good of the economy and people. Moreover, when it comes to their own diagnosis about why this growth has not reached the tribals and rural folks, the report is very clear that this problem has been created by the state due to its 'criminal neglect' and 'scorched earth policy'. If the tribals are being displaced, if they are not getting the 'good' rates for their land, if they are not finding employment, if the wages are getting depressed in spite of the growth, the spiralling corporate profits, and the increasing board room salaries, then still the report does not see any liability for the corporations in the increasing disaffection in the country at large. For instance read this with the recent debate on the draft Mines and Minerals (Development and Regulation) Amendment Bill. While FICCI and other business bodies have taken the standard position that 'this will lead to zero investments', some of them have gone further ahead, like Federation of Indian Mineral Industries and goes on to make patronising claims that "such a bill will breed lazy people, who will only drink and beat up their women" In fact the proposed bill suddenly makes FICCI worry about, of all the things inequality, and the general secretary of FICCI (and one of the authors of this report) Mr. Amit Mitra says : "The scheme would also lead to social and economic inequality as the people affected by the projects will derive benefits, while the rest of the population will not get any."

The report has no doubt that business has to continue doing whatever it does, putting up more ventures and making profits, and the genuine grievances will get resolved if only the state does its job well and if politicians were not corrupt and if the local 'vested interests' could be taken care of. The report has nothing to offer in terms of analysis of the implications of such growth for various sets of people and how these large scale mining, manufacturing and utility projects are going to affect especially the vulnerable sections who are resisting and protesting against such projects across the length and breadth of the country (according to a recent estimate such projects are going to displace 1 million people only in Jharkhand). The report does not see any contradiction between its own here and now symptomatic treatment of Maoists and its attempt to continuously exhort the state to indulge in long-term 'strategic thinking' and action. So does this mean that the report has nothing to offer in terms of concrete agenda? On the contrary, the substantive parts of the report are those where it proposes a detailed action plan for the state to implement – these are the parts where an elaborate military strategy has been worked out and specific recommendations have been provided for various parts of the state – the nature of command structures, the sophisticated technology that is required, the changes in legal regime, etc. We have summarised this aspect of the report in Part III and these appear to be the implementable aspects of the report likely to be picked up by the target audience.

It may not be a mere coincidence that, simultaneously when the report was being written and released, we began hearing about 'operation green hunt' (OGH), which according to the home minister has never ever been even discussed inside the inscrutable walls of North Block let alone existing in reality; yet OGH seems to be going strong for more than a year now. The purpose of the ostensible operation is to militarily 'destroy' the Maoists with all the unified might of the Centre and states, being led by central paramilitary forces, with state police and local militias like Salwa Judum in tow and assisted by the armed forces with UAVs, night vision, and so on. There appears to be uncanny similarity between what was proposed in the FICCI report in 2009 and what appears to have unfolded since then. The report are very clear about the task of the state, that is, to first be the advance party of business by doing literally the spade work, like getting the land and infrastructure ready; and second, when faced with 'security threats' like Maoists, to 'take care' of them, genuine or no genuine grievances.

That is the basic role of the neoliberal state and that is the function it is supposed to serve in spite of all the rhetoric of free markets and privatisation. That is why the model government is that of the Modi's Gujarat where all kinds of dissent can be squashed in the name of a 'vibrant Gujarat' and the state can be completely sanitised and made ready for business. No wonder that Forbes very recently called Gujarat the "most market-oriented and business-friendly" among Indian states.

This is the monolithic state that business wants to see, where there is no scope for plurality, democracy and dissenting voices, only a well oiled machine-like 'system', where the business is the prime engine and the job of the state is to fill-in the 'fault lines'. In fact where possible, business itself can take up the role of the state, like Blackwater in Iraq. It recommends a change in the statutes so that the private security agencies have the right to carry heavy weapons and also wants fewer regulations for such private security firms. Moreover, the report also sees civil society and the media as well in its own image and has an interesting take on these institutions. It repeatedly mentions how the two also need to be co-opted in its war on terror and exhorts them repeatedly to fulfil their duties and responsibilities. For instance it has a large list of do's and don'ts for the media: "information should be factual and responsible", "provocative media coverage must be avoided", "nothing should be done which helps the terrorists", etc. It also would like to see a 'code of conduct' for civil society groups and NGOs, of course meaning thereby that they should toe the business line, "and any of the organisations breaching this code should be brought to book mercilessly...". In order to implement proper monitoring, it also exhorts civil society to support laws that may even result in 'invasion of privacy'. In such a conception of society there is no place for citizens. One way of interpreting this report is that rise of Maoism in the country is an opportunity for big business to articulate their vision of a monolithic state devoid of citizens and voices. Needless to say, it does not necessarily mean that they will be able to attain their vision.

INDIAN NAXALS/MAOISTS TURNING INTO A GLOBAL THREAT

Once a peaceful city of Gadchiroli in the Maharashtra State of India is now facing a worst threat of Naxals/Maoists (NM) infestation. The signal is clear that Maharashtra is now going to become the part of Red Corridor very soon. Since long the threat of NM has taken all of the India into a strong grip. The hiding of reality and defying the questions of the media in this context made this menace reach the urban centres of the world's most emerging super power of the future. In comparison to Taliban of Pakistan that were focused by the world as they were believed to be reaching the Capital of Pakistan and capturing Nuclear Assets, the intensity of NM seems to be more lethal and devastating. India blames China for providing them weaponry and as usual it also raises finger on Pakistan's ISI but it is a reality that NM are building their fire power not only through alleged foreign help but most alarmingly creating their own Improvised Explosives Devices (IED) and other weapons indigenously. Following is the report suggesting that NMs are manufacturing their own weapons now!.

Giridh, Jharkhand The Naxals, who surprised everyone by using rocket launchers for the first time during the Lok Sabha polls, have already set up about four units to manufacture weapons and ammunition, say central security agencies. The Naxals, who usually target security forces with manual improvised explosive devices, are now slowly developing remote-controlled IEDs which can be activated from a distance with just the push of a button.

The improvement in fire-power is being supported by intensive training on the lines of regular forces, say sources. Central security agencies and local police sources say the Maoists have started two factories each in the dense forests and hills of both Jharkhand and Chhattisgarh. Sources say that though another such factory existed earlier in Bihar, the Naxals have dismantled it.

Early last year, a combing team of the CRPF and the local police had come across one such unit used for making small bombs and mortar shells in Jharkhand. The Naxals who are trying to improve their firepower have also come out with the deadly 'Claymore Mines', or what are often called 'directional IEDs'.

Unlike in the past, when IEDs use to be buried beneath the road in a small can, the Claymore Mines, which come with a thick aluminium plate, can be fitted to a tree.

The IED, when exploded, will deflect the shrapnels in a direction opposite to the plate, thus focusing them to a particular area as against conventional IEDs where the impact is in a circular area around the device. Certain blasts in Chhattisgarh have pointed to the possibility of remote-controlled IEDs being used but they are yet to become a standard strategy for the Naxals, say sources. "Naxals are constantly trying to improvise and have also set up factories for this. During searches by security personnel, they have come across few chips which suggest that they are trying to develop remote-controlled IEDs. If they succeed, it would prove deadly," according to a source. "The Naxalites also make their own guns besides those snatched from policemen and procured from outside. Their locally-made guns called 'pahar' can be used to severely injure a person if not kill him. The pellets break into pieces on impact and hence are deadly," the source says.

The left-wing extremists are known for using gelatin sticks in their explosives. They are sourced from mining areas, say sources. A source says that the Maoists also undergo military training similar to that of securitymen, which "suggests a possibility of ex-army or ex-policemen" helping in preparing training modules, whether due to force or their own wish.

One of the Naxal training CDs seized by security forces in Andhra Pradesh gives an insight into the training modules with the militants practising crawling backwards. Security forces have also come across abandoned centres of Naxals having rope climbing, ladder, crawling tunnels and other obstacles used for hard training. The Naxals have also hit upon an innovative way to store their ammunition by hiding it in branded plastic water tanks placed in the ground and covered with mud and stones. Sources said the logic behind it was that there are less chances of formation of moisture, which might damage the ammunition.

Indian security forces would not find it easy to stop NMs in near future because they have developed themselves into a parallel lethal army. Coming back to the main topic, the spreading of Mao Zedung's ideology throughout India is creating a greater menace for the world forces that are in support for free democratic system and the Capitalism. The world is looking towards India as a nation progressing with enormous pace, but the poverty level in majority of India displays a negative picture. NMs have the sympathies of the most thrown away and ignored people who are now becoming part of their movement. The NMs infestation when seen reaching the Urban centres of India raises the question that why these forces are not obstructed till now! There is a great understanding that Indian security forces and Army is not ready to encounter NM as they have reasonable fire power and ammunition to counter any attack initiated against them. It looks that within months most of the big cities would fall into NM's lap and the government could not move its shoulder then.

Another main reason for India's staying back from decisive action against NM is the staging of Common Wealth Games on 3rd October 2010 in Delhi. But to shock many NM have already reached the outskirts of Delhi. The witness's note of Delhi's train hijacked by NM forces as seen in the video aired by the media shows that the menace of NM is far more horrible than it is normally discussed. It would be a great risk for the participating players of different countries because, India cannot guarantee the safety of those who would come there to play with free of mind and without any fear. India's reluctance to initiate any action against the NM forces before the Common Wealth games also indicates that this opportunity would be capitalized by them and they would infest more urban areas beyond the Red Corridor.

The Government of India is now saying that they will start an operation against NM forces but they are not sure how intensified that operation would be because the moment this operation would be started the international media would jump quickly to highlight the developments. This can negatively affect the efforts of India to project itself as a safer nation. It would also strengthen the fear that Delhi's Common Wealth Games would be endangered due to the planned operation against the NM insurgents by not involving the regular Army. Following link proves that strong voice is raised inside India to keep the action against the insurgents on low profile as any intensity in the encounter would lead to collateral damage to the face of the progressing and safe India. The delay in taking action against NM forces is however creating a possibility that these insurgents would try to capture most of the territory in the coming days.

In an interview published in the weekly magazine, the Maoists Leader Mupalla Laxman Rao, better known as Ganapathi, said that any offensive might secure some early gains but insisted that the rebels would eventually triumph. The Rebel Leader who is quite confident to give Indian forces a tough encounter. In conclusion, the growing possibility of NM taking whole of India like a storm is nothing out of the reality. The present help by International media to India by not highlighting the real threat is seen as a criminal act because if the people of the world are not shown the clear picture, it may create a bigger catastrophe for many foreigners who are intended to visit India for either business or tourism. The recent threat by NM that foreigners would be kidnapped should also be taken seriously. Kidnapping motives by insurgents inside India prove that the situation is alarming and extremely dangerous. Recently, American Government has issued clear warnings to its citizens to revisit their plans to tour India as there is a growing threat to the lives of Foreigners working, touring and engaged in business deals inside India. The warning of American Government is taken very seriously.

Further, the recent cases of Uranium theft, leakages and explosions in the Nuclear Installations inside India also raises serious concern about the possibility of environmental catastrophe and the bad intentions of the terrorists who have obtained sufficient quantity of Uranium to make any kind of nuclear explosive device. It is now the responsibility of Global community to understand the intensity of problems attached to India which could lead to a devastating situation. From NM's insurgency to irresponsible attitude towards safety of Nuclear Installations may lead to immense danger to the lives of people living in India and for those who have any intention to visit to India in the near future. India should be pressurized by UN and United States of America in particular because the growing menace of Naxals/Maoists insurgency is leading to complete influence of Communists in India. The west had been united to diffuse the Red storm of USSR more than a decade back, but can they handle much bigger threat of people idealizing Mao Zedung and capturing India completely to make it another large Communist country like Russia and China. The time has come when this threat is to be seen with eyes wide open! The threat of a destabilizing India and drowning completely into insurgencies would create security threat for the neighbouring countries and the impact would be enormous and devastating to this region. If Indian Government would not realize it's responsibility to the International Community, then this wild fire of uncontrolled insurgencies would make this region a living hell.

THE NAXALITES'/MAOISTS' PROGRAMME

The programme of the CPI(Maoist), once the new people's democratic state is established, however, is one with which 'a large chunk of the Indian political class should have nothing to quarrel about'. The party proposes to redistribute land to poor peasants and landless labourers according to the slogan 'land to the tillers'; to ensure the land rights of women; 'to ensure all facilities for the growth of agriculture', including ensuring 'remunerative prices' for agricultural products'; to regulate working conditions and ensure that wages are adequate and equal between the sexes; to guarantee the right to work and 'improved living conditions for the people'; and 'to move towards the elimination of regional imbalances'. Much of this also appears in the Common Minimum Programme with which the United Progressive Alliance

(UPA), headed by the Congress Party, set out (also in 2004), while the major established party of the Left, the CPI(M), remains committed to the abolition of landlordism and radical land reforms. Contrary to what is suggested by some commentators, the CPI(Maoist) does have a coherent programme. The Maoists are not just armed bandits, as they are sometimes represented as being (as in the *Frontline* report from Lalgarh) and in spite of the history of attachment to violence that Simeon critiques. They are now seen increasingly as being more or less exclusively an armed movement with no concern for mass mobilisation has come about because state action against them leaves them with little scope for the latter, which has tended to shrink (as we saw from Balagopal's account from Andhra Pradesh outlined earlier) – or at least apparently so (close observers like Navlakha report that organising goes on wherever it is possible for the Party to do so).

The chances of land reform being carried out in India by intervention from above now seem remote. Neither is there significant pressure for such reforms from below in the major agricultural regions of the country. Moreover, the major left parties have chosen not to concentrate attention on marginal areas where the land issue still is alive. The Maoist/Naxalite organisations have filled the gap and Gupta argues that 'the major Naxalite contribution to Indian politics is that they have kept alive the agrarian demands of the rural poor through persistent but not always successful struggles'. Their emphasis, too, on armed resistance to oppression by bigger landowners and rich farmers who often still subject Dalits and *adivasis* to everyday humiliation has appeal to many of these historically oppressed people. Gupta thinks that it has a large mass following because 'no other political party in the country has taken up the cause of the rural poor with such single-minded zeal and devotion'. He thinks this even though he questions the priority that the Maoists themselves seem to give to the path of armed revolution, reinforcing the impression that theirs is a guerilla formation rather than a political party. Gupta also believes that their strategic-tactical line is quite inadequate in the context of present day India – as he says, most of India is not Dandekaranya (one of the major tribal-occupied forest areas of Chhattisgarh). Balagopal, similarly, has argued that 'the main reason for the wide popularity of the Naxalites in the entire forest region abutting the Godaveri river in Telengana, Vidarbha and

Chhattisgarh is the protection they gave to the forest dwellers for cultivation in reserve forests, the substantial increase they achieved in the payment for picking *tendu* leaf and the end they put to the oppressive domination of the headmen and *patwaris*'. The massive transfers of forest and agricultural land for infrastructural, mining and industrial projects that are either planned or are now taking place will lend even greater strength to the Naxalites.

THE NAXALITE CHALLENGE

Administrative heads and senior officials of 12 States, including Chief Ministers, Home Secretaries and Directors-General of Police, met in New Delhi under the auspices of the Union Home Ministry and decided to set up inter-State joint task forces to "facilitate coordinated and synergised anti-naxalite operations across State boundaries" and "strengthen intelligence networks" for this mission. Home Minister Shivraj Patil announced that "these forces would be made functional quickly", in the context of the developing situation in various naxalite-affected States. A number of politicians and security officials who attended the meeting rated the decision as historic, essentially because the "Union Home Ministry had for the first time accepted the need to raise a special joint task force that can operate across State borders to counter the naxalite threat". Even as the "historic", albeit somewhat contentious, decision was being circulated and officials of the administration and security agencies were working out the details of its implementation, Home Departments of various States received reports about scores of naxalite conventions across large tracts of forest land, stretching from Andhra Pradesh in south India to Orissa and Bihar in the east.

The professed objective of the conventions, which took place throughout the last week of September, was to observe the first anniversary of the Communist Party of India (Maoist). The CPI (Maoist) was formed on September 21, 2004, with the merger of two prominent naxalite outfits, the People's War Group (PWG) and the Maoist Communist Centre (MCC). The meetings, Home Ministry reports pointed out, were not confined to commemorating the formation of the party. They also considered plans to counter the proposed government offensive using the "military unit" of the organisation, the People's Guerilla Army (PGA). Catching up with a number of PGA cadre who attended the anniversary deep inside the Saranda forests of the Singhbhum region in Jharkhand, *Frontline* gathered that this was indeed the case. The PGA cadre said the celebrations "marked a resolve to continue with people's war against the Indian state, uphold the gains made so far, especially by protecting guerilla zones, where the party, its police, administration and army controlled day-to-day life, and counter the new aggressions that the state would make". The pronouncements of the Home Minister and the assertions of the PGA left little doubt that the "climate of accommodation and dialogue" that the United Progressive Alliance (UPA) government had sought to build up was over. In a sense, the new developments marked a significant dilution of the socio-economic-political approach, as opposed to a militaristic approach, promised by Prime Minister Manmohan Singh in tackling militancy-related issues. The earlier intent of the Congress-led UPA manifested itself in the form of discussions between the naxalite leadership and the Andhra Pradesh government in October last year. This had marked a major shift from the approach adopted by several State governments, including the erstwhile Telugu Desam Party (TDP) Ministry in Andhra Pradesh and the Bharatiya Janata Party (BJP) governments in Chhattisgarh and Madhya Pradesh, which had branded naxalites as mere lumpen outlaws causing harm to local communities and their development. These governments and their political leaderships highlighted how some naxalite leaders had become multi-millionaires through extortion and other criminal activities. The Congress obviously perceived that lumpenisation was not the dominant feature of naxalites, or that this trend was not as widespread as it was made out to be. The peace process in Andhra Pradesh did seem to make some progress before collapsing over two issues. One was the naxalite position that "the question of carrying arms and conducting armed struggle were non-negotiable". This assertion was in response to the government suggestion that the situation would be more conducive to talks if the naxalites gave up armed struggle.

The second was the inability and hesitation of the government to take up land reforms on the scale and in the manner suggested by the naxalites. The extremists had presented details of agricultural lands-including land on the outskirts of the State capital, Hyderabad, allegedly grabbed by industrial houses and influential persons, and demanded that the government distribute the 30,000 acres (12,000 hectares) among the landless. The State government rejected this demand. The fact that naxalites were continuing with their armed struggle in States other than Andhra Pradesh (they engineered landmine blasts in eastern Uttar Pradesh killing 15 policemen) and the political pressures they placed on the Congress also contributed to the failure of the talks.

It was in this context that Chhattisgarh raised the demand for inter-State joint security exercises. Chhattisgarh Chief Minister Raman Singh pointed out at the New Delhi meeting that his government had been stressing the need for a joint task force but the UPA government had consistently ignored the demand saying that the naxalite problem can and should be tackled by the affected States independently. In spite of their ultimate failure, the talks were apparently motivated by good intentions on both sides. Former Madhya Pradesh Chief Minister and Congress leader Digvijay Singh, whose tenure in power saw a number of naxalite operations, told *Frontline* in the context of the talks that no government committed to the welfare of the people could afford to ignore the growing influence of extremist political alternatives and their negative impact on mainstream polity. The leadership of the CPI (Maoist), including Ramakrishna, the head of the party delegation at the talks in Andhra Pradesh, had around the same time said that "it is wrong to classify naxalism as a problem, especially in the context of the faith and allegiance that lakhs and lakhs of oppressed and deprived people show towards us and our path" and added that his party was, in fact, more interested than any other party in peaceful solutions to the people's socio-economic problems

At a practical level, the Andhra Pradesh government, through the talks, sought to get some relief from the violence perpetrated by naxalites against the state apparatus, while the CPI (Maoist) made apparent an urge to spread its ideological and organisational influence by aggressively advocating land reforms and getting them implemented in various States, starting with Andhra Pradesh. It has been a rapid downhill trip after the collapse of the talks at the end of last year. Naxalite attacks on state machinery intensified through many of the affected regions. The CPI (Maoist) also complained that government atrocities had risen in various parts of the country affecting both its activists and its support base, which consist of "unarmed well-wishers". Statements released by the party leadership alleged that 150 activists and supporters were killed by various security forces in the past one year.

Notwithstanding these claims, naxalite attacks have been in greater focus throughout the past 10 months. Armed activists attacked security forces at several places during the Assembly elections in Bihar and Jharkhand in February. The Superintendent of Police of Munger district in Bihar was killed, and 38 Central Reserve Police Force (CRPF) and State Special Forces personnel were killed in April-June in the Dandakaranya forests in Andhra Pradesh. One of the most intense operations during this period took place in Madhuban town in north Bihar, close to the Nepal border. In a synchronised attack, over 150 naxalites hit various instruments of the state-the police station, banks, district offices and the house of Rashtriya Janata Dal (RJD) Member of Parliament Sitaram Singh. Closer to the September 19 meet, naxalites gunned down 15 persons in Jharkhand and triggered a landmine blast near Bijapur in Chhattisgarh killing 24 policemen, including 22 from the CRPF.

In the context of these developments, the Centre naturally assessed that naxalites had increased their strike power and influence. According to the Home Ministry's estimation, they have "9,300 hardcore underground cadre and they hold around 6,500 regular weapons besides a large number of unlicensed country-made arms". The naxalite infrastructure includes sophisticated weapons such as Kalshanikov rifles and Claymore landmines, modern wireless equipment and electronic gadgets. It has also been assessed that the naxalites' sphere of influence has spread in the past year and a half from 76 districts across nine States to 118 districts in 12 States. The security forces involved in anti-naxalite operations are convinced, especially in the background of the Madhuban attack, which apparently involved Maoists from Nepal too, that the CPI (Maoist) is steadily building up a wider network involving associates in neighbouring countries. The Home Ministry is of the view that the wider strategic motive is that of carving out a Compact Revolutionary Zone (CRZ) or what is called a "Red Corridor of armed struggle" spreading from Nepal through Bihar up to the Dandakarnaya region of Andhra Pradesh.

Obviously, these perceptions have contributed in a big way to the Union government giving up its reluctance to have unified inter-State anti-naxalite operations. However, as of now, the modalities of coordinating and carrying out such operations have not been worked out. Naturally, there is some uncertainty about the impact on the ground too. At the same time, the naxalite leadership is certain that the new plan of the government would not make much difference on the ground situation in the 12 States where the organisation has varying degrees of influence. A middle-level leader of the party, not actively involved in PGA operations, told *Frontline* that this assessment was based mainly on three factors.

One, the strike power of the party has increased considerably in the past year. Two, the socio-economic problems that have contributed to the steady growth of the party have only accentuated in vast parts of the country, especially in the rural, tribal and forest regions where naxalite influence is the most conspicuous. Three, in the background of the above-mentioned factors, the government's intelligence gathering would not be effective. All this, the leader said, would make the planned operations a non-starter. This confidence is indeed a reflection of the current balance of power dominated by naxalites. But the history of this Left extremist movement since 1967 has shown that an element of cocksureness has repeatedly brought stinging reverses. In the early 1970s, the movement seemed to be reaching the peak of its influence with the creation of vast guerilla zones from West Bengal to Bihar to Uttar Pradesh to Andhra Pradesh. But the might of the state machinery was able to disrupt all these within a couple of years. The PWG and the MCC did of course rebuild the movement, but the fact remains that the naxalites are facing opposition even from the common people in States such as Chhattisgarh and Bihar. The opposition has stemmed both from disagreement with their aggressive ideological positions and from the revulsion caused by the lumpenisation of some of the cadre. Given this background, the confidence about retaining the guerilla zones and support bases may not be entirely realistic. As some naxalite activists have pointed out, the task of retaining people's support is a daunting one in all guerilla activities. The larger view of the UPA government on the issue of extremism also emphasises the need to strengthen people's support to mainstream polity through effective socio-economic interventions. The September 19 meeting, which had representatives of State governments run by political parties of divergent views, too had pointed out that a lasting solution to Left extremist politics cannot be achieved without addressing the socio-economic factors that contribute to its rise and growth. Some of the measures identified by the Home Ministry in this context include, "strengthening of administrative machinery to make it more responsive, transparent and sensitive to facilitate effective redressal of public grievances", "development of an improved delivery mechanism aimed at accelerated integrated development" and "enhancing employment opportunities in naxalite-affected districts", especially to the local and indigenous population. Specifically, the government has mooted plans to raise a special tribal battalion with 1,200 members from the naxalite-affected areas.

But proclamations such as this have not, by themselves, generated any great hope about a turnaround. Prakash Singh, former Director-General of the Border Security Force (BSF) and the author of the book *The Naxalite Movement in India*, says, on the strength of his close observation of the movement as well as the initiatives to counter it, that successive governments have talked about this multi-pronged approach-combining security offensives with socio-political initiatives-since the 1970s without any concrete result on the ground. "Unless the governments and their leaders show the commitment to effect land reforms, weed out corruption and provide a semblance of fair and just governance in the interests of the poor, naxalite ideology will continue to grow," he told *Frontline*. According to a former Home Ministry official associated with anti-naxalite operations in the 1970s and 1980s, the only State government that steadfastly advanced socio-economic initiatives to counter Left extremism was the Left Front government in West Bengal, the State where naxalism originated. "That government, right from its first stint in office, consistently used the administrative and legal machinery to protect the rights of the tiller as opposed to the (absentee) landlord, and thus brought about far-reaching changes in the rural socio-economic set-up," he said. The results, he added, were there for all to see, in the form of the near-total collapse of naxalism in the State and the repeated return of the Left Front to power through the past two decades.

The appeal of the CPI (Maoist) evidently lies in the foibles of mainstream politics. Campaign material circulated by its activists in various parts of the country lampoons the mainstream as follows: "Maoists demand humanity for the poverty-stricken masses, not the dirty politicking of the mainstream. Maoists demand decent life for all, not just for the elite and their hangers-on that thrive on the mainstream. The vultures of the system demand that the Maoists give up not merely their guns, but their self-respect, humanity, sense of justice and the struggles for a decent existence. They want the Maoists to join the gutter mainstream." The conditions that exist in vast parts of rural India impart a special appeal to this kind of language.

In theoretical terms, naxalites justify their actions as the political programme to overthrow the Indian state, comprising the big landlord-comprador, bureaucratic, bourgeoisie classes and the imperialism that backs them, through armed struggle and establish a people's democratic state under the leadership of the proletariat. It states that the principal and immediate task of the present stage of the revolution is to arouse and organise people for agrarian revolutionary guerilla war in the countryside-specially in the remote countryside-and to build the people's army and a rural base through guerilla warfare. There are indications that the immediate manifestation of this theoretical projection would be in the form of struggles and strikes against the corporatisation of agricultural land. The specific demand for redistribution of land in Andhra Pradesh during the talks last year had this dimension. Jharkhand, where the National Democratic Alliance government is busy signing memorandums of understanding with industrial houses such as the Mittals, the Jindals and the Tatas for mining and related activities, could well become the next major naxalite target. There is a view in a section of observers that the current multi-pronged initiative against naxalites is linked to the efforts to "ensure safe passage" to liberalisation and globalization policies in large parts of rural India. If that is the case, the battle between naxalites and the state apparatus will acquire more intense proportions in the days to come.

5

Criticism of the Maoist

Maoists have been roundly criticized for their tactics and actions. While most of the criticism has been for their excessive use of violence, some critics have also pointed faults in other aspects of the movement:

- Unable to come to terms with the 21st century world reality: In a recent interview, the spokesperson of CPI(Maoist), Com. Azad, has dismissed the assertion that the 21st century world is different from the 20th century world. Referring to the technological advancements he said, *"How this unprecedented development has a bearing on the strategy of the revolutions in the 21st century or on the nature of democracy in the 21st century is not clear."* According to the party, the nature of oppression and oppressor has not changed in the past two centuries. Hence, there is no need to reorient strategies. The party has also failed to take into consideration the immense power that has accrued to the State. It is possible for them to even think of taking on the powerful security machinery of the government?
- Non-inclusion of dalits and tribals in the decision-making process: This is the most serious charge against the Maoist parties of India. Out of 22 or so central committee members of the CPI(Maoist) who chart out the party's course, not one is said to be a tribal, or a woman. The number of dalits in the top positions is also limited. With 60% of their cadres being women and around 70% of their supporters being tribals, it is incongruous that these sections are not represented in the central committee or the politburo.

- Mindless and brutal use of violence: A big charge against Maoists. It's the ordinary policemen, and petty informers who become the most common victims of Maoist violence, not those who represent the real "class enemies" of the movement. The Maoists are also alleged to have used brutal methods of torture. And they have been criticized for indiscriminate use of landmines, a abhorred weapon the world over.
- Not co-operating with the state to provide basic amenities to the tribal population: The state has blamed the Naxalites for hindering development. They block the building of roads as they are used to organize raids by police, they blow-up schools as they are used to house paramilitary forces. They don't allow the villages to access money that the government gives to panchayats. All this, in turn, increases the plight of the poor. The resources that the state can provide cannot be matched by the Maoists, and any attempt to seclude the people from the legitimate development support is a net loss for those men and women.
- Non-serious cadres: While it is true that many have joined the ranks of the Naxalites because of genuine grievances, the possibilities of people joining for the lure of guns and money cannot be ruled out. In fact the notorious "greyhounds" in Andhra Pradesh, the gangs that operate as anti-Naxal units backed by the state, are almost wholly populated by surrendered Naxalites. Former Naxalites have been accused of forming criminal gangs in AP. Some have been blamed for carrying out and supporting illegal mining activities in Karnataka. The Naxalites have to take extra care to ensure that their arms training comps do not become internship courses for criminals.

BACKGROUND TO THE MAOIST MOVEMENT IN INDIA

The first armed Communist movement in India took place in the Telengana region of present day Andhra Pradesh during the early fifties. It was brutally put down after great loss of life and unleashing of oppression against the poor peasants. The movement's leaders included several idealists, though they too committed heinous and unpardonable crimes. The Telengana region even today has produced the most dedicated and committed Maoist cadres and leaders in India.

During the late sixties and early seventies the Naxalite movement started and spread in many parts of India, most notably in West Bengal and Kerala. But within a matter of five to six years, this dangerous and anarchist ideology was effectively tackled by the State Police forces and many of those who had taken up arms were eliminated. Generally peace prevailed from the mid seventies onwards. Leftist ideologues continued their activities using democratic means and formed many regional splinter groups. However their mass influence and acceptance was minimal.

The States abdicated their authority over vast regions, as long as the semblance of normalcy could be maintained and the electoral interests of the dominant political party could be taken care of.

From the mid nineties many armed radical Communist Dalams became active in the common underdeveloped and adjacent forested areas of Bihar, Jharkhand, West Bengal, Orissa, Chathisgarh, Madhya Pradesh, Maharashtra and Andhra Pradesh. However it was the leaders from Andhra Pradesh who took the lead to unify these groups, formulate their common dogma and policies, start centralized armed training of core cadres, ensure an efficient arms and explosives procurement network, coordinate the intelligence gathering by over ground workers and sympathizers, and develop operational capabilities based on hitting weak targets with overwhelming local superiority followed by quick dispersal. They worked amongst the poor and dispossessed and acted frequently against the exploiters thus gaining a strong local following and acceptability.

Their morale also got a tremendous boost when the Nepali Maoist movement became very strong and entrenched against the oppressive and corrupt Royal rule there. Thus a great swathe of Maoist dominated influence came into being by the first decade of this century. Funds flowed into their coffers from the mining interests, contractors, and from illegal octroi collections. The States abdicated their authority over vast regions, as long as the semblance of normalcy could be maintained and the electoral interests of the dominant political party could be taken care of. However this facade had to crack one day, as the doctrine of power dictates that the superior entity has to keep on expanding in order to ensure its very survival, until a balance of power and human failings combine to dictate the limits.

We have presently reached this stage in our country. The Maoists, respective State Governments, and the Central Government have all become aware of each other's strengths, but are not yet ready to raise the stakes any further and go all out for the required push which is essential to achieve total victory.

THE SITUATION IN ANDHRA PRADESH DURING THE NINETIES AND EARLY PART OF THIS DECADE

The newly formed Telugu Desam had stormed to power in 1989 creating a world record for the shortest period after registration as a political party, for an entity to win an election. Many populist schemes were undertaken by NT Rama Rao during his first stint as CM, and he enjoyed vast mass support. During his next term in office after winning power again in the 1994 elections, many deviations and laxity of administration set in, besides family squabbles, which culminated in his being unseated and the reins of power going to N Chandrababu Naidu in 1995 who was an astute politician and a strong administrator. Simultaneously the Maoist organisations became strong all over Andhra Pradesh. Many youths flocked to this movement both as over-ground workers as well as in the ranks of the underground armed cadres. A parallel administration was created in many Mandals (Taluks). But Chandrababu Naidu also rose to the occasion and tackled the bull by the horns. Being not part of the Central Government, he did not expect much help from the Centre nor did he wish to be overly dependant.

The sustained campaign carried out by the Andhra Pradesh State Police during 2005 to clear the Nallamalla Hills region in the heart of Andhra Pradesh encompassing the adjacent forested areas of Kurnool, Prakasam, and Kadapa districts is a classic success story in counter insurgency operations in India...

After several brainstorming sessions with his close advisers and noted security experts, he decided upon a two pronged approach of re-establishing the writ of the civil administration and ensuring that developmental works are pursued, and secondly strengthening and revitalizing the Police Force whatever be the costs. The Andhra Pradesh Police Force underwent a total transformation in its work culture and level of accountability and within a year's time started showing results against the Maoists. They gained the upper hand against the entrenched Maoists who then either laid low or migrated to neighbouring States, or got eliminated.

This activist policy was continued by his successor YS Rajasekhara Reddy of the Congress who won the elections in 2004. YSR's entire focus was on the upliftment of the rural population. He spent the colossal sum of Rs 50,000 crores in setting up new irrigation schemes and improving the existing ones over a period of five years. Slowly the peasants became Kulaks and benefited from State sponsored subsidies like free power, land allotments, heavily subsidized housing schemes, scholarships, free emergency ambulance service, very low cost Group Health Insurance Scheme (Arogyasri) – where the costs of treatment in any private hospital for any serious ailment was fully reimbursed to the poor.

The oxygen of the Maoists got turned off, as here was a Government which was totally focused on rural development and upliftment of the poor classes, even though urban development and industrial sectors were gravely neglected compared to the previous Telugu Desam government. But at no time was security ever neglected. The Central funding components could be tapped to the fullest extent for various schemes, and this helped the State to usher in even larger budgets. Andhra Pradesh today has the largest state budget in India, even bigger than that of Bangladesh.

AP GOVERNMENT'S SUCCESSFUL METHODS AGAINST THE MAOISTS AND ITS POLICE TACTICS

The State Police's Intelligence Wing has been separated from the Police HQs and made an independent establishment reporting directly to the CM's Office. It does not have any rigid territorial restrictions and can follow up any leads. The intelligence setup has been provided with competent officers, ample funds, and necessary technical backup. Next, most of the Armed Reserve Police Battalions have been converted into Commando Units and they come under the Greyhounds Grouping having a separate IG. All new Police inductees have to spend their first four years of service in these Greyhound Units before getting their transfer to the District Police Establishments. Meritorious service with the Greyhound Units has been made a mandatory requirement to get accelerated promotions, including for filling up of Grade I Officer

Posts selection vacancies in the State Cadre. The lesson learnt is that there is no armed insurgency in India which cannot be put down within two years, if the right proportion of forces differential is created and sustained locally for at least a period of six months.

All Greyhound personnel serving in Maoist affected areas were given 50 per cent additional Commando Pay as incentive. The Greyhounds Training School was revamped and new Training Courses and Methodologies introduced, which are conducted with strict devotion and supervision. Suitable training facilities have been built up at each Greyhounds Unit location for imparting refresher training. The concept of keeping one Administrative and Security Duties Company and one Training Company at all times in the Battalion HQ has been strictly implemented. Most importantly the remaining six companies were deployed as three Joint Operational Bases (JOBs) consisting of two companies each. Experience proved that single company deployment was not giving optimum operational results nor providing the necessary nucleus for the civil administration to function safely and effectively in the Maoist affected regions.

These JOBs in the heart of Maoist affected areas were located within mutually supporting distances. It was normal for a complete Greyhounds Battalion to be deployed within 1-2 gravely Maoist affected Mandal (Taluk) areas, as then they could operate without fear of IEDs, ambushes etc. Each such Greyhound JOB also had two Home Guard Platoons who were recruited from amongst the locals. Over a period of time, they acted as guides, interpreters etc, besides performing most of the routine garrison functions, thus freeing the Greyhounds for 'area domination' and 'seek encounter' patrolling operations. Each Greyhound JOB could send out upto four platoon strength patrols out, at any given time. Hostel facilities were created within the JOB for the Government officials of various rural development departments as well as for contractors and their staff to stay and work in total safety.

Each Greyhound JOB always had a Dy SP/Asst SP ranked Class I Gazetted Officer as In Charge. This created a sea change in the environment and ensured accountability for maintaining sustained operations. Within a few months itself, the Maoists started feeling asphyxiated as their domination ended. Another important functional aspect was that the Greyhounds did not report to or work under the District Police set up. The Greyhound

Units reported to the Special DIG HQ In Charge for that Maoist affected Region, overlapping- several adjacent districts. Their operations were supplemented by adequate Technical Intelligence Teams working under this Special DIG HQ, which could intercept any wireless transmission made by the Maoists and do the Direction Finding Fix. With the advent of cellular phones, they also specialized in tracking down Maoist locations using fixes made from two or more cell phone Towers. This enhanced the accuracy of directed response, and reduced the time lag for the Greyhound patrol teams to make active contact with the Maoist Dalams. The credit for developing the Greyhounds' organization, selection, training and successful tactics primarily goes to their then IG Dr. Durga Prasad, who could out-think and outwit the well entrenched Maoists and also keep progressively adapting.

At this rate the Maoist problem will soon start pulling down the country's favourable GDP growth rate by at least one to two per cent.

The sustained campaign carried out by the Andhra Pradesh State Police during 2005 to clear the Nallamalla Hills region in the heart of Andhra Pradesh encompassing the adjacent forested areas of Kurnool, Prakasam, and Kadapa districts is a classic success story in counter insurgency operations in India, worth being emulated by even the Indian Army in J&K. The Maoist Dalams were well embedded in this region for over 15 years and nobody from the Government dared to go into these areas. Four Greyhound Units working under a single Special DIG HQ established 13 JOBs covering the mountainous and forested terrain of approximately 5000 sq km. This works out to an area coverage of approximately 400 sq km per JOB at the peak of operations. The Maoists reacted very violently with great stealth, IED blasts, assassination of locals, and planned ambushes. But within a matter of six months, the weekly attrition rates started taking their toll and their cadres got demoralized, as they had to keep running in the jungles constantly without getting shelter and sufficient help from the habitated areas.

The Greyhounds went on improving in their tactics and morale. Their losses were few and were immediately replaced in both men and equipment. After a year's time there were no more Maoists left in this area and they were forced to give up this legendary bastion. Thereafter the Greyhounds strength there was reduced to one half of the original deployment. After the period of active operations was over, the Greyhounds deployment in the JOBs was never brought down to below Company strength for very sound operational and functional reasons, and the Maoists have so far not ventured to come back into this erstwhile 'liberated' zone. The relieved Greyhound Units have been redeployed onto the other Maoist affected interstate border areas, where they have repeated their operational successes and driven the Maoists out of AP. The neighbouring States then started requesting the Greyhounds to operate across the border.

The lesson learnt is that there is no armed insurgency in India which cannot be put down within two years, if the right proportion of forces differential is created and sustained locally for at least a period of six months. After wiping out the insurgents in a particular area, 50 per cent of the Security Forces can be redeployed to another area to create the right Forces differential there. The French treatise 'Pacification Operations in Algeria' written in 1963 by Col David Galuta clearly summarized counterinsurgency as "80 per cent protection of the civil population by cutting down 'unrisky access' to them by the insurgents, and the balance 20 per cent of the effort to be directed in maintaining a steady and sustained attrition rate – on weekly and monthly basis." At no cost should the first cleared target region be left totally denuded of Security Forces deployment, otherwise within a matter of a few months, insurgency conditions will be back to previous levels, and the hard won gains would have soon got frittered away.

The Economics and Good Governance Aspects of the Anti Maoist Offensive in AP

What Chandrababu Naidu perfected as the new Police methodology to tackle and root out the armed Maoist groupings, this has been exceeded in far greater measure and significance by his successor, the Late YS Rajasekhar Reddy (YSR) in his epochal shifting of the direction of State spending towards the Rural Sector, creation of additional irrigation potential (Jalayagnam Scheme), and several Poverty Alleviation Programmes never before seen in India since Independence. The total allocations for Rural Sector activities are double that of for all the Urban Sector – Infrastructure Development, and Industrial Promotion activities combined. This approach had not only brought rich political dividends, but also has knocked the winds out of all Maoist and Naxalite 'ground level organizers' even in the most remote hamlets.

The popular saying goes that though the roads in Andhra Pradesh may still be full of potholes, and the urban areas perhaps the dirtiest, but in the rural areas there is not a single member of a poor household who has not benefited from at least three of the following freebies – viz seven hours of assured and free electricity for agricultural activity, free low cost house, 25 kg of heavily subsidized rice for each household, Very Low Cost (and all encompassing) Health Insurance Scheme (Arogyasri), Reimbursement of Higher Education Fees for low income families, and anyone type of Social Welfare Pension for the Aged or Destitute. YSR never gave the least opportunity or space to his political detractors to exploit any popular resentment, and he was always found touring and checking the progress of development activities in all the districts of this vast State.

CAPITALIST DEVELOPMENT AND MAOIST DOGMA

The basic problem with the conceptual framework of Maoism as has been elucidated by the Indian Maoists lies in their inability to come to grips with the need for evolving with the changing situation and grasping the concrete situation in the society where they are working. Thus the basic analysis of the Indian State of the 40 year old CPI (ML) programme in the wake of the Naxalbari movement is retained by the Maoists, failing to draw any lesson from the complete splintering of the ultra Left movement into myriad factions and groups.

In carrying out an analysis of the Indian state the Maoists have not moved an inch from the earlier programme authored by the CPI (ML) in 1970 in the wake of the Naxalbari movement. Almost 40 years back, an understanding that Indian independence is fake and formal with Indian rulers subservient to an imperialist order which is in a state of imminent collapse persuaded them to believe that an armed struggle involving the rural areas to 'encircle' the cities will deliver the 'revolution' in quick time. Slogans like 'decade of the seventies –a decade of liberation' appeared in Naxalite wall writings in the streets of Kolkata. That the objective experience did not substantiate such an assessment-ought to have triggered some degree of introspection. But, obviously it didn't. The naxalite understanding was that the Indian ruling class was a "comprador bureaucratic bourgeoisie". A comprador bourgeoisie defined by the Communist International (6th Congress of the Comintern) is one which subserves imperialism by exporting raw materials and importing finished products. It is a bourgeoisie that does not seek an independent development of capitalism in its country. It is a mere puppet of imperialism. Such a bourgeoisie, therefore, is one which does not command a social base of its own. Overall, this would then be as fragile as a house of cards-requiring a gentle push to bring down the edifice like a domino.

The CPI (M) understands that the Indian ruling classes consist of an alliance between the bourgeoisie and the landlords which is led by the big bourgeoisie. The big bourgeoisie, in turn, increasingly collaborates with international finance capital. At the same time, the CPI (M) recognizes that the Indian bourgeoisie, as a whole, has a dual character. On the one hand, being part of the world capitalist system and seeking to develop capitalism in India, it collaborates with imperialism and international finance capital. On the other hand, in order to preserve and expand its economic domain from being encroached upon by global capital, it also has conflicts with imperialism. Such conflicts, however, get resolved not by confrontation but through compromise, pressure and bargain.

This dual character finds its most visible expression in the economic and foreign policies of the Government. Without understanding the complexity of the process of capitalist development in India and mechanically presuming an exact resemblance with China has led the ultra Left in India to remain clueless in explaining what has happened in all these years. Heavy industry, infrastructure like railways, power, science and technology in advanced areas like space, nuclear, knowledge based industries like bio-technology and information technology and of course-manufacturing-these have developed in India as part of the overall development of capitalism. The indigenous capacities built over the years are unthinkable had it been spearheaded by a "comprador bureaucratic bourgeoisie".

Mindless Militarism: Unconnected to People's Issues

The practice of the Maoists has little to do with issues of livelihood and socio-economic justice. For example, there are a large number of daily issues which are connected with the rights and access to forest wealth of those very people who inhabit those areas where the Maoists are active. But far from raising the question of the mining laws of the country which displace the tribal and other forest dwellers, the Maoists are only talking of a violent armed revolution. This is as if just by talking of a long drawn armed struggle the people can be attracted and changes will take place only after the 'revolutionary' government is established. Similarly, despite their shrill anti-imperialist rhetoric, when it comes to taking up issues and mobilizing people against imperialist dictated policies – there is a deafening silence. The Maoists have never spoken on the disastrous impact of financial liberalisation and speculative activities in the economy. Neither have they raised their voice against the complete withdrawal of public investment in agriculture which has been one of the main reasons for the severe agrarian crisis in the country which has led to thousands of farmers committing suicide.

The cult of the gun – the firepower of the so-called people's guerrillas and the discourse on military tactics has completely overwhelmed the Maoists. They seem to be paying no heed to the exhortations of Mao against mindless militarism in many of his writings on the strategy, tactics and experience of the Chinese revolution. The biggest danger of such mindless militarism lies in the fact that they provoke repression from the state which not only eliminates the so-called 'revolutionaries' but also exposes innocent rural poor to repression, demoralizes them and impacts adversely on their potential to organize and fight for their rights. The rural poor thus continue to remain victims of exploitation and depredation. A glaring instance of this phenomenon can be seen in Chhattisgarh, where the tribals today are caught in a vicious cycle of violence and counter-violence by the Maoists and the state-sponsored militia, Salva Judum. In the process, the Maoists manage to disrupt the emergence of a strong democratic movement which raises the level of revolutionary consciousness of the poor and the exploited. We have seen that happen earlier in West Bengal and subsequently in Andhra Pradesh.

What can happen as a result of such mindless militarism is evident from the large material which has now been brought out in the public domain by those who had been in the past participants and fellow travellers in the activities of the People's War Group of Andhra Pradesh and who constitute the main component of the present Maoist party. Dr. Balagopal, who recently passed away, had brought out in graphic detail the degeneration of the Maoists in his essays in the *Dark Angles.* He has described several heinous and ghastly acts of the Peoples War Group bringing out the sadistic character which should otherwise be alien to a revolutionary movement. In order to make immediate tactical and military gains, the PWG had not even flinched from having unholy alliances with landlords and other ruling class elements. Strange as it may seem, in their document "Post Election Situation Our Tasks", the Maoists have admitted that "in the last government, where it had a smaller number of seats, the Congress was totally dependent on its various allies in order to continue in power and the Left too exerted some amount of pressure on Manmohan Singh government for almost four years." And they conclude "the result has given scope for the UPA government to enact more draconian legislation". But yet, because of their failure to oppose the very policies of that very government they end up in attacking the Left and embracing the second largest component of the same government – the Trinamul Congress in West Bengal. They have ended up being the armed mercenaries of the Trinamul in the forest areas of West Bengal which borders Jharkhand. This is a classic demonstration of the effect of indulging in 'armed struggle' intended to usher in 'revolution' without any connection with the peoples issues.

Uncomfortable With Democracy

Communists the world over are vigorously engaged with the question of democracy. The urgency of this has intensified after collapse of Soviet Union. We in the CPI (M) have done this not only in our struggles for defence of democratic rights in the wake of emergency or in the face of depredations of communal fascist forces; but also in understanding the deficiencies that existed in Soviet Union and which contributed in no small measure to its eventual collapse. We had noted in our document entitled "On Certain Ideological Issues"-"as the socialist system and the state consolidated and correlation of class forces changed in its favour, opportunities for widening democracy and opened up. Unfortunately incorrect assessments of the reality led to the earlier methods of running the state machinery being carried over into the subsequent period. This led not only to distortions such as growing bureaucratism, violation of socialist legality and suppression of individual freedom and liberty. The movement to higher phases of the form of the dictatorship of the proletariat implies the progressive enrichment of socialist democracy."

The Maoists in Nepal have also realized that the struggle for socialism in the 21st century cannot be successful merely through an emulation of the 20th century struggles. They have thoroughly debated and discussed the question of democracy in the 21st century. At the Rolpa Plenum, held in May-June 2003, the CPN (M) adopted a document *"The Development of Democracy in the 21st Century"*. Baburam Bhattarai writes: "After making a critical review of the experiences of revolution and counter-revolution in the 20th century, the document advocated the need to ensure the supervision, intervention and control of the masses over the Party, army and the state in order to march along the path of continuous revolution after making the revolution, and for this advanced the concept of practicing a multi-party competitive system within the stipulated constitutional framework.

This was a new milestone in the development of revolutionary ideas". (Baburam Bhattarai *Epochal Ten Years of Application and Development of Revolutionary Ideas*, The Worker, #10, May 2006) On the tenth anniversary of the launching of the peoples' war in Nepal, Prachanda commented in the special interview quoted at the beginning: "One has to be clear about one thing, that our Party is talking about the development of people's democracy in the 21st century after having learnt from the experiences of the revolutions and counter-revolutions of the 20th century, and accordingly has accepted multi-Party competition within an anti-feudal and anti-imperialist constitutional frame."

Indians Maoists have, however, remained blissfully oblivious about such an overriding demand to respond on the question of democracy. Well-meaning liberal intellectuals have been rightly stressing the need for respecting human rights in dealing with the Maoists. But even they seem to be overlooking the fact that the mindless killings that the Maoists indulge in have to be dealt with firm administrative action. If the Maoists commit a crime they have to be prosecuted and tried independently with full freedom for defending their actions. The liberal opinion also legitimately emphasizes that the State should not indulge in fake encounters and campaigns like Salva Judum in Chhattisgarh. Because, these actions of the State completely undermine the basic principle of natural justice and assumptions of innocence until proven guilty-this is the underlying premise of our jurisprudence.

However, the major problem of the Maoists lies with the methods that they employ in dealing with whom they perceive as their 'class enemies'. Designating individuals as the class enemies and terming them lackeys of feudal exploiters or police agents is a purely subjective exercise. Often they degenerate into holding of kangaroo courts under the shadow of the gun where a death penalty is pronounced against ordinary policemen, school teachers or agricultural workers. Here the Maoist squad leader functions – as a complainant, a prosecutor, a judge and finally the executioner all rolled into one. Often, the trouble of going through such cumbersome procedures is also discarded conveniently. Putting up a poster declaring the dead man a class enemy next to the dead body would suffice! It is almost as if, if you are not with the Maoists, you are a class enemy – a perverted version of the Bush doctrine. Therefore, this obvious discomfiture on the question of democracy becomes evident. And this is a question which will also have to be answered by all the well-meaning liberals who rightly question the government's record on human rights.

The CPI (M) believes that the battle against Maoists cannot be carried out successfully merely on the strength of security forces. Banning them is not a solution to tackle violence and the spree of killings that Maoists armed squads indulge in. The CPI (M) will also continue to oppose the draconian provisions of the Unlawful Activities Prevention Act (UAPA). The CPI (M) also points out the urgency in addressing the questions of socio-economic backwardness which dog those very areas where the Maoists operate. But the Maoists response is clearly marked by visible discomfiture on eschewing violence, not to speak of giving up arms. Why this discomfort? The Maoists themselves have to realise that the observance of human rights cannot be a one-way traffic.

THEORY AND PRACTICE OF MAOISM

However, there's something even more exacting — in the very long run, Marxism has to be judged by the fruits of its project of taking humanity along the road towards equality, cooperation, community, and solidarity. The whole purpose of constructing and re-constructing its distinctive intellectual structure to understand the world was and is so that this exercise may lay the basis of changing society for the better. This is stated most succinctly in Marx's 1845 *Theses on Feuerbach*: "The philosophers have only *interpreted* the world; the point however is to *change* it." But integrating theory and practice (developing a strategy and a set of tactics for changing the world for the better and implementing them) is far more difficult and messy a project. Marx and Engels wrote *The Communist Manifesto* in December 1847 and January 1848, but they never even attempted to define, let alone provide any blueprint of the transitional society (their followers called it socialism) which would in time — that was the expectation — evolve asymptotically towards communism, never really reaching it. As Sweezy has it, in Marx and Engels' conception, the transitional society ("socialism") would begin its existence as "primarily a negation of capitalism which would develop its own positive identity (communism) through a revolutionary struggle in which the proletariat would remake society and in the process remake itself" (1983: 2-3).

But, frankly, the proletariat in the developed capitalist countries, for reasons already mentioned, was increasingly losing its quality as the source and carrier of revolutionary practice. The development of the working class, the advance of human capability — always at the very centre of the forces of production — was not perceived by the workers as being hindered by the relations of production; the latter was not discerned as intolerable by the workers as long as they were able to extract better terms from capital through their struggles (strikes, etc) within the confines of the system. Why should they then bear the risk of losing what they were gaining in the present when what they could gain by revolting against the system was highly uncertain and far away in the future? In other words, Marx and Engels didn't blame the workers for the lack of a revolutionary consciousness; the objective conditions weren't there for its germination.

What then of early Marxism (it was not called Marxism is Marx's time, but for convenience we are designating even that period within its scope) in its mistaken expectation, drawn mainly from its analysis of the living and working conditions of the working class (in Engels' *The Condition of the Working Class in England*, written in late 1844, early 1845 when he was 24) and the logic of Marx's the famous 1859 Preface to *A Contribution to the Critique of Political Economy* that, that class in the advanced capitalist countries would eventually, sooner or later, revolt and emancipate itself? The, at first spontaneous, and later on, organised struggles of the workers, led by the parties of the left, were eventually able to force the ruling class and its political representatives to bring in the factory laws and various social legislations, and implement them, which convinced the workers that things could get better even within the confines of capitalism. In this, no doubt the surplus from the toilers in the colonies/neo-colonies/semi-colonies/ dependent countries (the "periphery"), shared not only between the local elites and the ruling classes in the "centre", but also to an extent, by the working classes there, helped provide part of the cushion. As a result capital at the "centre" got richer and stronger too.

Marx and Engels didn't take all of these developments into account and so proved wrong in their expectations of a socialist Europe. But, to his great credit, Marx did brilliantly take account of — besides the massive expropriation in Britain through the enclosures — capitalism's pillage, in its mercantilist phase, of what later came to be called the "periphery" or the third world, in Part VIII of *Capital*, Volume 1, entitled, "The So-Called Primitive Accumulation".

He also did not ignore "unequal exchange" — through siphoning a part of the surplus created in production via funds used by a distinct class for trade in commodities (merchant capital) — with the periphery, in the competitive phase of capitalism. Basically, merchant capital played a crucial role in the periphery, albeit as an appendage of industrial capital at the centre. Marx had not the opportunity to re-orient his theory of accumulation to take account of what had begun to happen at the end of his life, the emergence of capitalism as a global system with the ushering in of monopoly capitalism. But, we have it from Sweezy that he was fully aware of the causal relationship between the development of capitalism at the "centre", in his day, in Europe and the development of underdevelopment in the "periphery". Early Marxism however proved inadequate in elaborating a theory of accumulation on a world scale that would explain the functioning of capitalism as a global system. All the same, Marx suggested a way of analysing capitalism — how capital got its wealth from the pillage of the "periphery", from expropriation through the enclosures, from the surplus labour of workers in the past, and from the acquisition of smaller and weaker units of capital; how the superstructure (the state, the legal system, the dominant ideology and culture) was adapted and modified to facilitate all of this; and with what potentialities. That method was "materialist dialectics", which was applied by the best of his followers — two of whom were Lenin and Mao — to understand the ever-changing world and to intervene to change it for the better.

Meanwhile, the parties leading the various working class movements in Europe, members of the Second International, continued to pay lip service to the cause of proletarian revolution. But, soon they were exposed for what they really had become when in 1914 they supported their respective governments in the war, an act demonstrating nothing less than the self-destruction of internationalism, and the quashing of many a hope of proletarian revolution. With the possibility of the workers making significant economic, social and political gains within the confines of capitalism at the "centre", Marxism was "revised", re-fashioned by Eduard Bernstein and others to empty it of its revolutionary content. Of course, this was not Marxism anymore, but given the objective conditions in Europe, the "revisionist" doctrine took the place of the revolutionary one there.

'MAOISM': THOROUGHLY MISPLACED CONCEPT

'Maoism' in India is a crude distortion of the theory and practice of Mao Ze Dong. Maoists hardly realise that by blindly imitating the particular path of Chinese revolution that the Chinese people traversed under the leadership of Comrade Mao – they are in fact undermining the very contribution of the great Chinese revolution and the success of the widespread national liberation struggles in the wake of the great victory over fascism led by the Soviet Union. These two momentous developments had changed the alignment of political forces in the aftermath of the Second World War. Ignoring this, the Indian Maoists continue to believe in what the Naxalbari movement propounded that Indian independence is fake and that India continues to be a semi-colonial state in the new millennium. Revolutionaries, whose essential hallmark is to usher in change, cannot remain oblivious of big changes at the global and national level and fail to assimilate their implications. The present secretary of the CPI (Maoist) Ganapati, in an interview to their own mouthpiece *People's March* admitted that in the CPI(ML) People's War Group which is a component of the present Maoist party had a debate over the use of the word 'Maoism' in their literature and understanding. He had, of course, branded those who opposed this new nomenclature as an 'opportunist clique'. But the fact remains that the very notion of 'Maoism' is misplaced.

This was made clear by the Communist Party of China itself that "Mao Zedong Thought is the integration of the universal principles of Marxism-Leninism with the *concrete practice* of the Chinese revolution". To try and replicate the path of the Chinese revolution in India, lock, stock and barrel, is nothing but a denial of the Indian realities. The CPI (ML) which emerged during the Naxalbari movement articulated unrealistic slogans like "China's Chairman is our Chairman" and "Chinese path is our path".

Contrast this to the opposition of Mao himself against the general line of Communist International in so far as China was concerned. It was Mao who asserted, and correctly so, that the Chinese revolution could not follow the same trajectory as in Russia. Similarly, the Communists in India have to chart their own road to the revolution on the basis of a concrete analysis of Indian conditions. Wholesale borrowing of the path followed by the Chinese Communist Party before the revolution in China in the name of 'Maoism' is against the very grain of Mao Zedong Thought. The Indian Maoists would do well to learn and assimilate the experience of the Nepalese Maoists. In spite of the fact that Maoists in Nepal commanded a major support through its armed peasant warfare in large parts of the country, they realized that their movement would be unable to go further forward unless they participated in the task of developing a constitutional multi-party democracy replacing the archaic monarchy. In this background the Maoists had entered into a historic agreement with the seven party alliance with other Left and anti-monarchy bourgeois parties.

This ensured that they were recognised by the Nepali people as a major force in Nepali politics. Rather than learning from the Nepalese Maoists, the Indian Maoists virulently opposed and criticized them. The content of the open letter that the CPI (Maoist) wrote to the Communist Party of Nepal (Maoist) is the most outrageous document that a party calling themselves communists could have issued given the principle of proletarian internationalism associated with communism.

MAOIST BOYCOTT: PARTICIPATION BY OTHER MEANS

Lenin opposed "passive rejection, abstention, evasion of elections" and advocated "active boycott... as a declaration of open war against the old regime, a direct attack upon it", immediately adding, "unless there is a broad revolutionary upswing, unless there is no mass unrest which overflows, as it were, the bounds of the old illegality, there can be no question of the boycott succeeding." Really, there is no question of the boycott tactic succeeding — in a Leninist sense — in conditions generally obtaining in present-day India.

But our clever friends have found a way to claim success. They want us to believe that the passive abstention of a large section of the people from elections shows that their boycott slogan is correct, conveniently forgetting that people who do not go to the polling booths are not generally involved in any "broad revolutionary upswing". Going by their logic, the weapon of boycott would seem to be more successful in those advanced capitalist countries where polling percentages are even lower! However, to themselves they concede that the importance of Parliament and State legislatures as the seat of political power cannot be wished away and that they too have a stake in which party forms government. So they cannot avoid taking part in electoral politics. But they do so in their own distorted ways: indirectly, secretively, conspiratorially, usually by supporting one reactionary party against some narrowly conceived "main enemy" — another reactionary or "revisionist" party. This tactic-turned-strategy was most 'successfully' implemented in Andhra Pradesh in the 2004 assembly elections.

They enforced one-sided boycott on TDP and BJP while canvassing in favour of Congress candidates and the 'success' lay in the fact that Chandrababu Naidu, whom they had earlier tried to eliminate by pure 'Maoist' means, was now removed from power by parliamentary means and a friendly Congress government installed. It is another matter though that after some apparent progress in the talks that ensued, the friend suddenly turned hostile and launched a repressive campaign even more ferocious than that of Chandrababu Naidu. In Bihar, during the Laloo era Maoists were widely known as "RJD during the day and Maoists by night". In many places they used to mobilise votes and manage booths in favour of RJD candidates while trying to damage the prospects of rival contestants, ML nominees in particular. Acting in collusion with the then ruling RJD and the local police administration, they attacked the CPI (ML) office at Paliganj, Bihar, in August 2004 — barely 6 months before the February 2005 assembly elections — killing five comrades in their sleep at the dead of night and officially justified the killings. In Jharkhand, where the erstwhile MCC already had a long and nasty record of killing our comrades, CPI (Maoist) squads allowed themselves to be utilised by the ruling BJP and the notorious SP of Giridih in gunning down comrade Mahendra Singh during election campaign in January 2005.

Such examples in their stronger areas have been replicated even in West Bengal in a somewhat different manner as demanded by the very different conditions obtaining there. They have had clandestine local level deals with both the CPI(M) and the Trinamool Congress (mostly with the latter) in different areas at different times to suit their own convenience. In many CPI(M) strongholds including Nandigram and other areas they used their firepower to clear the ground for the entry of TMC; subsequently too, they have trained their guns mainly on CPI(M) cadres. The Maoists have even gone beyond this to express their open preference for Mamata Banerjee in no uncertain terms. In September this year Kolkata's Ananda Bazaar Patrika and some other dailies published Politburo member Kishenjee's detailed views on why he thought Mamata Banerjee was the fittest person to replace Budhhadev Bhattacharya as the Chief Minister. In recent months Ms Banerjee, now that her purpose has been served and she finds herself within striking distance from the coveted seat of power in West Bengal, has started distancing herself from Maoists; but that only proves her cunning - not any principled position on the part of CPI (Maoist). Even if we set aside the aspect of secretive, indirect participation, abstention from politics - particularly from participation in elections - always boils down to subordination of the working people to bourgeois politics and constitutes a basic feature of anarchism.

This is so because you just cannot cut yourself off from crosscurrents of dominant politics of the day, which can only be bourgeois politics in present conditions. And this subordination can happen in either of two ways: when the masses are left to the mercy of bourgeois electoral propaganda alone (since the 'revolutionary party' is absent from the scene) or when the latter, rather than fielding its own candidates and contesting independently, supports parties like RJD or Congress with an eye to some temporary gains for itself. The Maoists are masters of both methods. The utter Maoist indifference to the task of combating bourgeois politics with revolutionary politics, especially in the arena of elections, can also be seen in the emerging phenomenon of 'ex-Maoists' joining the electoral fray in Jharkhand. It started initially as Maoists contesting the polls as independent candidates before Kameshwar Baitha, an erstwhile commander contested on BSP ticket from Palamau LS (SC) seat in a by-poll in 2006. Baitha finished second in that election and in 2009 he contested as a Congress-backed JMM nominee and won the polls. The Assembly polls in November-December 2009 saw a whole contingent of Maoist leaders contesting the polls in the state, most notably in the Palamau region, and almost all of them are JMM nominees.

In the 2009 LS election we had put up a former Maoist leader from the Chatra LS constituency, but by the time of Assembly election we found him migrating to the RJD! The CPI(M) too caters to the same subordination of the working class to bourgeois politics by means of all sorts of pacts with the latter, but they do so often with a different set of logic, like defeating the 'main enemy' and securing a few seats in the process, whereas Maoists want quid-pro-quo with dominant local leaders/major state parties/state governments. Subordination to bourgeois politics thus expresses itself both as social democratic parliamentary cretinism and anarchist "boycottism" (to borrow once again from Lenin, who said 'left' phrase mongers reduced the politics of Bolshevism to this narrow concept),with the CPI(M) taking pride in having the longest-running state government or the biggest contingent of left MPs (never mind the recent reversals) and the CPI (Maoist) complimenting itself for upholding what is commonly perceived as one of the most distinct hallmarks of pure, unadulterated Naxalism.

But this is a patently superficial and one-sided perception. Depending on assessment of situation, Charu Mazumdar advocated utilization of elections for the sake of revolutionary advance and he called for a boycott when that assessment changed radically. In the penultimate article of his celebrated Eight Documents written less than six months before the Naxalbari uprising he asked revolutionary communists "to take advantage of these elections to propagate our politics... the politics of New Democratic Revolution... of worker-peasant unity under working class leadership, of armed struggle ..." After the first UF government was formed, he wrote: "communists may join an alternative government with only one purpose - to create conditions for launching movements, and not to protect or uphold constitutional obligations.

But if, instead of advancing along this path, calls for struggle are given on one hand and on the other the owning classes are assured that they have nothing to fear, the whole perspective of the struggle gets lost. The target of struggle itself gets blurred. This line inevitably leads to the path of class collaboration." Clearly, he was not against participation in an alternative government on principle; his debate was on how to utilise such government for the advancement of class struggle. It was only before the mid-term elections that was held after the implosion of the first UF government, that CM advanced the slogan of boycott. In late 1968, with the CPI(M) spreading constitutional illusions under the slogan of another UF government and communist revolutionaries longing for a direct assault on the state in a context of rapid upswing of revolutionary peasant movement, the question of choice of the path of struggle assumed decisive importance. The latter, much like Russian Bolsheviks in 1905, felt it necessary to fight constitutional illusions "with the utmost demonstrativeness. And that meant refusing to take part, abstaining oneself and holding the people back, issuing a call for an assault on the old regime instead of working within the framework of an institution set up by that regime." On behalf of AICCR, CM wrote:

"In the present era when imperialism is heading towards total collapse, revolutionary struggle in every country has taken the form of armed struggle; Soviet revisionism, unable to retain its mask of socialism, has been forced to adopt imperialist tactics; world revolution has entered a new higher phase; and socialism is marching irrepressibly forward to victory ... the slogans 'boycott elections' and 'establish rural bases and create areas of armed struggle' ... remain valid for the entire era." Boycott elections and build base areas/areas of arms struggle – this integrated call was clearly premised on the assumed existence of a whole era of worldwide revolutionary upswing and rapid advance of socialism.

This arguably proved to be a case of overestimation, but the lesson that must be learnt here is that the tactic of boycott is premised on the assessment of situation and employed not negatively but as a positive weapon so as to lead the people along a more direct course of action towards seizure of power. But to delink the boycott tactic from these basic conditions or to imagine that such conditions obtain permanently in a country like India is a clear travesty of Marxism-Leninism, or Maoism if you will. Ostrich like, our Maoist friends bury their heads in the sands of the past because they lack the political courage to wield the difficult weapon of parliamentary struggle and continue to play with the great Leninist tactic of boycott.

This does not mean that communists should opt for the polar opposite – the parliamentary path. It is entirely possible and absolutely imperative to keep up the revolutionary spirit and uphold the revolutionary perspective even while participating in elections and waging parliamentary battles, as Lenin observed after the failure of the first Russian Revolution of 1905: "since the accursed counter-revolution has driven us into this accursed pigsty [the Duma – AS], we shall work there too for the benefit of the revolution, without whining, but also without boasting." It is in this spirit that true heirs to the legacy of undivided CPI(ML) has been developing a principled policy framework for parliamentary struggle: (a) take parliamentary forms of struggle as supplementary and subservient to extra-parliamentary forms, (b) participate in elections for the basic purpose of organizing powerful political campaigns with a view to projecting alternative policies in different spheres and heightening the political assertion of the working people as an independent force, (c) measure success mainly by our ability to integrate our election campaign with the basic movement of the people and raise the level of popular mobilization (d) where elected, raise the voice of popular movements within these bodies (from panchayats up to the parliament) and play the role of revolutionary democratic opposition vis-à-vis higher authorities, (e) reserve the boycott tactics for exceptional circumstances marked by, inter alia, an unmistakable upswing in revolutionary struggle.

6

Marx, Marxism and Maoism

The point of departure for this essay is the exchange in *Modern China* between Andrew G. Walder, Stuart Schram and Frederic Wakeman. It is extremely useful since it shows, clearly if I am right, what is wrong with most discussions of the very important matters it addresses. The direct motivation for this is the current work of a number of my students.

Some obvious problems

First, while all of the writers would acknowledge problems in understanding Marx, all have a view and, if I am right, none of them have got it quite right. The point here is not merely to challenge readings of Marx, but to emphasize that one cannot talk about Marx without having *some* view and that these days, there are more options available than these scholars suppose. (Missing, critically, is the view propounded by 'realists,' Roy Bhaskar, Derek Sayer, Norman Geras and others).

Second, it is critical to separate Marx, Engels, and Marxism. That is, not only have interpretations of Marx proliferated, but so too have interpretations of Engels. At issue is th e relation of 2nd International Marxism to both of these. Mao could hardly have appreciated the problems here, since most of the materials which provoked this fairly recent debate were not available when he was attracted to Marxism. Of course, Mao knew some central texts, e.g., *Capital*. But he read these through the eyes of a combination of first, 2nd International Marxism, which was powerfully influenced by 'positivism' and Darwinian naturalism, second, 'Leninism,' third, Stalin's understanding of Marx and Lenin—and, finally, of course, he understood all of this through the eyes of his own Chinese experience. 'Leninism' is in quotation marks, because, as above, the issue is not what Lenin believed, but what people came to understand what he believed. As with Marx, some key texts were not available, e.g., Lenin's notes on Hegel, and after 1917, Lenin had little time to refine or clarify his doctrine. None of these writers seems sensitive to these issues. None recognize the problems of reading Engels against Marx or of Engels against Kautsky or Plekanov. None seems sensitive to the context of the debates and the texts written in response to them. Walder, who is very close to getting Marx right, fails to see the problems created by Engels's later interventions, and, as Schram points out, he is especially impervious to problems of Leninism. Schram, as everybody, conflates Lenin and Leninism.

Third, Walder, but not Wakeman or Schram, seems to forget that Mao is Chinese. But none of them make much effort to say what this means.

Walder attacks 'the China field' for assuming a dualism between 'determinism' and 'voluntarism.' The 'China field' referred to seems to be mainly English-speaking writers on China. There is European literature on these topics, but we take it that these do no much figure into the relatively small circle of debates among those who constitute 'the China Field.' It would be worthwhile to explore the sociology of all of this.

Walder's formulation of the way that the 'voluntarism' issue is articulated seems to me be an accurate characterization. He writes: 'Voluntarism'—in this case denoting a social analysis and revolutionary strategy stressing human will as the primary causative agent in producing desired social change—is thus a commonly accepted characterization of Mao's thought (1: 103).

The key problem in all of this is the failure to come to grips with causality, both generally and in human affairs. Put bluntly, we need, first, to reject thoroughly empiricist readings of causality and second, we need to acknowledge firmly 'agency' and the fact that everything that happens in society is caused by what we do, even if outcomes are not intended.

We can begin by getting clear about 'determinism': Broadly, in Western philosophy, 'determinism' refers to assumptions regarding causality, that everything is caused. Moreover, and critically, causality takes the form of lawfulness: 'Whenever this, then that.' I call this, (following Bhaskar) 'regularity determinism.' It owes primarily to Hume but is now taken for granted,among all empiricists. Critically, empiricist philosophy of science thoroughly dominates thinking about science.

Because science must assume that everything is caused, the 'will,' strictly speaking is not 'free.' Thus, acts are determined if they are caused. But on a regularity determinist understanding this implies that the agent 'could *not* have done otherwise.' If we knew enough, then we could predict acts, just as we predict the location of planets in the solar system. We may 'feel' that we are free ('subjectively'), but 'really' ('objectively') we are not. More generally, then, determinism in social theory means that what happens *had* to happen, that human 'will,' ultimately, is irrelevant. Seeing the problems of the determinist view, the 'voluntarist' resists. He thinks that 'will' can make a difference. 'Objective' conditions are 'determinative,' but we can overcome these. Yet it is not only 'voluntarists' who are caught in the 'free-will/ determinism' chestnut. Almost all writers accept the bifurcation then opt uncritically for some mix of the two. Our acts are caused, but somehow we are still 'responsible' for what we do.

The 'free-will/determinism' dichotomy, however, must be rejected and reformulated. Thus (to go too quickly): 'agency' requires that agents 'could have done otherwise.' But this is not incompatible with causality. On the one side, one needs to reject ontological dualisms (Descartes' or Kants') and put humans squarely in nature. Second, one needs to reject regularity determinism and accept a 'realist' conception of causality. Causes are 'productive powers' which are always operating complexly. Thus unpredictability is a fundamental feature of the world because outcomes are complexly caused by continually changing configurations of things.

Third, humans, while part of the natural world, have emergent powers, among them, the power to choose. ('Reasons' are causes, even if one can explain them.) On this view, then, our *choices* (as Aristotle argued) are part of the causal nexus which includes existing 'materials at hand.' (These matters are more fully developed in my *A History and Philosophy of the Social Sciences*

To return to Walder: In 'the China field,' there are, he continues, two 'distinct and integrally related senses' (of voluntarism.) 'The first,' a development of the foregoing, 'refers to the relative emphasis Mao places on subjective (sic) human effort in activist politics over objective (sic) economic forces to produce (sic) social change. In this sense Mao is said to inverted Marx's dialectic (sic), so that in his method of analysis "superstructure" rather than "economic base" is the primary, if not sole factor' (ibid).

This is very typical and presupposes, of course, a bifurcation of 'base' and 'superstructure.' The language of 'objective forces' is common, but never critically unpacked. This is the problem of agency and the sense in which we 'make' history. To anticipate, 'economic forces' are the economic outcomes (e.g., unemployment) intended, but usually unintended, of decisions made by people acting with materials at hand. Or they are 'imperatives' in terms of which people act, in which case they are either 'system requirements,' holding either absolutely and therefore 'determining' what we do, or conditionally. If absolutely, they *must* obtain. Thus we must *act* in accordance with them. This nonsensical view is typical of functionalist accounts, a feature of much Marxism. It issues in a fatalism: we are all but pawns of "forces." But "forces" are plausibly construed conditionally. If so, then, they may or may not obtain. For example, it is a system requirement of capitalist reproduction that surplus be absorbed. Not only may it not be, but if it is, it is because persons have done something—which, critically, they may not have done. They do not, of course, need to have been intended to do that which, in fact, has the effect of absorbing surplus.

Walder's formulation betrays most of these problems. Thus, agency—the acts of persons—has been replaced with a dichotomy between 'subjective' and 'objective' in which perhaps, the former is 'in the head,' 'reflex,' perhaps epiphenomenal and epistemologically suspect and the later is 'real' (causal), 'out there' and knowable. Political activity (superstructure) is thus 'subjective' since presumably, it is merely 'reflection' of what is 'objective.' One thinks here of Don Quixote.

There is a way, to be sure, to rescue the idea of voluntarism so that is a genuinely useful idea. Thus, voluntarism it plausibly denotes a social analysis and revolutionary strategy which largely ignors enabling and constraining factors with which people, inevitably, act. This simple and obvious way to put the matter has enormous implications, as I shall argue.

Worth mention, it seems to me that the 'subjective'/'objective' dichotomy is more frequent in Chinese Marxism than elsewhere, but perhaps not. It would useful to pursue this issue within the framework of variations of Chinese thought. In the second sense, Mao is voluntaristic in wanting to 'speed up' 'stages through emphasis on politics' (*ibid.*).

This involves, of course, assumptions regarding Marxist 'stage theory'—the logical consequence of any 'determinist' reading of history, along with the usual bifurcation of base and superstructure. It is interesting that Walder does not say that a 'voluntarist' might try to skip or omit some stage and that he does not bring Lenin here? Surely this is also a characteristic theme of much discussion, at least outside 'the China field.'

Walder insists that 'voluntarism/determinism' dichotomy depends on views that Marx did not hold. Walder is clearly correct in this. But one needs to see how Marx escapes this and how, if I am right, Walder does not.

Walder offers a 'dialectical' reading of Marx. The problem is what, in clear terms, this means. Because he is unclear about causality, both generally, and in human affairs (and thus assumes part of the framework of the views he is opposing), Walder's view is at least confusing, if not on the edge of inconsistent. This is why both Wakeman and Schram feel sympathy with it and why both feel that they have been misrepresented. No one is sufficiently clear about the issues. (To repeat, they have not been much represented; the problem lies elsewhere.)

All Marxists appeal to 'dialectic' and everybody who tries to analyse Marxist thought therefore must assume something about what it means. Unfortunately, it is employed in a wide variety of contexts including: the relation of individual to society, the relation of 'factors' to other 'factors,' including the relation of 'base' to superstructure,' to anything containing contradictions, including 'reality,' 'consciousness' and their relations, to a particular method which involves one to grasp process, and finally (and vaguely, to a 'way of looking at the world.' Bhaskar helpfully suggests a way to organize these various contexts, e.g., into ontological, epistemological and relational dialectics, divisions which, then, can in turn be divided, but I do not pursue this here. Marx, we must emphasize, was not in the least helpful.

In a famous text in the Afterword of the 2nd Edition of *Capital* he wrote: The mystification which the dialectic suffers in Hegel's hands by no means prevents him from being the first to present its general forms of motion in a comprehensive manner. With him it is standing on its head. It must be inverted to discover the rational kernal with the mystical shell.

Unfortunately, however, 'Marx never realized his wish "to make accessible to the ordinary human intelligence, in two or three printer's sheets, what is *rational* in the method which Hegel discovered and at the same time mystified'

But, as Bhaskar as observed, 'dialectics' is 'the most contentious topic in Marxist thought and his 'two metaphors, the inversion and the kernel—have been the subject of almost theological speculation.' The reason for this clear. 'Dialectics' raises 'the two main issues on which Marxist philosophical discussion has turned, viz.,. the nature of Marx's debt to Hegel and the sense in which Marxism is a science.' The implications of this are too little appreciated and thus, it cannot be too strongly emphasized. Not only is it difficult to see what Marx did with Hegel's dialectic, but we need to appreciate that there are at least three very different conceptions of a human science at issue, a 'dialectical' *and* an 'undialectical' version of naturalistic positivism and, little noticed, a naturalistic, realist version which also is 'dialectical' (in some sense).

Some history: I have elsewhere argued that after Marx and Engels made clear their philosophical position *vis a vis* Hegel and the Hegelians—in *The German Ideology*, they turned away from philosophy. This text is surely the key text as regards the general philosophy of Marx (and at least at this stage, Engels), and its relation to both Hegel and to the question of what constitutes a human science. Unfortunately, this text was not published until after Marx died. To this day, most people read only Part I, on Feuerbach, and ignore both rest and the context of their treatment.

In the intervening years, however, socialists who were materialists (in the classical sense) were insisting that Marx and Engels make clear their relation to Hegelian philosophy and make clear why *their* socialism was 'scientific.' It was important to represent one's position as 'scientific,' but the conception of science was not settled. (For example, Marx often used 'dialectical' as a *synonym* for 'scientific.') These issues were a critical feature of the debates and struggles within the First International and within 'left' parties, particularly in the German speaking parts of Europe. For example, Duhring, an old-fashioned materialist and Ernst Mach, a phenomenalist (and later object of Lenin's polemics) were both socialists who had important conceptions of science.

Engels responded in two main tracts: *Ludwig Feuerbach and the Outcome of Classical German Philosophy* (1886; 1888) and *Herr Eugen Duhring's Revolution in Science* (1877;1888). (*Dialectics of Nature* was not part of the initial historical argument since it was not published until 1927.) Engels's *Socialism, Utopian and Scientific* (1892) is three chapters from *Anti-Durhring*. Engels introduction to the English edition (1892) perhaps finalized the codification of 'dialectical' and 'historical materialism.' The latter term was introduced in this text. Thus, Plekhanov, speaking in 1908 for the mainstream of the 2nd International (founded in 1889 and controlled by 'Marxists'), asserted that with the *Anti-Durhring*, Marxist doctrine has taken 'its final shape.'

Engels had answered the Hegelians and materialists by insisting (to make a long and complicated story short), that Hegel is an idealist; Marxists were materialists; but the 'old materialism' could not overcome two problems: restricted to the science of mechanics, it could not treat chemical and organic processes (it was 'reductionistic) and it could not 'comprehend the universe as a process—as matter developing in an historical process.' 'Old materialism' was surely reductive.

But Engels's remark that matter develops 'in a historical process' should put us on our guard. Engels needs to avoid materialist reductionism. The three 'dialectical laws' presumably make this possible. Presumably, mind and matter are 'opposites,' joined 'dialectically' but with matter primary. (Bodies can exist without minds; minds cannot exist without bodies; cf. base and superstructure, where the same relationship is thought to hold.). Thus, 'dialectical materialism'—a term probably used first by Plekhanov in 1891.

Lenin added his powerful force to this view with his *Materialism and Empirio-Criticism* (1908), a track directed at the anti-realism of the Machists who had come to dominate thinking about natural science. But despite Lenin's best intentions (and here following Engels), a defence of realism is not necessarily a defence of materialism, dialectical or otherwise. Briefly, all 'realists' are in agreement that 'nature' exists independently of mind. They are anti-idealist. But 'materialism' almost always implies a great deal more. Thus, not all naturalists are materialists.

Dialectical materialism, of course, became the official philosophy of the Soviet Union and thus appeared in all the standard texts. When we consider the hundreds of millions who have cut their teeth on this—including, of course, the Chinese, our sensitivity should be aroused. For better or for worse, Mao's writings are full of terms and formulae which have all the look of the 'orthodox' view. To the extent that 'diamat' texts are thought to represent Engels and to the extent that Engels is thought to have put into final form Marxism.

This is not the place to offer an extended criticism of 'diamat.' We can note, however, that as regards the mind/body problem, it must accept either epiphenomenalism, eliminating mind as causal or it must be a dualism, and accept some sort of mind/body interaction with body 'primary.' This has been, the more comfortable view for Marxists. It is betrayed, as noted, by the 'objective'/ 'subjective' dichotomy—a dichotomy rooted in Western philosophy in Descartes, the outstanding influence on 'French materialism.' (Cf. Marx and Engels: *The Holy Family*.)

As regards science, Engels aimed 'to show, in effect, that Marxism could formulate laws of nature and that a single ontology could embrace nature and humanity'. This was never a project of Marx, who, as noted, having 'settled issues' with Hegel, Feuerbach, etc., abandoned philosophy after 1848.

Engels does this with his three dialectical laws. They are, he says, *generalizations* from 'nature, history and thought.' They are, accordingly, exactly on a par with Spencer's evolutionary generalization that there is a 'change from an incoherent homogeniety to a coherent heterogeneity, accompanying the dissipation of motion and the integration of matter.' They conform fully with the naturalistic monism which had been profoundly accelerated by Darwin and which was eagerly picked up by materialists, e.g., Ernst Haeckel and by 'agnostic' naturalists like Spencer.

There are many difficulties with Engel's version of 'naturalism,' but one is obvious: At some level of abstraction the 'three laws' catch the idea of process (as, of course, does Spencer's famous 'law') and, perhaps, they give us a way of looking at the world. But at this level of abstraction such generalizations are entirely vacuous. There is, accordingly, a tendency to hold everything that happens or could conceivably happen is 'explained' as an outcome of the three 'laws'—without even making the effort to grasp the concrete causal mechanisms involved. (Natural selection, for example, is a mechanism realizing Spencer's 'law.') On the other hand, if change is truly to be explained, 'dialectically,' as the outcome of contradictory processes, then one needs to theorize the relevant mechanisms. It was just this, of course, which Marx did in *Capital*. On the other hand, based on everything that Marx wrote, both 'early' and 'late,' absolutely no doubt that he was not a 'dialectical materialist,' indeed, that the philosophical naturalism sketched out and presupposed in the *German Ideology* was a (successful) effort transcend the idealist/materialist dichotomy.

What of the bearing of the foregoing on 'historical materialism? Engels's *Feuerbach* contains an extensive account in criticism of Hegel's philosophy of history. What is most critical is his argument (following Hegel) that 'the many wills active in history for the most part produce results other than those they intended—often quite the opposite; their motives therefore in relation to the total result are likewise only of secondary significance.' Both propositions are true and important and as Engels rightly has it, the second is a consequence of the first. But it is not, then, a premise. With Marx in the *18th Brumaire,* Engels is clear here that people make history, even while they do not make it the way they want to. However, in rejecting Hegel, Engels's is drawn directly into a reductive materialism. He asks: '...what are the historical causes which transform themselves into these motives in the brains of actors?' But this is exactly the wrong question. We do not need a materialist account of person's motives for these are not 'the ultimate causes of historical events.' He had given the right argument: If the unintended consequences are the stuff of history, then appeal to the motives, reasons or intentions of people is largely irrelevant. What is relevant is their actions and the consequences of these. As Marx so famously remarked), we make history but not with materials of our own choosing. The problem for the historical materialist (as is clear enough in the *German Ideology*) is explaining the materials, 'materialistically.'

It is not clear when agency got lost in 'historical materialism.' Kautsky, it seems, had something to do with it. Neither Plekhanov, Lenin or Bernstein were insensitive to the problem, although none of them, burdened by *The Communist Manifesto*, a 'determinist' reading of the 1859 Preface and perhaps by Engels's remarks (above) had a fully adequate grasp. Bernstein, influenced by Kant, was also sensitive to the issue; but his account is, ultimately anti-naturalistic.

Engels's two critical books were followed by a series of now famous letters (to Conrad Schmidt, Bloch and others) in which Engels spoke directly to the problem of 'base' and 'superstructure.' To Mehring, he repeated the position of the *Feuerbach*, but confessed that he and Marx 'were bound to lay the main emphasis at first on the derivation of political, juridcial and other ideological notions, and of the actions *arising* through the medium of these notions, from basic economic facts' (1, 110). He defended the theory against the charge that it assumed an 'undialectical conception of cause and effect as rigidly opposite poles,' and thus completely disregarded 'interaction.'

This language must be emphasized. It seems, at least, to treat dialectics as a version of empiricistic causality. (I have argued that it was just during this period that empiricist versions, came to dominate. One critical holdout was Hermann Helmholtz, who held out for a strongly realist view of *Kraft* ('forces') and Ursache ('cause'). Similarly, to Bloch, Engels wrote of 'the interaction of two unequal forces: on the one hand the economic movement, on the other the new political power...which having once been established, is endowed with a movement of his own.' Here agency seems to have disappeared and 'forces' are causes. Since presumably, the economic was temporally prior and of greater force, 'the economic movement' was 'the ultimately determining factor.'

This is perhaps familiar enough, but we need to see here that on the natural reading, Walder's characterization of the view of writers in the 'China field' fits this quite exactly. In summarizing their views, he writes:

Superstructure and economic base are...considered, in the fashion of dominant positivist social sciences, as distinct separable factors or independent variables reacting on one another (1, 105).

It is easy enough to argue that, either in some particular case, or generally, some 'factor' is more important. Indeed, that is just what multiple regression is all about!

Walder is adamant in rejecting *this* view. But he *also* argues that Engels 'spent in the waning years of his life a significant amount of time correcting the common misinterpretations of..."orthodox Marxists" who systematically ignored the important role Marx attributed to all aspects of the superstructure' (1, 110). He quotes just the letters already noted to support this. But he shows no awareness of the context and relevance of Engels's books, nor of the rather plain meaning of Engels's words, including the likely significance of the remark to Bloch, frequent in Engels, to the effect that 'political, legal, philosophical theories, religious ideas and their development into systems of dogma' are 'reflexes' in 'the brains of combatants.' To sure, these 'reflexes,' 'derived' from 'basic economic facts' 'exercise influence' and even, 'in many cases

predominate in determining their *form*' (1, 112). Unfortunately, this last clause is anything but clear. On one natural reading, at least, 'form' contrasts to *substance* —reality as it really is?

Walder is unhistorical. There are no 'orthodox Marxists' until later. Engels is responding to 'ideologists,' who say that Marxists fail to give a role to ideas in history, to good old fashioned undialectical materialists and to sympathetic readers of Marx who, influenced by the famous introduction to the Preface (1859) think that in history there is but a *one-way causal street.*

Engels's letters are open to the reading Walder gives to Marx, and it may be that Engels was not far from the Marx which Walder wants to recover. But even if this is the case, in the absence of clarity between them of the critical issues, we shall never know. But it can hardly be denied that an empiricistic, causal/interactionist understanding is the conventional wisdom on Engels.

What, then, of the point that the base is 'ultimately determining.' On the view causal/interactionist view just sketched, this becomes an empirical question: Which factors ('forces') have the greater causal weight. One might just be dogmatic here and insist that the 'economic' is always 'primary.' Or one might, as with Engels, offer that it is only 'ultimately' primary or decisive 'in the last instance.' But it is not clear what this could mean? Is it a temporal question?

Since the 'economic' is first, what is 'derived' from it is 'determinined' by it even if it is 'determining?' But either these other 'factors' are 'relatively autonomous' (as must be assumed for there to be interaction) or they are not. If they are, what remains of the priority?

These problems, of course, are familiar and most recently were treated by Althusser who tried desperately to reformulate historical materialism so as to save 'the primacy thesis.' There are, features of this analysis worth preserving, but 'structure in dominance' is not one of them. (Geras's account in Bottomore, *Dictionary*, is judicious.)

By contrast, G.A. Cohen can rightly claim to represent the 'orthodox' view. Basing his argument largely on the *Preface,* he succeeds completely in saving the primacy thesis. But then one needs to reject even Engels and accept Cohen's unabashed technological determinist reading of Marx. On his reading, there is no question that history is a one-way causal street.

We argued that there are problems in giving a consistent reading of Walder. We have already suggested that he accepts and rejects an (empiricist) causal interactive model. The problem is Engels, of course. Was his reading of 'dialectics' Marx's? But we look at some of these problems from the other side. Walder points out that Marx (and Engels) have an 'organic view.' Marx undoubtedly speaks of 'organic unities.' But so as to put oneself on guard, so do positivists, e.g., Comte, Spencer and Durkheim. Marx's unities are, presumably, 'dialectical.' Thus: superstructure and economic base [are] merely different aspects or sides [why not 'moments'?] of a single unit or conceptual structure (1, 105).

This is much enriched in the second part of his essay where his account draws heavily on the work of Bertell Ollman.

Marx, he argues, conceives of society relationally. Many people, of course, say this; but the idea has is a very clear and precise meaning in Marx. This is most vivid in *Capital* where 'capital, labour, value, commodity, etc. are all grasped as relations, containing in themselves, as integral elements of what they are, those parts with which we tend to see them externally tied' (Ollman, p. 15).

We can distinguish 'externally tied' (or 'related) and 'internally related:' A relation 'aRb' is internal if both a and b are what they are by virtue of standing in the relation aRb. By contrast, a relation 'aRb' is external if 'a' and 'b' are what they independently of R.

Undoubtedly, there are internal relations (especially in society). 'Father of' is one. So, too, in Marx, is capitalist and wage worker. One cannot be a wage worker unless there are capitalists (and conversely), one cannot have capitalist production unless, within the sphere of exchange, labour power is commodified. Ollman demonstrates that many of Marx's key concepts are internally related. Moreover, it is clear that, for Marx, this is an empirical matter. There is only one to know if a relation is internal or external: one must look and see!

As Ollman says, it is in this context that we must place Marx's (confusing) use of 'determines' (*Bestimmungen*). For people socialized into an empiricistic understanding of causality, '*a* determines *b*,' means that '*a* is the cause of *b*'; and this means (in standard Humean terms), 'if a, then b.' Critically, however, on standard (Humean) readings of causality, *a* and *b* are externally related. If so, their relation is contingent (not necessary). Moreover, if so, it is hard to see how if *a* determines *b*, *b* can also determine *a*. (If it does, *a* and *b* are 'extensionally equivalent' or they have the same 'truth conditions.' E.g., 'a bachelor is an unmarried male.' Such sentences are said to 'analytic,' true 'by definition,' but, in consequence, empirically vacuous: They tell us nothing about the world. If, however, *a* and *b* are internally related, *a* and *b* can be mutually determining, necessary *and* empirical. A change in either *a* or *b* is *necessarily* a change in the other. To say, then, that '*a* determines *b*' is to focus on one side of the relation and to say that *b* could not be what is unless in stood in relation R to *a*, that there is something about *a*'s relation to *b* which makes *b* what it is. It does mean that *a* is an efficient cause, temporally or logically prior. Nor does it mean that it is a sufficient condition. It is, of course, a necessary condition. Indeed, Marx often uses 'condition' *(Bedingung)* in just such contexts.

It is easy to see the confusion and why also Walder translates '*bestimmt*' as 'presupposes' and others, e.g., Sayer, as 'entails.' Indeed, both '*a* presuposes *b*' and 'a entails *b*' are renderable as 'if *a*, then *b*;' but then, 'if, then' is a necessary relation!

The forgoing is nicely illustrated by Walder's account of apparent inconsistency in a long text from Marx's 1859 *Critique* in which Marx discusses the 'links' between production, consumption, distribution and exchange. 'First, [Marx] writes that production "determines" all the others and is "decisive," then he asserts that those aspects "determined" by production in turn determine it' (2, 131). Putting aside for the moment Marx's assertion that 'production is the decisive phase', it is clear that Marx is talking about the effects of change on these 'inner-related' (*not*, misleadingly, *inter*-related) processes. Thus, 'if the market, or the sphere of exchange expands, then the volume of production grows and tends to become differentiated.' While the relations of these factors is necessary in the sense that capitalist production requires commodification in the sphere of exchange (and conversely!) Marx is not talking about changes in the relations themselves. (If a female is divorced, she is no longer a wife.) Indeed, Marx also says, intelligibly, that 'production is, finally, determined by the demands of consumption.'

There is nothing terribly mysterious about this, even if one must be clear about what is being said. (Indeed, the simultaneous equations of modern general equilibrium theory are best understood in these terms. Its failure lies elsewhere, in particular in its failure to get under the empirical relations and to analyse the causal mechanisms which make capitalism what it is.) That is, there is an 'organic unity' to capitalist reproduction. It was precisely to task of *Capital* to spell out the causes—in the sense of mechanisms—which gave capitalism the (essential) 'organic' character it has.

If then we apply this to historical materialism, it is clear that the base/superstructure dichotomy must be *in toto* rejected. Thus to quote Ollman's summary:

If we accept that Marx's theory requires a separable determining factor carefully distinguished from what it is supposed to determine, we arrive by a process of elimination at productive technology, not because it satisfies all the conditions but because it does so better than other possible factors. What is popularly known as 'economic determinism' becomes on this interpretation technological determinism...The sustaining model for [this] interpretation is supplied by Marx's claim that 'The hand mill gives you society with the Feudal lord; the steam mill society with the industrial capitalist'. Indeed, as Ollman and then Sayer (both *Marx's Method* (1979) and *The Violence of Abstraction* (19) demonstrate, a wealth of texts show that we must reject that assumption (or accept with Marx's critics that no theorist was sloppier with his concepts). Thus, even in the *locus classicus* of the empiricist view, the Preface, it is hard to see how property relations, which presumably are juridical and thus superstructural can also be essential to constituting the mode of production, which then also 'determines'—in the empiricist sense—the superstructure.

There are, however, still several huge problems, including a positive conception of historical materialism, the primacy thesis, and the concept of dialectic in Marx. We should begin, however, by recalling what Marx was arguing against.

Philosophically, as noted, it regarded the opposition between idealists and materialists. Although Engels (and following him, Lenin), were to insist that these were only alternatives, Marx saw virtues in both. Although we cannot develop this here, nor defend the assumption that Marx never abandoned these originating ideas, in writings versus Hegel, Marx sketched an alternative 'naturalism.' Some long texts will give the taste of his resolution:

The outstanding achievement of Hegel's *Phenomenology*...is, first, that Hegel grasps the self-creation of man as a process, objectification as loss of the object, as alienation and transcendence of this alienation, and that he therefore grasps the nature of *labour*, and conceives objective man (true because real man) as the result of his *own labour*. The *real*, active orientation of man to himself as a species-being (i.e., as a human being is only possible so far as he really brings forth all his *species-powers*.

Idealism sees that humans are self-creating and that this process and the *realization* of human powers requires society. It was precisely the materialist incapacity to deal with historically constructed 'human sensuality' that was expressed in Marx's first thesis on Feuerbach.

The chief defect of all hitherto existing materialism (that of Feuerbach included) is the the thing, reality, sensuousness, is conceived only in the form of the *object or of contemplation*, but not as *sensuous human activity, practice*, not subjectively. Hence, in contradistinction to materialism, the *active* side was developed abstractly by idealism—which, of course, does not know real, sensuous activity as such. Feuerbach wants sensuous objects, really distinct from the thought objects, but he does not conceive human activity itself as *objective* activity.

Marx here rejects the Cartesian epistemological problematic of 'subject' and 'object,' the problematic which generates the idealism/materialism dichotomy. (It is of some significance to scholars in the 'China field' that John Dewey totally shared in rejecting this problematic.) Idealism correctly sees 'the active side,' the role that socially constituted human consciousness plays in constituting the experienced world. Materialism, which recognizes the independence of objects from thought is unable to adequately deal with this. But the idealist collapses 'reality' into 'reality as known.'

Hegel, Marx says, made 'a double error.' First, he conceives of 'entities alienated from the human being' 'only in their thought form.' The consequence was the reconstitution of reality as 'absolute knowledge.' This is the defining feature of absolute idealism. Second, 'the vindication of the objective world for man...appears in Hegel as the recognition of *sensuousness, religion,* state power, etc. as *mental* phenomena, for *mind* alone is the true essence of man'. Thus the Hegelian 'dialectic' is a dialectic of 'the Idea:'

Universal history...shows the development of the consciousness of Freedom on the part of Spirit. This development implies a graduation —a series of increasingly adequate expressions or manifestations of Freedom, which result from its Idea.

Putting these points together, we can see what Marx was up to when he asserted: We see here how consistent naturalism or humanism is distinct from both idealism and materialism, and at the same time constitutes their unifying truth. We see also that only naturalism (sic) is able to comprehend the process of world history.

Man is directly a *natural being*. As a natural being, and as a living natural being he, on the one hand, endowed with *natural powers* and *faculties,* which exist in him as tendencies and abilities, as *drives*. On the other hand, as a natural, embodied, sentient, objective being he is a *suffering,* conditioned and limited being, like animals and plants. The *objects* of his drives exist outside of himself as *objects* independent of him, yet they are *objects* of his *needs,* essential *objects* which are indispensable to the exercise and confirmation of his faculties...

But man is not merely a natural being; he is *human* natural being. He is a being for himself, and therefore a *species being* and as such he has to express himself in being as well as thought. Consequently, *human* objects are not natural objects as they present themselves directly, nor is *human sense,* as it is immediately and objectively *given, human* sensibility and human objectivity...And as everything natural must have its *origin so man* has his process of genesis, *history,* which is for him, however, a conscious process and thus which is consciously self-transcending.

The Preface and opening pages of Part I of *The German Ideology,* 'Feuerbach: Opposition of Materialist and Idealist Outlook' provides the transition to the problem of history.

Until now men have constantly had false conceptions of themselves, about they what they are and what they ought to be. They have related themselves to one another in conformity with their ideas of God, of normal man, etc. They, the creators, have been bowing to their creations.

This is, of course, Feuerbach's criticism of Hegel—and, so far, Marx agrees. The problem, however, is that in the Young Hegelians' fantasies all the relationships of men, of all their actions, their chains and their limitations are products of their consciousness. Consequently they give men the moral postulate of exchanging their present consciousness for human [Bauer], critical [Feuerbach] or egoistic [Stirner] consciousness to remove their limitations. This amounts to a demand to interpret what exists in a different way.

Indeed, 'a clever fellow once got the idea that people drown because of they possessed *the idea of gravity.* Cf., of course, *Thesis 11: 'The philosophers have only interpreted the world in various ways; the point is, to change* it. For this we need to understand history.

Marx continues: 'Not one of these philosophers [i.e., neither Hegel nor his 'materialist' critics] ever thought to look into the connection between German philosophy and German reality, between their criticism and their own material environment'. The section which follows, then, is the heart of what we now call 'historical materialism.' Its point was to show that the 'chains and limitations' cannot be removed short changing the social world which we have made—along with, to be sure, those forms of consciousness which are its historical product.

Marx (and Engels) will begin with 'real individuals, their actions, and their material conditions of life, those which they find existing as well as those which they produce through their actions.' This is the 'first premise of all human history,' a premise which 'can be substantiated in a purely empirical way.' The first act of these individuals is that 'they begin to *produce their means of subsistence*. The first fact to be established, then, is the physical organization of these individuals and their consequent relationship to the rest of nature...All historiography must proceed from these natural bases and their modification in the course of history through the actions of men'. There is no clearer statement of 'the primacy thesis.' Indeed, even if, as above, there is no 'separable, determining factor,' if we are understand history, we must establish this 'first fact.' Moreover,

> In each particular instance, empirical observation must show empirically, without any mystification or speculation, the connection of the social and political structure with production.

There is here no *a priori* commitment to the *nature* of this 'connection' and no concern for efficient causality, for what causes what. The primacy thesis holds only that the social and political are 'connected' to production and that this must be our first concern. The contrast is to 'ideologists' and, if you will, to the social scientists who still today think that 'ideas' of political forms or forms of the family, etc. have *independent* histories, unconnected to what is produced and how it is produced.

Indeed, failure to fully appreciate that, for Marx, in capitalism these 'connections' are very different than they were in pre-capitalisms has contributed to confusion over the base/superstructure bifurcation. In *all* societies, including capitalism, 'superstructural' elements are involved in the very constitution of the mode of production. In some, there is no 'state' and, e.g., as Durkheim demonstrated, religion is often *constitutive* of production modes. Marx, of course, offered but sketches of the 'connections' in pre-capitalist societies. He concentrated on capitalism. It is, however, a critical part of his analysis that *only* in capitalism is there a bifurcation of 'civil society' and the state, of 'bourgeois' and 'citizen.' Only in capitalism is there, strictly speaking an 'economy.' It was thus easy to think of the 'base' as 'the economy' and the state, etc. as superstructure, separate from it (and 'determined' by it).

Marx's emphasis on the activities of real individuals makes his view strongly agency centered. It assumes the philosophical naturalism of the earlier criticism of Hegel, an account which is expanded, in 'dialectical' terms, in a section which repeats the claim that 'as far as Feuerbach is a materialist he does not deal with history, and as far as he deals with history he is not a materialist'.

The language shifts to 'moments'—aspects of an internally related (dialectical) process. There are four: (1) the production of means to satisfy biological needs; (2) the production, attending this, of new needs; (3) their reproduction; (4) the 'appearance' (manifestation) of a double relationship regarding production and reproduction. That is, the relation manifests itself, on the one hand, as 'natural' (i.e., as quite inevitable, and *not* 'conventional) on the other as 'social.' Marx explicates 'social.' 'The latter is social in the sense that individuals co-operate, no matter under what conditions, in what manner, and for what purpose.' 'Consequently,' Marx continues, 'a certain mode of production or industrial stage is always combined with a certain mode of co-operation of social stage, and [NB!] this mode of co-operation is itself a "productive force"'. It is not wrong to say, I think, that the mode of co-operation is the *essential* relation for Marx. It quite literally *defines* the 'mode of production.' Contrast here, of course, the slave mode of production with capitalism in which co-operation is mystified 'freedom.'

All of this *presupposes* consciousness. Following Rousseau (if not directly?), 'language, like consciousness, only arises from the need and necessity of relationships with other men...The animal as no *"relations"* with anything...Its relation to others does not exist as a relation. Consciousness is thus from the very beginning a social product and will remain so as long as men exist'. Of course, animals are related; but they are not *socially* related. Social relations require consciousness: shared meanings, self-awareness and awareness of others—a 'species-life.'

But, 'in direct contrast to German philosophy, which descends from heaven to earth...,' 'the production of ideas, of conceptions, of consciousness is directly interwoven with the material activity [i.e., production in satisfaction of need] and the material relationships of men [i.e., social relationships constituting the organization this production]; it is the language of actual life.' That is, 'consciousness does not determine life, but life determines consciousness'. In contrast to the 'ideologists' ideas have no independent existence—the key insight of any serious sociology of knowledge.

Moreover, 'the ideas which these individuals form are ideas either about their relations to nature, their mutual relations, or their own nature' *and* 'it is evident that in all these cases these ideas are the conscious expression—real or illusory—of their actual relationships and activities, of their production and commerce, and of their social and political behavior'. We need to keep in mind here that people do not have one 'consciousness' when working, another when arguing about politics and another when praying or playing with one's family. That is, ideas about themselves, their relations to one another, and to nature are implicated in all their activities. And we need to emphasize that these ideas need not be true. Indeed, with the division of material and mental labour, consciousness can really boast of being something other than consciousness [real or illusory] of existing practice, of *really* representing something without representing something real. From this moment on consciousness can emancipate itself from the world and proceed to the formation of "pure" theory, theology, philosophy, ethics, etc..

This sketch of an explanation of 'ideology' and the distinction between real and illusory forms of consciousness, is perhaps the most distinctive feature of Marxian social science. We can, at this point, consider some other issues usually confounded in discussing the 'base/superstructure' metaphor. We see some of these in Wakeman's response to Walder. Wakeman is rightly concerned that Walder's account smacks of Lukacs's Totalitat in which 'the totality of relations' overwhelms those it 'enmeshes.' Then, he continues, 'truly critical consciousness would be obliterated, and mere idealism or false consciousness would prevail. The Marxian dialectic, in other words, would yield to a Heraclitan [Parmenidean?] or Taoist conception of interaction within what is given.

From the present point of view, it is not clear whether Walder's account is vulnerable to this difficulty. But such a collapse is quite impossible if we keep firmly in mind Marx's criticism of Hegel, or alternatively, the naturalistic ground for distinguishing real and illusory forms of consciousness. Marx, ever the epistemological realist, holds that we can come to an understanding of *actual* practices of people and of the *real* relations which obtain in these.

Our ideas about these may be either true of false. Indeed, it may well be that some of our activities, at least, require that we have *false* beliefs (false consciousness). This includes, of course, religious practices—criticized by Feuerbach, et al. But as Marx insisted, this does not go far enough. It includes, as well, political practice and the social relations themselves. Again, take it that this is the fundamental burden of *Capital*, Vol. I, but especially the account of the fetishism of commodities, a necessary precondition for the commodification of labour power, and a necessary condition for capitalist reproduction and thence, of a host of other practices 'connected' with these. This an example of 'dialectics.'

In his account of the 1859 Preface, Wakeman sees this, but misconstrues it. Lodged in the causal/interactionist model, he argues that if there is to be 'critical consciousness,' one must give causal priority to 'the real foundation' ('the hard material core of Marx's economic reductionism'). He quotes Marx:...it is always necessary to distinguish the material transformation of the economic conditions of production, which can be determined with the precision of a natural science, and the legal, political, religious, artistic or philosophic, in short, ideological forms in which men become conscious of this conflict and fight it out'.

This is, admittedly, a puzzling and confusing text. But the main message is clear enough: 'ideological forms' refers precisely to those beliefs which people have—including beliefs about the social relations of production. Some may be true and some false. That is precisely why there is conflict. (It suggests also that it would be wrong to identify 'ideology' with 'false consciousness.')

Sayer (*Marx's Method*) offers that in the Preface Marx's bifurcation is meant to distinguish between 'essential relations' ('economic structure') and their 'forms' of manifestation ('superstructure'). This is useful, but easily misunderstood. Lenin got it right. And Wakeman misunderstood. Lenin wrote:...Just as material causes underlie (*Ursache:* which means, as Helmholtz had said, 'that which lies hidden behind the changes we perceive') all natural phenomena [what is manifest], so the development of human society is conditioned (sic) by the development of material, productive forces. On the development of the material, productive forces depend the relations into which men enter with another in the production of the things required for the satisfaction of human needs. And in these relations lies the explanation of all the phenomena [what is manifest] of social life, human aspirations, ideas and laws.

One reads this an 'economic reductionism' only if one reads 'conditioned' and 'depends' in empiricist causal terms: 'forces' cause 'production relations' which cause beliefs. But it would be very hard to deny that the development of human society is not 'conditioned' by the development of productive forces. Similarly, the development of productive forces 'depends upon' social relations. Notice, please, that he does not say that social relations depend upon 'productive forces'! Finally, Lenin says, rightly, that we can explain beliefs in terms of *real social relations*, relations which are constitutive of what is produced and how it is produced, including, then, not simply the relation of capitalist to wage worker, but the juridical and political relations which are implicated. Again, compare Marx's effort to *explain* 'price' or 'free wage labour' in *Capital*—an effort in 'critical dialects'!

As noted, this is precisely the place to see the pertinence of 'dialect' in Marx. As noted, 'dialects' in Marx shows up on many contexts. This has led some writers to argue that it mostly (at least) a way of looking at the world. What way? Roughly, it is an anti-empiricistic, atomistic way, which is the way of Hume, Russell, Wittgenstein of the Tractatus and of logical positivism—and thus of most mainstream social science (and 'theory' of science). By contrast, then, a 'dialectical' approach emphasizes wholes, unities, relations, *trans*action, epigenesis, process, emergence. This is quite right, but first, as above it is very vague and second, it does not in any way require the materialist dialectics of Engels. Indeed, in my view, this is likely to be either a dodge or a straightjacket. We can, in any case, be more specific than this. Bhaskar argues that in Marx, we can distinguish his *critical* from his *systematic* dialectics.

Critical dialectics takes the form of 'a triple critique of (1) the economic conceptions of everyday life which are uncritically appropriated by political economy; (2) a critique of political economy as considering only phenomena as 'given': positivism (NB, the subtitle of *Capital*) and (3) a critique of an existing mode of production (capitalism) which renders these conceptions necessary for the agents who actions constitute, reproduce) and, eventually, transform it.

Marx's systematic dialectics, then, provides the theoretical grounds for his critique. As Bhaskar writes: 'Ultimately...all the contradictions of capitalism derive from the structurally fundamental contradictions between use-value and the value of the commodity, and between the concrete useful labour and abstract social aspects of the labour it embodies'. As above, these are '(i) real inclusive oppositions, in that the terms or poles of the contradictions existentially presuppose one another and (ii) internally related to a mystifying form of appearance. That is, the 'dialect' appears in two way: first in the structural conditions of capitalism as a system and second, in the analysis of the connection between 'consciousness' and its conditions.

In sum, Marx transformed Hegelian dialectic 'naturalistically,' so that it became a way to grasp 'the causally generated presentation of social objects and their explanatory critique.' For Marx, this involved recognition of those conditions of activity which make humans natural beings and those conditions of activity which, depending on activity, are historically specific. While he concentrated on the latter, he never forgot the former. For Marx 'contradictions' were neither necessary truths (as in Hegel) nor metaphysical postulates (as in Engels). Rather, he aimed his guns at the specific contradictions of capitalism, an analysis which, as Bhaskar says, neither entails or presupposes a 'dialectics of nature.'

7

Rise of the Maoist Movement

Nepal has been suffering from the worst crisis of its history since 12 February 1996. Since the onset of Maoist insurgency — (the Maoists call it 'People's War')- more than 7000 people — including state forces, insurgents and innocent civilians — have lost their lives and many thousands are internally displaced in violent conflicts in the country. The conflict was initiated from socially and economically deprived western hills of the Kingdom, but the web of violence swept through the entire country rapidly. On 26 November 2001 the state of emergency was imposed in the country. The government has deployed the Royal Nepal Army (RNA) to remote areas considered to be strongholds of the insurgents. However, several 'successful' attacks by the insurgents on many district headquarters and government infrastructure suggest that almost a year of SOE was anything but successful in curbing the violence in Nepal.

High profile visits to Nepal by the U.S. Secretary of State (January, 2002), followed by inspection of insurgency areas by the U.S. Ambassador to Nepal and U.S. military officials (April, 2002) "to evaluate the military needs of Nepalese government," highlight the international importance of the conflict. These activities will have direct repercussion on Nepal's relations with its two giant neighbours- China and India. Political analysts fear that such international involvement and the severity of the ongoing civil war could be an indication that Nepal is fast becoming a 'failed state' and thus a playground of geopolitical actors.

GEOGRAPHY OF THE KINGDOM OF NEPAL

Located strategically between China in the North and India

in the East, West, and South, the small landlocked country of Nepal has a great variety of topography ranging from high mountains in the north to a narrow strip of a flat land in the south. Nepal comprises the middle third of the long sweep of the Himalaya, stretched between upper Indus River in Pakistan to Tsang Po and Brahmaputra Rivers in Tibet and India, respectively. Due to vast topographical variation, Nepal has extremely diverse biogeographic belts of subtropical, temperate, subartic, and even desert-steppe environments in its cross-section. As a result the country is blessed with a unique bio-diversity.

For administrative purposes, Nepal is divided into five development regions: Eastern, Central, Western, Mid-western, and Far-western; and each region is then divided into three ecological sub-regions: Mountains in the north, Hills in the middle parts, and Terai (flat land) in the south. Similarly, there are 14 zones in the country and each development region consists of two or more zones. Fragile highlands and mountains occupy two third of the country. In such harsh environmental and climatic conditions live more than 23 million Nepali people.

A Brief Political History

Until recently Nepal was considered a peaceful Himalayan Kingdom. Apart from occasional tales of the Everest-conquering brave Sherpas and fearless Gurkha fighters, the country mostly remained in anonymity - a mysterious Shangri-la to the rest of the world. Unlike many of its counterparts in the subcontinent, Nepal did not have to endure the postcolonial trauma, as it was never colonized by foreigners. However, it had to go through a painful period of the autocratic Rana regime that lasted for 105 years and its borders remained virtually closed for the first half of the 20th century. Although this isolation ended in 1951, it left the country with a devastating legacy of severe poverty, illiteracy, and backwardness, which hurt the kingdom even today.

The demise of Rana regime and a multiparty democracy, however, did not lead to a bright start for the country. The country made little progress in terms of tangible development. After almost a decade of power struggle and political experimentation, in 1959 a new constitution was finally promulgated and general elections for a national assembly were held in which the social democratic Nepali Congress (NC) Party held absolute majority. However, the political leadership could not take advantage of this unique opportunity. Instead, the political wrangling intensified in the kingdom, providing the monarchists with an opportunity to speculate that being an extremely poor country with a very low literacy rate Nepal still lacked political sophistication to remain a multiparty democracy. In addition, the Tibetan revolt against the Chinese in 1959-60 made the entire region politically volatile.

Conservative forces went on to speculate that in such an externally volatile situation, Nepal would not remain a unified, non-aligned and independent state unless the king intervened to provide political stability and strong leadership.

Consequently, on December 15, 1960 King Mahendra dissolved the parliament, disbanded all political parties, and new multitiered pyramidal party-less *Panchayat* System of governance was introduced, which was subsequently formalized by a new constitution in 1962. The constitution established the King as the head of state with sole authority over all governmental institutions, including the Council of Ministers and the parliament. Three decades of absolute monarchy, however, made little progress in dismantling the feudal structure of society; bringing development to the needy people of remote areas; and finding political reconciliation in the country.

During the autocratic *Panchayat* era "the top-down, donor-driven planning process lacked a connection with the local population in remote areas. Development projects were selected on an ad hoc basis, depending on the availability of external aid without regard to their overall integration, socio-economic justification, or long-range sustainability". Such an ad hoc arrangement of development, often made by autocratic and feudal bureaucrats, created disparities among the regions. The development gap between the mountains and the Terai regions, the eastern and western regions, and the urban and rural populations of the country widened. Forty per cent of the population was below the poverty line in 1975-76 and the proportion increased to 43% in 1984-85.

Thus, the three decades of *Panchayat* System of governance, "tailored made to suit Nepalese condition and traditions", as the Panchayat leaders loved to proclaim, miserably failed in both political and economic fronts. Outlawed political parties, such as

Nepali Congress (NC) Party and several left parties united under a common banner of the United Left Front (ULF) continued their struggle to restore democracy, which culminated in a huge mass movement across the country in 1990. The *Panchayat* system was thus abolished and a shift to constitutional monarchy was achieved.

The country proclaimed the 1990 Constitution of the Kingdom of Nepal, drafted within a few months by representatives of the NC and the left parties. This is the legal base of Nepal's current political system and it not only enshrined fundamental human rights, but also brought sovereignty finally to the people. The constitution proclaims, "Nepal is a multiethnic, multilingual, democratic, independent, indivisible, sovereign, Hindu and Constitutional Monarchical Kingdom". Despite being the most democratic constitution the country has ever had, it was a result of a tripartite agreement and a series of compromises between the monarchists, NC and the ULF. It ignored the voices demanding a constitutional assembly and failed to recognize many distinct ethnic identities by institutionalizing a common culture of Hindu hegemonism.

The NC won the first elections held under the new constitution and United Marxist-Leninist (UML) became the formidable opposition in the parliament. The enthusiasm of the early 1990s was short-lived partly because expectations for political and economic progress were extremely high and partly because political leadership proved to be utterly unprepared and corrupt. All political permutations and combinations of governance among radically different political parties were experimented in the following 12 years in Nepal. All together Nepal has changed 11 governments in the last decade. Even the UML party formed a minority government in 1994, becoming the first communist party in the world to form a government in a monarchy. Amidst such political instability, economic development had to take a back seat. Donor-driven economic reforms and liberalization were conducted in great rush, which yet again proved to be devastating. NC was blamed for abandoning its socialist agenda and rapidly moving towards a market economy. Hasty experimentation with market reform, however, did not help alleviate endemic poverty of the country.

Prosperity remains as elusive as ever. According to the World Bank, almost 50% of the Nepalese population survives below

US$1 a day. The GDP growth rate in 2001 was below 1%. The country remains dependent largely on subsistence agriculture. The share of manufacturing in the total economy is less than 10 percent of GDP. Increasing reliance on foreign assistance became the hallmark of successive and ineffectual governments. Economic inequality among various social groups in Nepal became wider and deeper. Leftist scholars in Nepal argue that the richest 10 percent of the population has control over 50% of the national income. To cope with abject poverty nearly one-third of the total labour force, especially from high mountains and hills, is forced to emigrate to India and other countries for low-paying jobs and some for services in Indian and British armies.

Rationale

The Maoist insurgency in Nepal has commonly been presented as a political and socio-economic problem. Endemic and persistent poverty, inequitable distribution of wealth and lopsided regional policies, social injustice or political disparity, as well as chronic failure of governance at the center are perceived as the most visible and significant precursors of the armed insurrection in Nepal. There is no disagreement that destitution has been a major cause of numerous civil conflicts in many developing economies. However, political analysts generally limit their argument within these proximate issues and tend to ignore other causal linkages. Acceptance of political and socio-economic factors as ultimate causes of deprivation and conflict generally fails to provide tools much needed by the state to defuse a conflict. Since provision of physical infrastructure (classical interpretation of 'development') becomes the dominant strategy, policy makers fail to follow whether the lack of 'development' is the primary factor of persistent poverty, and hence rebellion, or are there underlying environmental issues that are often not elevated to the realm of 'high politics'?

Ecologists and some scholars in security studies have argued that environmental degradation is the ultimate cause of civil strife in many parts of the world. However, their analyses are often not empirically grounded in the domestic politics of a region, and hence have not been widely accepted in policy-making circles. Anne Ehrlich et al. describe the pre-existing social, political, or cultural cleavages, regime types, and economic circumstances, as 'intervening variables' of the conflict, and analysts often interpret them as the conflict's immediate causes. Political commentators both from Nepal and abroad on Maoist insurgency have concentrated only on these intervening variables. A web conference on the current crisis in Nepal organized by the Program on Humanitarian Policy and Conflict Research at Harvard University identified political and legal, social and ethnic, economic and regional and international political factors as the most significant aspects of insurgency in Nepal. Similarly, one of the eminent political thinkers of Nepal, Nilamber Acharya, who was involved in the preparation of current constitution of Nepal in 1990, thinks that the Maoist rebellion is basically a political movement created by extreme poverty in rural Nepal and sustained by organizational skill and economic strength of Maoist.

Exclusion from larger social, economic and political institutions may be a necessary but not sufficient cause of a conflict. In the context of Nepal, such analysis often fails to appreciate the complex inter-linkage between environmental degradation, prosperity, and poverty in the hills. Homer-Dixon hypothesized that "environmental scarcity simultaneously increases economic deprivation and disrupts key social institutions, which in turn causes 'deprivation' conflicts such as civil strife and insurgency". Moreover, according to him such civil conflicts particularly affect developing countries because of their over reliance on environmental resources. The history of deprivation conflicts around the world indicates that rebellions are likely to occur in remote and marginalized regions, which are often plagued by erosion, resource degradation and depletion and hence increasing scarcity of renewable resources. With numerous examples of conflicts in many parts of the world, Myers noted that a decline in the environmental underpinnings of agriculture was a major or strong contributing factor of violence. In fact, agricultural degradation is linked to the decade-long violence in one of the most prosperous states of India. Vandana Shiva traces roots of the Punjab tragedy — commonly presented as an outcome of ethnic and communal conflict between two religious communities— to the high political and ecological demands of the Green Revolution in India, which left the prosperous state with overextraction of natural resources, diseased soils, pest-infested crops, waterlogged deserts and disillusioned farming community that went violently against the centralizing state.

In this paper we explore the causes accelerating the degradation of the environment that threatens the livelihoods of millions of poor people in the hills of Nepal. We argue that such environmental degradation coupled with demographic changes widened socio-economic disparities especially in the form of access to sufficient food and land among peoples in the Mid-and Far-western development regions of Nepal and indirectly led to the Maoists insurgency in these regions. Mounting massive anti-insurgency campaigns may provide an immediate relief from the present Maoists, but the mechanism that creates the phenomenon of red rebellion will continue to exist unless the root cause of the conflict is identified and addressed properly.

Methodological constraints

Generally, social conflicts are the result of a series of causes, which are often inter-linked and trigger each other mutually. Hence, they cannot be explained with a mono-causal rationalization. As explained earlier, although environmental degradation plays a major role, it mostly remains at the bottom of a long chain of a cause-effect scenario of violence. Although the effects of ecological degradation on poverty and conflicts have long been debated, the evidence has been fragmented, owing in part to the poorly understood complexities of the issue. Moreover, it is difficult to establish an independent variable of the degradation with respect to which other variables change with time and finally lead to violent conflicts. Therefore, a quantitative demonstration of a direct link is hard to achieve. It is even more complicated in a country like Nepal, where micro level studies are

rare and very limited number of research resources are available on the environmental degradation of the conflict zone. In absence of independent studies and reliable time series data, one has to rely on government statistics, the quality of which is not always fully reliable.

THE MAOIST INSURGENCY

An ostensible alternative to the present predicament arose on 12 February 1996, when the Communist Party of Nepal (Maoist) or CPN-Maoist launched its so-called "People's War" (*Jana Yuddha* in Nepali language) in the Mid-western hills to eliminate "feudalism and bureaucratic capitalism" from Nepal- a country which the Maoists think is still under "a semi-feudal and semi-colonial dispensation and thus has a *revolutionary objective situation*".

The insurgency was started with a 40-point demands presented to the government as a prerequisite for negotiation. The ultimate goal was to "turn this beautiful Himalayan country into an invincible 'red-fort' and a shining trench of world proletarian revolution.". The experience of Sendero Luminoso in Peru seems to have provided many strategic lessons to the Himalayan Maoists. Emulating the 'Gonzalo Thought' of the Sendero Luminoso movement, Nepalese Maoists - through their own 'Prachanda Path' (named after the leader of the movement Pushpakamal Dahal, a.k.a. 'Comrade Prachanda')- called for the "prolonged people's war" that first liberates the poor villages from "a handful of ruling parasitic classes" and eventually surrounds and defeats the cities. This was precisely the kind of revolution that was employed by Mao in China. It is important to note that the Mao's original cultural revolution had appalling environmental consequences and indeed nature was abused quite perfidiously in that context, and hence we should not transpose any lessons from the Nepalese Maoist struggle to the original Maoist movement in China.

Initially, the insurgents chose the Mid-western hills of Rukum, Rolpa, Salyan, Jajarkot and environs to begin their war because the location is remote and far from the capital and an oppressed ethnic population as an easy recruitment option for the Maoists exists in the region. While according to Nilamber Acharya even prior to the insurgency there was nominal existence of the state in that area and that could be the main reason why the violent struggle started from there.

Armed assaults on police stations in rural districts, confiscation of property from oppressive landlords, and punishment of local 'tyrants' were the initial strategies that made the insurgents popular among the poor. Although the ethnic composition of the insurgents is not known, available evidences of the involvement of various ethnic liberation organizations such as Tharu National Liberation Front in the Terai region, Khumbuan Liberation Front in the eastern mountains, Newa Khala in the capital Kathmandu, and numerous faces of dead insurgents suggest that many Mongoloid ethnic groups (considered to be traditionally exploited by upper castes Brahmin and Chhetri or Thakuri) such as Magar, Rai, Limbu, Tamang, etc. and Tharus of Terai make up the core fighting cadre of the Maoist movement. Surprisingly, however, out of forty people recently listed by the government as the "top terrorists", twenty-nine belong to the in the words of Comrade Prachanda "....[Western Nepal was chosen because] *geographically, there are no transportation facilities, there is no electricity, and communication is also very weak for the ruling classes.... people here are more oppressed by the ruling classes, and the government in Kathmandu is very far from here. And in western Nepal there are the Mongolian ethnic groups.... These nationalities are so sincere and such brave fighters-historically they have had this kind of culture. And upper caste chauvinism and feudal ties do not prevail in these nationalities"*.

supposedly "oppressor" Brahmin and Chettri castes, including the supreme leader 'Comrade Prechanda' and one of the main ideologues of the movement Dr. Baburam Bhattarai.

Interestingly, just like 'Comrade' Gonzalo of Sendero Luminoso movement, Nepalese Maoist leader Bhattarai has a doctoral degree from a reputed University. It indicates the involvement of highly educated middle-class Brahmins in the movement. Like Sendero movement, women and young people make up the core of Maoist militants. It is significant that observers think women now constitute a third of the Maoist movement in some of the most affected districts.

Armed struggle by leftist parties is not a new phenomenon in Nepal. Inspired by the 1967 peasant uprising at neighboring Naxalbari in Darjeeling district of West Bengal, India (popularly known as the 'Naxalite' movement), many young leftist activists in the Eastern Jhapa District initiated the 'class elimination of bourgeois'. Land reform was a core issue of that violence. However, the armed rebellion was quickly suppressed. Nevertheless, in spite of having a tradition of factionalism the communist movement survives and grows in strength in Nepal, because the slogan of utopian and egalitarian society remains highly appealing to illiterate and extremely poor masses of the country, especially in remote areas.

However, poverty and disenfranchisement are penultimate causes and we argue that ever-increasing environmental degradation is the ultimate cause of the creation of the so-called 'revolutionary objective situation' in Far- and Mid-western regions for Maoists insurgents to grow and multiply.

ENVIRONMENTAL DIMENSION OF POVERTY

Although the degree of reliance on the environment for survival varies from place to place, there is no ecosystem, which is "free of pervasive human influence". Human dependence on the environment is clearly pronounced in the hills of Nepal. Being a land-locked country with two-third of its area covered by geologically young mountains severely constrained by rugged terrain and limited resources, the lives of many Nepalese people living in remote and hilly areas totally hinge on natural resources that the surrounding ecosystem offers. Almost 80% Nepalese population is rural and subsistence farming is the major occupation. Hence, constant modification of the environment is inevitable. However, mountains and hills are sensitive to any changes because of their "specificities" such as inaccessibility, fragility, marginality, diversity, human adaptability and unique niche advantages. Sensitivity to changes tends to increase with increasing altitudes in mountains.

Environmental carrying capacity of mountain regions is extremely low and, therefore, with repeated, high-intensity use of limited resources the chances of irreversible damage to the environment remain high. Proximate causes of depleting limits of fragile mountain habitats in Nepal could be a variety of human interventions, such as overextraction of mountain resources, overcropping and overgrazing, disappearing traditional techniques of agriculture and dwindling niche advantages. As a consequence, deforestation and soil degradation, erosion, flooding, landslides are becoming frequent, while necessary crop yields are declining.

Ever increasing demand for food for growing population exerts tremendous pressure on available land. Little agriculture is possible in high mountains, while the middle mountains occupying more than 60% of Nepal's total land area offer only 35% of cultivated land. Possibilities of farming in Nepal are limited by physical factors such as inadequate precipitation, low temperature, the mountains terrain, and thin and infertile soils. Scarcity of irrigation water and poor soil quality limit the prospect of cropping intensification in many parts of the country. Some recent data suggests that more than 20% area of the country is already under cultivation and it is estimated that approximately 33% of land area could be potentially cultivated if irrigation and soil fertility management facilities were provided. However, provision of irrigation in many parts of the country is financially not practical and available irrigation facilities are rudimentary. Hence, agriculture in Nepal remains heavily dependent on Indian Monsoons, which result from complex interacting phenomena and are thus highly unpredictable. Expansion of agricultural land is practically not feasible anymore, as most agriculturally suitable lands have already been brought under cultivation. Hence, encroachment of forests remains the only available option.

Deforestation

The livelihood of rural poor completely depends on forests and hence forests of Nepal are one of the heavily exploited natural resources. Population growth, growing livestock numbers, and poor management are all contributing to forest degradation in Nepal. Historically forest management was not a priority of the state since the population was small and forest resources were abundant. In the hills the conversion of forests into farmlands was encouraged and remaining forests were managed by the local populations through various arrangements developed indigenously. User rights, consensus on resource use, control of access by humans and livestock, and a balance between protection and utilization were the common characteristics of indigenous forest management systems that had effectively ensured a sustainable use of natural resources in the country.

Available literature on the rate of deforestation in Nepalese hills is conflicting. Despite spending a large chunk of budget on forestry management, the country still does not have an exact figure of forest resources and the rate of their disappearance. The most widely used 1986-Land Resource Mapping Project (LRMP) survey is too old to be useful. Deforestation in Nepal, however, is generally regarded as quite alarming. The 'State of the Environment 2001' report published by the United Nations Environment Program indicates that within the last 15 to 16 years the country has lost 24 per cent of forest coverage. Respective figures for Mid- and Far-western regions are higher at 28 and 31 per cent. Only 38 per cent of forests in the Mid-western region are physically reachable by local people.

Rural populations depend on forests for fuelwood and fodder supply, and during the time of severe food deficit forest provides coping means to earn money or barter food. In 1998, approximately

80% of energy demand of the country was fulfilled by fuelwood. People are more dependent on fuelwood in the hills. Per capita fuel wood consumption in the Hills is estimated to be 640 kg/person/year, much higher than that in the Terai at 479. Similarly, between 1985 and 1998, the overall population of livestock in the country increased by 20%. Grazing areas, however, remained constant in the same period putting more pressure on available forests. In the hills and mountains of Nepal, from 1984 to 1996, the population of cattle, buffaloes, and goats increased by 5.77, 8.30, and 9.37%, respectively, while that of sheep declined by 2.53%. It is estimated that forest feed used by livestock in hills and mountains are 42 and 33%, respectively.

Due to these reasons, the pressure on forests in all parts of Nepal increased sharply over the years. According to an estimate only about 29% of the total area of Nepal is under forest coverage at present. The forest area declined considerably since 1966, while at the same time the area of shrubs or degraded forests increased remarkably. The annual deforestation is estimated to be 2.3 per cent in the hills, and 1.3 per cent in the Terai. The change in forest coverage in Mid- and Far-western development regions of Nepal is alarming. The UNEP report indicates that within 15 to 16 years these two regions lost 31 and 28% of their forest coverage, respectively. Both these records are higher than the national average of 24%.

Soil Degradation

A direct consequence of high population growth is rapid expansion of agriculture in environmentally sensitive and marginalized steep slopes and former forest areas. And also it causes constant fragmentation of agricultural lands as discussed earlier. Cultivation in numerous, fragmented and terraced plots in hills and mountains are not suitable for agriculture and can yield very little. Already in the 1960s Bishop had observed rampant erosion from fields carved from hillsides that had an angle of slope of more than 40° at elevations as high as 3700 meters in Karnali. Erosion of soil from poorly managed slopping terraces was reported to be 20 to 100 tons per hectare a year. Expanding area of shrubs is an obvious example of land degradation in Mid- and Far-western mountains of Nepal. Increasing livestock population in the hills exerts tremendous pressure on grasslands, shrubs and degrades forests. A study conducted in 1985 suggested that soil erosion rates in over grazed hills below 1000 m were more than 200 tons/ha/year, which means a huge amount of organic matters, minerals, and nutrient loss and thus a big loss of potential grain production. Five tons per hectare of soil loss is equivalent to 75 kg/ha of organic matter and 3.8 kg/ha of nitrogen. It is estimated that from entire Karnali River catchment basin, 1.7 mm of topsoil is removed annually. Back in 1960s, Bishop had found that farm soil in Karnali had decreasing pH value and thus increasing need of lime application. In high mountains of western and mid-western Nepal overgrazing is the major cause of soil erosion and desertification.

Demographic changes and shrinking per capita cultivated land

Demographic changes in Nepal are astounding. The country has witnessed almost three-fold increase in its population since 1952/54 – from 8.5 million in 1952 to 15 and 18 millions in 1981 and 1991, respectively. The 2001 census shows that it has crossed the 23 million mark with a doubling time of just 29 years. The current population growth rate is 2.24%. At a fertility decline scenario similar to the median experience of many Asian countries, Nepal's population is expected to reach about 60 million by the end of the next century. In addition, a very high in-migration from northern India facilitated by a common culture and an open border further raises the growth rate of the population in southern Nepal. Being a country with limited resources, Nepal certainly does not have the means to cope with such a Malthusian increase in population.

Terai bears the major burden of country's population with a constant migration of upland people, but the demographic changes in mountains and hills are also significant. In almost half a century since 1952/54, the hill and mountains witnessed a 100 percent increase in population. Currently, the population distributions in mountains, hills and Terai are 7.3, 44.3, and 48.4%, respectively. The distribution of population in ecological regions of Nepal. Although demographic changes in Mid-western and Far-western hills and mountains is not alarming (total 12.9%), rugged mountains and harsh climate limit the area suitable for habitation and cultivation in those regions. Yet the regions are heavily dependent on agriculture. In the three western most regions farm population constitutes some 95% of the total population. Hence, it is necessary to view population density in relation to arable land. The area of arable land in Nepal increased from 2,287,500 hectares in 1981/82 to 2,323,400 hectares in 1991/92. During the same period the population increased from 15 million to 18.5 million and the average land holding size declined from 1.13 ha to 0.96 ha. Farm sizes are much smaller in the western part of the country. In districts like Achham in the Far-western hill, the average land holding size is incredibly small at just 0.28 ha. An agricultural holding is equivalent to a farm household and the average farm household in rural Nepal as per the 2001 census is 5.7 persons, whereas in Far- and Mid-western region the sizes are 6.19 and 6.22, respectively.

The arable land area in the mountain increased from 115,700 ha in 1981 to 162,300 in 1991, while during the same period it increased from 856,500 to 871,300 ha in the hills. The 1991 agricultural census shows that more than 43% of land holdings were less than 0.5 ha and more than 69% were less than 1 ha. The per capita agricultural land declined from 0.16 ha in 1980 to 0.13 ha in 1999. Bishop's research in Karnali zone (comprising of Humla, Jumla, Mugu, Dolpa and Kalikot districts in Mid-western Development Region) showed that due to very high population growth the per capita *khet* (irrigated land on which paddy can be grown) holding was only 0.1 ha/person in 1968. The current value is considerably lesser than that.

Consequences of environmental degradation for mountain population

Increasing population and constant loss of renewable resources has a huge negative impact on mountain people. It exerts high pressure on stagnant or declining production system, which in turn changes resource use pattern with adverse effects on the environment. That leads the vicious cycle of 'environmental degradation and overextraction'. As discussed earlier, in the hills of Nepal agriculture is constantly being extended to steeper and fragile slopes and to far and marginal lands previously kept under forests or pasture. Food production, however, is declining.

Although agriculture sector in Nepal has been the first priority sector of development since the initiation of planned development in the mid-1950s, land productivity remains stagnant indicating land degradation and excessive use of natural resources. Since possibility of agricultural expansion is limited due to above-mentioned reasons and available technology is primitive and at subsistence level, food production in Nepal has not kept up with the population growth. Expansion of agricultural to marginal lands did manage to increase the total production of major crops, but their yields declined or remained stagnant over the years. In the early 1960s, the per hectare yields of Nepal's major crops such as paddy and wheat were significantly higher as compared to those of other South Asian countries, while at present the scenario is just opposite. Rice and wheat yields are slowly increasing but they are mostly grown in Terai region. The stagnant maize production is of concern for residents of the hills.

In the mountains and hills the deficit is particularly severe. Out of 16 mountain districts, 13 districts had negative food balance in 1985 that increased to all 16 districts in 1995. Due to endemic food deficit, most of Karnali zone and the hilly parts of adjacent Mahakali zone suffer from regular famine like situation during the winter. As compared to previous year the crop production in Bajura district is said to have declined by 60% in 2002. The situation in other districts most affected by the rebellion is also not different. In aforementioned districts- Accham, Bajhanng, Dailekh, Kalikot, Rukum, Mugu, Rolpa, and Jajarkot- the per capita food production in terms of caloric values (adjusted for adult equivalence) are 1197, 1060, 1556, 1270, 2966, 1773, 1845, and 2189 kilocalories/capita/day, respectively which are among lowest in the Kingdom. The recommended adult caloric requirement for the Hills and the Mountains is 2,340 kilocalories in Nepal. These values clearly indicate that excluding Rukum all other districts cannot produce minimum required food for survival. People in Far- and Mid-western hills and mountains are forced to spend the major part of their income on food.

Prior to the population explosion of 74,000 in 1920 to 132,000 in 1950 in Karnali zone, people used to have three meals (0.568 L each) of milled grain per day, which gradually decreased to two and some communities were forced to have only one daily meal during the period of preharvest even in the late 1960s. The entire zone produced only two-third of grain required for human consumption and the calorific requirement of an adult male was barely met. In 1992, more than 30% of high mountain population was undersupplied, while in the hills and Terai, the figures were 47 and 23%, respectively. Even in relatively prosperous Kaski district in the western hills, 41% of households surveyed (356) were less than six months self-sufficient and only 8% were found to have food surplus. A study conducted in 1996 found that over 63% of households in mountains and 55% in hills reported that their food consumption as less than adequate. Due to severe food deprivation, malnutrition is prevalent among the children of low-income groups in the mountains and hills of Nepal. Five out of six children suffer from stunting in mountains. However, in addition to ecological degradation, the insurgency itself plays a detrimental role in declining land productivity as physically active population has been gradually migrating from the region to escape the terror from both the Maoists and government forces.

For people in mountains, livestock is second only to land resource for it provides a source of income, fertilizer, assistance in agriculture and transportation in some places, as well as means of coping in time of food deficit. During the time of severe food deficit, many communities trade their cattle for food grains. That is why the livestock population increased in the hills and mountains of Nepal. However, researchers have shown that the local mountain communities are not benefited by the increasing livestock population. According to Tulachan "the *White Revolution,* in fact mostly benefited the comparatively well-to-do livestock rearers who happened to be located

in dairy areas in the plains and had access to modern technology". Both men and animals compete for the same limited space available in the mountains. Livestock management is poor with overstocking and overgrazing as the dominant mechanism that again put more pressure on forests and pastures. Declining sheep population in high mountains might be a direct consequence of degrading pastures.

Depleting forest has a serious impact on women who are forced to spend more time in collecting firewood and fodder, which means less time available for agriculture and other income generating jobs. In some parts now firewood collection takes one day trip from farmstead. In many other parts of Nepal, since firewood is no more available, poor people are forced to burn animal dung at the expense of their fertilizer needs. It has a huge negative impact on food production. As a consequence of soil erosion, subsistence farmers are regularly forced to abandon their farm terraces in many parts of hills. Forest depletion and soil degradation have intensified natural calamities such as flooding and landslides throughout the hills of Nepal. As compared to other hilly countries in the region, economic and human losses due to natural disaster are much higher in Nepal. Since 1990 to 1998, deaths due to natural calamities were 60 persons per ten million population in India. In Pakistan, China, Bhutan, and Myanmar the figures were 70, 30, 20, and 20, respectively, while in Nepal it was 350. Apart from reducing the productivity of already poor lands, floods destroy infrastructure such as bridges that often disconnect an entire mountain region for months.

Due to extremely concentrated rainfall (up to 93% of annual rainfall occurs during June to September), devastating floods occur in the central Himalaya of Nepal during the monsoon months of June through September. Destruction of footbridges that often provide the only link between remote mountain villages; demolition of irrigation diversions, mass-wasting by undercutting of steep, stream-adjacent slopes; and damage to floodplain agricultural land by erosion and sedimentation are some forms of damages caused by floods. On the other hand the Mid- and Far-western regions of Nepal regularly suffer from drought and famine-like situation. Compounded by all these factors, poverty in Nepal is endemic, widely varied among the regions and persistently increasing.

Situation of poverty across geographical regions of Nepal

Much has been written on the situation of poverty in Nepal. The Human Development Report 2001 published by the United Nations Development Program (UNDP) recognizes Nepal as a country with "low human development". Life expectancy at birth in 2000 was only 59.5 years and almost 51% of adult population was illiterate. Furthermore, 47% of children under age 5 are underweight and almost 23% of them may not survive beyond the age of forty. Both infant and maternal mortality rates in Nepal are very high. In summary, Nepalese people ".... continue to suffer from low life expectancy, low literacy and living conditions that deny them dignity. In short, Nepal's levels of human development remain among the lowest in the world". That, however, is the national average. Poverty level is higher in mountain districts (56%) followed by Terai (42%) and hills (41%). The picture becomes gloomier in remote hilly areas of Mid-western and Far-western Development Regions. According to a study conducted using a composite index of 39 indicators covering Poverty and Deprivation; Socio-economic, Infrastructure and Institutional Development; Women's Empowerment; and Natural Resources Endowment and Management, etc. in all 75 districts showed that 17 of the 25 least developed districts fall in the Far and Mid Western regions. Wide variation in literacy rates, infant mortality rates, etc. were observed between Kathmandu and districts of Karnali Zone in the Mid-western region. Karnali zone still does not have motorable road, which greatly hinders the economic development of entire northern part of Mid-western region. The hills and mountains of Far- and Mid-western development regions have one of the lowest HDI in the country (0.201-0.274); the GDP much lower than the national average and life expectancy ranges between 42 to 46 years. These two regions have the lowest per cent of cultivated area (3-15%), but the possibility of its expansion is not possible because of rugged terrain (as indicated by the percentage of areas with slopes more than 30° and slopping terrace areas) and very high infant mortality rates due to severe malnutrition. Far from power center, they hills of Mid- and Far-western Development Regions remain neglected with a very low human development, deep gender disparity, high illiteracy and low life expectancy, low investment that inhibit their participation in economic, social, cultural, and political life.

Poverty in Nepal is a complex phenomenon varying not only spatially, but also socially. Social aspect of poverty among various groups of people is a significant factor of stagnation in Nepal. Caste and ethnicity are two such strong factors. Ethnic diversity in Nepal is represented by Mongoloid tribal groups from the north-east, who speak Tibeto-Burman languages, and Caucasoid caste people from the south-west, who speak Indo-Aryan language. Among the latter, lower caste people (*Dalits*) are generally the poorest and most vulnerable group of society, which does not have access to enough resources in most parts of Nepal. Population of *Dalits* below poverty line is more than 65%. According to Bishop, in Karnali zone in 1969-70 the upper two castes (Brahmin and Chhetri) had control over 87% of irrigated *khet*. Similarly, among indigenous people, the proportion below poverty line varies from 45 to 71.

Lower caste and indigenous people are often small land holders who gradually transform into landless workers relying on scarce wage employment. This tendency adds to the number of the rural poor. The correlation between landless and marginal farm households and HDI in all districts of Nepal (excluding the three districts of Kathmandu Valley). The districts with lowest HDI have the highest number of marginal farmers and these are the districts where the insurgency was originated from and where the concentration of lower caste and indigenous people is the highest in the country.

Indications, therefore, are there to suggest that the environmental degradation of the fragile hills and mountains could be the hidden and hitherto unnoticed ultimate cause of the Maoist rebellion in Nepal. The ecological degradation widened resource scarcity especially in the form people's access to sufficient fertile lands in the Mid- and Far-western regions. When the resource is limited and widespread deprivation is prevalent, other socio-economic variables — such as land tenure issues, resource capture by local privileged few, gender, caste and ethnic equations — intervene. Such gradual loss of livelihood made people vulnerable to the exploits and rhetoric of Maoists, who offered an alternative (albeit violent). Policy interventions, therefore, should be directed towards rectifying the ultimate factor. Poverty cannot be alleviated without eradicating its ecological roots. The state needs to take immediate steps to identify and correct the causes of deforestation and soil degradation in the hills so as to restore agricultural productivity and create food security for mountain communities. Large-scale infrastructure development, as many researchers argue, does little help to mountain people because it is economically expensive and environmentally hazardous. Application of indigenous knowledge and appropriate techniques of natural resource management with due attention to mountain ecosystems would be instrumental in alleviating such stresses. We also recognize that the evidence presented thus far needs further analysis amidst multiple causality. Indeed, environmental degradation might be a necessary but not sufficient cause for conflict in this case as well. Nevertheless, the prevalence of these factors is certainly making the conflict more intractable and any lasting resolution effort will be well-served by considering environmental criteria.

MAOIST INSURGENCY ROCKS INDIA

The Indian society is suffering from simmering religious and ideological dissensions that have the potential to jeopardize the economic development of the country. Moreover these fissures area reflection of betrayal of secular character of Indian polity. The successors of the founding fathers have failed to accommodate the legitimate grievances of diverse communities inhabiting India. In late May 2009 the Naxalites (Maoists) took up arms against the communist government in West Bengal and threw out the police personnel occupying the Lalgarh police station. The state operation started in early June to regain control of the area involved police repression in the form repression in the form of alleged torture, illegal detention and arbitrary arrests. The Maoist leader claimed in a recent interview the mass Naxalite movement in 2009 aimed at creating a 'liberated zone' and that they 'will have an armed movement going in Calcutta by 2011'. The genesis of the Maoist insurgency in India lies in the peasants' movement and the agrarian discontent.

The movement began in March 1967 when a group of revolutionaries led by Charu Majumdar launched an uprising at Naxalbari, a small village of West Bengal, after a hapless tribal youth was attacked by local landlords over a land dispute. In its early stages the movement had its centre in West Bengal but now it has spread into less developed areas of rural Central and Eastern India such as Chhattisgarh and Andhra Pradesh. Now The Maoists have a presence in 40 per cent of India's geographical area and are especially concentrated in a region commonly known as 'Naxal belt' comprising 92000 square kilometres.

In 1969 the Naxalites organized themselves into the Communist Party of India (Marxist-Leninist). The CPI (Maoists) was formed in 2004 with the merger of two prominent Naxalite outfits, the People's War Group (PWG) and the Maoist Communist Centre (MCC). In the early 1970s, the movement seemed to be reaching the peak of its influence with the creation of vast guerrilla zones. Some years later the movement was split into several opposing factions. By 1980 it was estimated that around 30 Naxalite groups were active, with a combined membership of 30 000. A 2004 home ministry estimate put numbers at that time as "9,300 hardcore underground cadre... [holding] around 6,500 regular weapons beside a large number of unlicensed country-made arms". The Naxalite infrastructure includes sophisticated weapons such as Kalshanikov rifles and Claymore landmines, modern wireless equipment and electronic gadgets.

Today some groups have started participating in parliamentary elections while others are determined to continue with their guerrilla armed struggles. The government of India has declared above 200 districts out of total of 620 as the 'Maoist-infested'. In recent attacks during the last two months the Maoist rebels killed almost 110 policemen in Chhattisgarh. The Indian PM Manmohan Singh has described the Maoist uprising as 'the biggest internal security challenge ever faced by our country' as several states, like Chhattisgarh, Jharkhand, Karnataka, Andhra Pradesh, Maharashtra and Madhya Pradesh, are facing terrible internal insurgency by Naxals. The writ of the state has been given a serious blow in Lalgarh area where the Maoist People's Committee is in full control of everyday affairs. The Maoists in Chhattisgarh recruit adolescent girls as a stepped-up drive to increase the membership of the women's wing.

They also induce minor children to join their cause as it is easier to brainwash them and infuse their minds with extremist ideology. The security experts have dismissed the view that the insurgency is just a law and order issue. Political exclusion and socio-economic underdevelopment lay beneath the estrangement of the peasants. The vicinities in which the Naxalites operate are in dire need of economic development and rural elevation. The local villagers view the new development with suspicion as they are not sure whether the economic benefits will accrue to them. The majority of the populace considers economic projects simply an excuse for 'rapacious developers' to seize land from farmers without adequate compensation. The Naxalite rebellion has serious implications for India's energy security as the affected areas have vast coal reserves required for industrial boom of India. The media reports suggest the five states in which the movement is the strongest account for 85 per cent of the coal reserves. The toll in Naxal related violence was 231 in 2008. The Indian government has so far formulated no concrete plan to deal with the Naxal problem. The political parties do not seem reluctant to appease the Maoists for the sake of votes. The Central government passes the buck of responsibility for fighting such elements to the states and the latter lack financial resources, trained forces as well as the weaponry to suppress the insurgents. The Maoists claim to be fighting on behalf of the rural poor and the landless peasants.

They justify their actions as the political program to overthrow the Indian state, comprising the big landlord-comprador, bureaucratic, bourgeoisie classes and the imperialism that backs them, through armed struggle and establish a people's democratic state under the leadership of the proletariat. It states that the principal and immediate task of the present stage of the revolution is to arouse and organize people for agrarian revolutionary guerrilla war in the countryside-specially in the remote countryside-and to build the people's army and a rural base through guerrilla warfare. The unfortunate civilians are also victims of insurgency because of brutal, forced membership campaigns. In many states, the private armies and vigilante groups have been sponsored by the government to counter the Maoists. Tens of thousands of civilians have been displaced by the fighting between Maoists and counter-insurgents. In one of the worse affected states, Chhattisgarh, over 40,000 tribal people have been moved to the inadequate government camps.

The security forces engaged in anti-Naxalite operations are convinced that the CPI (M) is steadily building up a wider network involving associates in neighbouring countries. The wider strategic motive of the Maoist rebels is to carve out a Compact Revolutionary Zone (CRZ) spreading from Nepal through Bihar up to the Danakarnaya region of Andhra Pradesh. Prakash Singh, former Director General of Border Security Force (BSF), is of the view that the successive Union governments have mooted multi-pronged solution to resolve the problem but without any concrete result on the ground. The government authorities must show their commitment to implement land reforms, weed out corruption and provide people just and responsive governance in order to deprive the insurgents of their fodder. The Central Government of India has been planning to set up National Security Guards (NSG) hubs all over the country to promptly respond to terrorism but no strategy has been outlined to train state police force to confront the Maoist threat.

The Naxalite leadership is certain that the newly launched operation of the government would not make much difference on the ground situation in the 12 States where the organisation has varying degrees of influence. A middle-level leader of the party, opined that this assessment was based mainly on three factors. One, the strike power of the party has increased considerably in the past year. Two, the socio-economic problems that have contributed to the steady growth of the party have only accentuated in vast parts of the country, especially in the rural, tribal and forest regions where Naxalite influence is the most conspicuous.

MAOISTS TAKES ROOT AMONG RURAL POOR

He's 30 years old, speaks English and is conversant in the language of e-mail and the Internet. Friendly and self-confident, he could be a manager in a call centre, or perhaps a software engineer on one of India's gleaming high-tech campuses. But "Comrade M," as he asks to be called, prefers a different line of work: waging war on the Indian state. Armed with a battered Lee-Enfield rifle that he laughingly describes as "senior to me," the university graduate in an olive-drab uniform with a red star on the breast was one of about 30 Maoist guerrillas encountered recently in this remote forest in east-central India. Drawing recruits and support from indigenous tribespeople known as *adivasis*, the ragtag band of young men and women is part of a larger revolutionary movement whose audacious, if anachronistic, goal is to replace India's parliamentary democracy with a communist system straight out of Chairman Mao Zedong's Little Red Book. Once dismissed as little more than an irritant, the Maoist movement is gaining ground in this country of more than 1 billion people, feeding off anti-government hostility in some rural areas and highlighting the uneven nature of India's unprecedented economic boom.

Analysts say the movement consists of about 10,000 regular fighters, with several hundred thousand supporters. The rebels are known as Naxalites, after the eastern town of Naxalbari where the movement began in 1967. During the recent encounter with the rebels in the state of Chhattisgarh, a visitor witnessed a rally of at least 2,000 tribal supporters, many armed with axes and bows and arrows, gathered next to a concrete plinth topped with a hammer and sickle. The rally took place in a stand of tall trees about six hours' walk from the nearest paved road. The Maoist commander in the area, who goes by the name Kosa, said the movement had not been deterred by the triumph of capitalism in China and other formerly communist countries. "When a scientist doesn't get the desired results from an experiment, he doesn't just abandon the experiment," he said. "Every movement has its ups and downs. There are defeats as well as victories. We should learn from the failure of Maoism in China and move ahead." Following a long period of relative quiet, the Naxalites in the past several years have expanded their presence to 13 of India's 28 states, according to official estimates, spurring talk of a "red corridor" extending from Nepal, which is battling a Maoist insurgency of its own, down through the wooded heartland of central and southern India.

The Maoist rebels in India and Nepal have acknowledged ideological ties, and security officials suspect logistical collaboration as well. Equipped with homemade bombs and rifles looted from police stations, the Indian rebels have staged increasingly bold attacks, such as seizing a passenger train for 12 hours in the eastern state of Jharkhand in March. They function in some remote districts as a parallel government, complete with makeshift courts and police. Their violent tactics have turned parts of Chhattisgarh, among other states, into virtual no-go areas for the government, thwarting plans for corporate mining operations in forests that many adivasis regard as their own. Last month, Prime Minister Manmohan Singh described the Naxalite movement as "the single biggest internal security challenge ever faced by our country" — no small claim in a nation with many insurgencies, including the long-running Islamic rebellion in Kashmir. Singh said the rebels draw strength from "deprived and alienated sections of the population" and "are trying to establish 'liberation zones' in core areas where they are dispensing, or claiming to be dispensing, basic state functions." He called for redoubled efforts to promote development and better governance, as well as better intelligence-sharing among Naxalite-afflicted states and improved training and equipment for police and paramilitary forces.

The Naxalites are proliferating despite the rapid growth of affluence in the country. Driven by industries such as software and outsourcing, the boom has helped expand the middle class, its aspirations reflected in such entertainment fare as "Who Wants to

Be a *Crorepati* ?" — India's version of "Who Wants to be a Millionaire?" The streets of major cities are clogged with new cars, and developers are gobbling up surrounding fields for shopping malls and housing developments. But the boom has bypassed much of rural India, where more than 70 percent of the country's 1.1 billion people live. Though some rural areas, such as the fertile agricultural states of Punjab and Haryana, are doing reasonably well, others — especially in the central and eastern parts of the country — are beset by water shortages, poverty and caste discrimination. Against that backdrop, the death toll from Naxalite violence has jumped from 483 in 2002 to 669 last year, according to the Home Affairs Ministry.

In Chhattisgarh, the Naxalite movement has found abundant recruits among adivasis angered by police harassment, dismal or nonexistent government services and collusion between corrupt officials and criminals engaged in illegal logging. According to government data, 165 people died in Naxalite-related violence last year, and the bloodletting has continued: Last month, Naxalite rebels abducted 50 members of a pro-government militia called the Salwa Judum, then murdered 13 of them by slitting their throats, police said. "They're absolutely ruthless killers," a senior Chhattisgarh security official, B.K.S. Roy, said by telephone from the state capital, Raipur. "I've never seen this kind of brutality in my life before, the way they strike and kill Salwa Judum members.

They're hacked to death, heads severed from bodies." Roy said the Naxalite movement's numbers were growing in Chhattisgarh, where the state last year set up a school to train police in jungle warfare and counterinsurgency tactics. "A thousand commandos are already ready for operations," Roy said. "We want a big striking force." Human rights monitors have also criticized the Naxalites' methods, accusing them of forcible recruitment, extortion and the abduction and killing of "class enemies" and villagers suspected of colluding with the state.

At the same time, they have denounced members of the Salwa Judum, which means "Peace Initiative," as vigilantes who rape, torture and kill villagers thought to be sympathetic to the rebels. Contacted through intermediaries, the Naxalites agreed to meet with a foreign reporter and several Indian journalists in the heavily forested Bastar district, where the rebels maintain a large presence. Youthful Naxalite supporters met the visitors at a prearranged point and guided them into the woods. Winding through dry, scraggly forests, the route occasionally passed clusters of grass-roofed huts, many with crude animal pens fashioned from tree branches. The hike eventually ended in the rebels' camp, which was littered with weapons, sleeping rolls and solar panels for charging batteries. Fighters greeted their guests with a handshake and a "red salute" — a clenched fist raised to the temple. They were under the command of Comrade Kosa, a swashbuckling figure with a warm, if wary, manner and a folding-stock Kalashnikov assault rifle.

Members of the group asked to be identified only by first names. Kosa, 48, was the only fighter in civilian dress, which he accented with a Calvin Klein baseball cap adorned with a red metal star. He said he had been with the movement since 1977, when he dropped out of a technical institute where he had been studying in the neighbouring state of Andhra Pradesh. He has been fighting in Chhattisgarh for 26 years, he said, and now commands a force of about 700 guerrillas, nearly half of them women, supported by several thousand tribal militiamen. Kosa holds a political title, secretary of the Dandakaranya Special Zonal Committee, a state-level body that answers to the Central Committee of the Communist Party of India (Maoist), the Naxalites' banned political affiliate. In honour of their guests, the rebels had erected a small bamboo enclosure decorated with hand-painted slogans such as "Down With Salwa Judum" and "Stop Corrupting Adivasi Culture to Make it Market Culture Under the Guise of Tourism." Uniformed cadres sang a song that included the line "America and Japan are big exploiters of this country." Despite their isolation in the woods, Kosa and his aides keep abreast of current events by listening to shortwave radio broadcasts.

Sanjeev, 35, a university dropout who has been with the movement since 1987, asked reporters for advice on how to "upload" Naxalite propaganda onto the Internet, to which he said he had occasional access. The visitors were provided with CDs purporting to contain evidence of Salwa Judum atrocities. The rank and file was made up mostly of adivasis, several of whom said they joined the movement out of anger toward local authorities. "I've never seen a hospital in any of these villages," said Nirmala, a slender, short-haired woman in her twenties who joined the movement four years ago and now serves as one of Kosa's bodyguards. "There are schools, but there are no teachers. The government says the adivasis, my people, have no rights over the forests."

Another adivasi rebel, Neela, said she was radicalized at the age of 12, when police arrested her father for illegally clearing a small patch of land and imprisoned him for three years. A broad-faced woman with a ready smile, the 25-year-old Naxalite said she spoke only her local tribal dialect when she joined the movement a decade ago. Fellow cadres taught her how to read and speak Hindi, she said, and eventually she joined the movement's military wing. A member of a nine-person squad who carries a walkie-talkie and a single-shot rifle, Neela said proudly that she had taken part in 10 military operations, including one in which a mine was detonated beneath a vehicle carrying paramilitary troops. Four of them died, she said. "They come into villages, beat up men, rape women," she said of the paramilitaries.

Comrade M, the university graduate and a squad leader, said the rebels typically laid ambushes for "our friends in khaki uniform" using mines triggered by camera-flash devices. Military operations aside, the Naxalite rebels also engage in small-scale development projects, such as digging wells and small reservoirs and training villagers in rudimentary health care, according to Kosa and his aides. They maintain an active political and propaganda wing, publishing a newsletter and holding rallies. At the massive forest gathering, women from a Naxalite cultural troupe swayed and sang. Then Kosa and several other speakers addressed the crowd over a makeshift public address system powered by car batteries. Watching from the sidelines, Neela, the Naxalite foot soldier, said she had "complete confidence" that the revolution would one day succeed.

ON THE INDIAN MAOISTS AND THEIR SYMPATHISERS

As the Maoists continue with their violent and disruptive activities, sections of the intelligentsia are openly expressing sympathy for their cause. Although the sympathy is often couched in rhetoric against the state and its security offensive against the Maoists, what distinguishes the Maoist sympathizers from a broader community of intellectuals and civil rights groups, who are skeptical of the intent and apprehensive of the efficacy of the Union Government's anti-Maoists operations, is their stubborn refusal to condemn the anarchic violence and mindless killings by the Maoists.

On 4th October 2009, the Bengali daily Anandabajar Patrika carried an interview of CPI (Maoist) Polit Bureau Member Koteshwar Rao alias Kishanji where he said that Union Railway Minister Mamata Banerjee is their preferred choice for being the next Chief Minister of West Bengal. He even justified Maoist support to the Trinamul Congress by hailing Mamata Banerjee's capacity to rise above class interest and adopt pro-people positions. One wonders what Kishanji and the Maoists' take is on Mamata Banerjee's Railway Budget passed by the Parliament few months back, which is replete with proposals of Private-Public Partnerships in developing railway stations and freight terminals to logistics parks and cargo centres. What do they have to say about the thousands of acres of land that is proposed to be acquired for the Railway freight corridor project in Uttar Pradesh and Bihar? Perhaps the Maoists also consider the FICCI Secretary General Amit Mitra, who was appointed by Mamata Banerjee as head of an expert panel to draw up business plans for the Railways, as not a part of the "comprador-bureaucratic bourgeoisie", which according to their Party Programme rules over India. Mamata Banerjee's "interactive session" with the corporate bigwigs in Kolkata on 22nd August may also have been perceived by the Maoists as an enclave of the "national bourgeoisie" who have come on board their "new democratic revolution".

This rank opportunism of the Maoists has gone hand in hand with their devious game of turning themselves into henchmen of Trinamul Congress under the façade of pseudo-revolutionary rhetoric and joining in the massacre of CPI (M) cadres in West Bengal. Over 130 CPI (M) activists have been killed by these forces since March 2009 across the state, with more than half of them killed in the West Midnapore district alone. The victims were mostly poor peasants or agricultural workers from dalit or adivasi families.

The Maoist sympathizers justified this mayhem as elimination of "class enemies" and celebrated the violence against the CPI (M) in Lalgarh as a revival of Naxalbari. The Trinamul Congress, on the other hand, aided and abetted by sections of the media, indulged in stupendous double-speak. They started by attacking the State Government for failing to control Maoist violence and questioned why the Maoists were not being banned in West Bengal. When the Central Government banned the CPI (Maoist) and the State Government started joint operations with central security forces, the Maoist sympathizers initiated shrill rhetoric against state repression. The Trinamul Congress obliged by shifting its stance and opposing the anti-Maoist operations, calling for a withdrawal of Central security forces.

The hypocrisy of the Trinamul Congress and the Maoists is further borne out by the protests against the arrest of Chhatradhar Mahato, the leader of the People's Committee against Police Atrocities (PCPA) of Lalgarh, who was arrested by the police in end-September 2009. Besides charges of murder and attempt to murder of CPI (M) activists, arson, demolition of police outposts, waging war against the state etc. under various sections of the IPC, charges have also been framed against him for raising funds for a terrorist outfit, attempting to murder police personnel and conspiring against the state. All these charges are prima facie credible. While Chhatradhar Mahato was a one-time Trinamul Congress activist, his brother Shashadhar Mahato is an active member of a Maoist armed squad. Since November 2008 the Maoist backed PCPA, which was led by Chhatradhar Mahato blockaded the Lalgarh area, making it out of bounds for the police and administration. This "liberated zone" was used by the Maoists to launch a series of attacks against the CPI (M) activists and others like activists of the Jharkhand Party (Naren) and election commission personnel, killing over 80 persons in the Lalgarh area since November 2008. Several Trinamul Congress leaders, including Mamata Banerjee visited Lalgarh during this period and expressed open solidarity with Chhatradhar Mahato.

After his arrest, Chhatradhar Mahato has started disclosing several facts to the police regarding the Maoists' activities, their nexus with Trinamul Congress, their sources of funds, etc. This has embarrassed the Maoists, who have now started adopting desperate tactics. First came the kidnapping of the OC of Sankrail police station by the Maoists, through which they secured the release of some of their arrested supporters. Then the Bhubaneshwar Rajdhani Express was held hostage for several hours by the Maoists and the activists of the PCPA near Jhargram on 27th October, in order to pressurize the State Government to release Chhatradhar Mahato. With the situation getting out of control, Mamata Banerjee and other Trinamul Congress leaders have started leveling outrageous allegations against the CPI (M), that the hijacking of the Rajdhani Express was a conspiracy hatched jointly by the CPI (M) and the Maoists in order to malign the Railways. The day is not far when she is going to allege that even the killings of CPI (M) activists is also a CPI (M) conspiracy!

The brouhaha over state repression in West Bengal is complete bunkum. On the contrary, the Left Front Government has continued to adopt a democratic approach towards the problem in Lalgarh. Following the complaints of police harassment of some adivasis following the assassination attempt on the Chief Minister in Salboni in November 2008, which had sparked off the Lalgarh agitation, the administration had negotiated with the agitators, transferred the culpable police officials and released several arrested persons. Since then there has not been a single reported instance of atrocity by the State police or the Central security forces, even as the Maoists have continued with their killing spree. Can the State Government be faulted for taking steps to arrest the culprits of murder and arson? Had the alleged links between Chhatradhar Mahato and the Maoists been fabricated, why has the court remanded him to custody? After all, he is not being tried in a kangaroo court. Why should he not be prosecuted? Why should he be released only to return and continue with the murders and mayhem against the CPI (M) activists?

It is time for the Maoist sympathizers in West Bengal to deeply introspect about their role in these developments. Blind hatred for the CPI (M) have driven them into such frenzy that even wanton killings of poor CPI (M) activists seem justifiable to them. They have no qualms in supporting Mamata Banerjee and the Trinamul Congress, which is a reactionary force allied to the Congress, the ruling party at the Centre today. Mamata Banerjee will never sever her ties with the Congress because the only thing she is interested in is power, not only at the Centre but also in the State. In the ultimate analysis, the Maoist sympathizers are only playing into the hands of the rightwing anti-democratic forces. The restoration of peace, dignity, justice and socio-economic development is what the adivasis want in Lalgarh and elsewhere in the State. This cannot be attained unless the Maoists stop their brutalities and targeted assassination of CPI (M) activists. Far away from the political theatre of West Bengal, where the Maoists are on a rampage, some Maoist sympathizers based in New Delhi have chosen to raise the pitch. Prominent among them is celebrity activist Arundhati Roy, who appeared on CNN IBN news channel few weeks back, facing an unusually genteel Karan Thapar, to express her outrage at the planned security offensive by the Union Government – "the army of the rich" – against the "the army of the poor", the Maoists. She argued that free market democracy in India has failed to deliver justice to the poor, especially the adivasis, and the State has deliberately ignored peaceful protests against those injustices. What is the choice left for the adivasis, dispossessed of their land and livelihoods by big corporates and tortured and raped by the State, but to take up arms in self-defence, she asked? Her advice to the Union Government: withdraw the armed offensive, hold unconditional talks with the Maoists and do things like, "for example", making public all the MoUs signed by the Government with mining companies, which according to her is a "key issue".

What strikes one immediately is that the media savvy CPI (Maoist) leadership, whose interviews galore nowadays from TV channels and websites to newspapers and magazines, has neither cited any MoU signed by any Government as their "key issue" nor made any demand to make those MoUs public. When Roy does so, is it because she perceives the question of mining and displacement in the tribal inhabited areas to be the root cause of the Maoist problem? Or is it because of her difficulty in providing a truthful account and reasoned justification for the activities and beliefs of the Maoists, whose cause Roy has chosen to espouse?

The explanation that the roots of the Maoist insurgency lie in the systemic deprivation and exploitation of the adivasis by the Indian bourgeois-landlord state suffers from several infirmities, because it is entirely ahistorical. The Naxalite movement of 1967, from which the present day Maoists originated, was supposed to be the beginning of a protracted armed struggle; to wrest State power from the hands of the "comprador-bureaucratic" bourgeoisie who had kept India as a "semi-colony". The experience since then has shown that such a road to revolution is not only inappropriate in Indian conditions where parliamentary democracy has taken roots, but such sectarian politics in a diverse society like India, inevitably leads to alienation from the people and degenerates into mindless violence and anarchy. Eventually, the Naxalites reached an ideological dead-end as domestic and international developments completely overtook their shallow and confused understanding of Indian society and polity. The failure to make any advance in pursuing such an erroneous path led to innumerable splits within the Naxalite movement in the 1970s and 1980s. In practice, the basic debate within the Naxalites have always been on whether their activities would remain to be based on individual assassinations of "class enemies" (the infamous "khatam line") or to reorient their work prioritizing mass activities and participating in the democratic process. Several Naxalite groups, like the CPI (ML) Liberation and the CPI (ML) New Democracy, eventually realized the futility of their adventurist path, abandoned armed struggle and joined the parliamentary democratic process. However, some of the groups like the CPI (ML) Peoples' War and the MCC continued with their violent tactics and eventually merged in 2004 to form the CPI (Maoist). The documents of the CPI (Maoist) clearly enumerate their "central task" as "seizure of political power by armed force".

It is this historical background which celebrity activists like Arundhati Roy are now seeking to suppress by constructing a new narrative of poor people and adivasis taking up arms to defend their lives and livelihoods in the face of ruthless exploitation by free market capitalism, after their peaceful protests have been entirely ignored by the State. The effort is to portray the security offensive as one between the State and the adivasis. But this is so deceptive. The Maoists can hardly claim any contribution in the struggle against the exploitation and deprivation of the adivasis. The Left parties like the CPI (M) and CPI and several independent adivasi organisations have been fighting in these areas for the land and forest rights of tribals and against their exploitation since decades. A major achievement of that struggle was the enactment of the Forest Rights Act for the tribals and other forest dwellers, during the tenure of the previous UPA Government. What has been the contribution of the Maoists in this struggle?

The adivasis have also been increasingly dispossessed of their lands and forests, in the post-liberalization period, which has seen foreign and domestic big capital being allowed to exploit forest and mineral resources in a reckless manner, especially in States like Chhattisgarh, Jharkhand and Orissa. The socio-economic development in tribal inhabited areas has been grossly neglected by the Central as well as the State Governments. The Left parties and adivasi organisations have been struggling against these policies. The Left ruled States like West Bengal, Kerala and Tripura have successfully implemented land redistribution programmes in the adivasi inhabited areas. While much remains to be done in terms of ensuring comprehensive socio-economic development, the Left led Governments have been steadfast in defending the land and forest rights of the adivasis as well as protecting their culture and identity. The Maoists have never been found agitating on these issues. In fact, much of Maoist violence is directed against the railways, roads, power and telecom facilities and even medical teams, which expose their anti-development vision.

Far from any concern for the socio-economic development of the adivasis, the Maoists have chosen to focus on the tribal inhabited forests mainly out of military-tactical reasons, because it is easy to conduct guerilla warfare and set up their "liberated zones" in these areas given the near absence of the administration in those places. The typical tactics of the Maoists have been to build their base areas in forests near tribal habitats and establish their control over the area through the force of the gun, eliminating or terrorizing all other political parties and adivasi organisations into submission. The hapless situation of the adivasis can be seen in Chhattisgarh today where they are caught between the vicious cycle of violence between the Maoists and the state-sponsored armed militia, Salva Judum. In Orissa, thousands of Christian tribals had to bear the brunt of Bajrang Dal orchestrated violence, after the Maoists executed VHP leader Lakshmanananda Sarawati in August 2008 and fled from the scene leaving the tribals to fend for themselves.

The experience in the States like Chhattisgarh, Jharkhand and Orissa shows that mindless violence by the Maoists and repression unleashed by the state using the pretext, invariably leads to a cycle of violence and counter-violence, shattering the lives and livelihoods of the poor tribals. In this violent milieu armed Maoist gangs get a free hand to indulge in extortion, robbery and mayhem. Under the garb of pseudo-revolutionary rhetoric against the Indian constitution and the election process, the Maoists also forge opportunistic links with bourgeois political parties for patronage and protection. Having witnessed how people decisively reject their poll boycott calls by turning out in large numbers, they have started issuing directives to people on who to vote for. Kishanji's statements endorsing Mamata Banerjee reflect this trend. They are also involved in booth capturing, threatening and even killing representatives of one political party on behalf of another. For instance, JMM MP Sunil Mahato was killed in Ghatshila by the Maoists in March 2007. They also made assassination attempts against former Andhra Pradesh Chief Minister Chandrababu Naidu in 2003 and West Bengal Chief Minister Buddhadeb Bhattacharya in November 2008.

The Maoists do not represent any democratic movement. In their "liberated zones", no political activities other than their own are permissible. They conduct kangaroo courts and summarily execute political opponents labelling them as "police informers". Their presence outside their base areas in the forests is negligible. Politically, they are totally absent in the countrywide movement against imperialist globalization and neoliberal policies, be it working class actions like strikes or peasant struggles on agrarian issues. They have failed to draw any lesson, either political or economic, from the experiences of building socialism in the twentieth century. If anything, they have become even more dogmatic over time, articulating a development vision, which seem eerily similar to Cambodian Khmer Rouge under Pol Pot. To romanticize these nihilist anarchists as a revolutionary force fighting for justice to the adivasis is nothing but utter travesty.

CONCEPTION OF MAOISM

Let us start with the understanding of the task force about Maoism. To begin with there is little surprising here and we find some of the regular stuff. The primary reason for the spread of Maoism is the genuine, longstanding and unattended grievances of the tribals and landless arising from their "political, economic and social hardships". It declares that, "unemployment, poverty and unbridled exploitation of the poor are all a reality in large parts of (the) Indian rural landscape." Further, such lack of development initiative is leading to "increased urban-rural divide". The task force accepts that the issues raised by the Maoists are "people-centric and have certain legitimacy in the eyes of the common people" as states like Andhra Pradesh and Bihar have yet to implement even minimal land reforms. It goes on to say that since India lacks social security mechanisms, "the Maoists have tried to exploit such (policy) gaps to increase their influence".

Thus it rues the fact that the "Maoists have virtually unlimited supply of potential recruits given the huge numbers of Indians living in poverty and (that) most of India's social problems (are) related to (unaddressed) caste issues."

But it also adds that many of the cadres are there not due to any ideology, but "to take advantage of the power that a gun can draw in a lawless land." There is repeated emphasis on the magnitude of the 'Naxal problem' and vast territory under their influence-that they enjoy wide support and have a "growing mass base in rural areas" and thus constitute the "single biggest internal security threat" to the country. It further states that the "Maoist threat appears to be overtaking all other insurgencies in the country" which is "more complex... to fight than any that (the) Indian security forces have fought until today." At several places the report also comments on the modus-operandi of the Maoists. It warns that, "there is no grievance that (Maoists) *do not* identify with, however *unjust* that may be, and there is *no* Indian institution that the armed movement is appreciative of (30, emphasis added)."

In its assessment, they have been "building a counter state by exploiting the genuine grievances" and have worked up that anger against the state to their advantage. But the primary purpose of the Maoists is not to address the immediate grievances but to further their strategy of "isolating the enemy" by mobilising the masses. It further states that the Maoists begin with "destroying the 'state control' through propaganda, destruction of symbols of governance like schools, hospitals, government offices, railway lines, assassination of government officials, members of elected local bodies, caste enemies, and raids on isolated police pickets."

The military formations of the Maoists contain "well-coordinated, trained, *ideologically brainwashed* cadres and ancillary units" and induction of women soldiers and propaganda personnel add value to the movement and allows it easy access to the *homes and hearts* of the vulnerable people." The task force also believes that the Maoists have the "ability to out-think and out-fight the state" and the idea of a liberated zone (it takes Lalgarh as an example of a liberated zone in 2008) is a sample of the brazenness and defiance of the Maoists. Moreover, the protracted face off with the state gives them an opportunity for rapid radical political mobilisation. It emphasises that the Maoists are following the "textbook strategies" of guerrilla warfare and also have a sophisticated intelligence apparatus. Unlike 'jihadis' they attack mainly 'hard targets' like police stations and paramilitary posts. In its assessment, all this is made possible due to "the magic spell of Maoist Mass Control" that the militants are able to weave. It explains that such a spell is constituted of a propaganda machinery that is "based on folklores woven around Sido-Kanu, Birsa Bhagwan, etc." with Mao thrown in for good measure; thus "Mao has started replacing Sido-Kanu and Birsa in various tribal strongholds of the Maoists."

The report also warns that Maoists have an imminent plan for encircling and capturing cities and will find sympathy amongst students and unemployed. What the FICCI task force assesses to be the character of the 'Maoist threat' for the Indian business, economy, and polity can be best summed up below by three brief quotes from the report: India's emergence as a hot growth market depended at first on the tech outsourcing boom in Bangalore and elsewhere. Now the world is discovering the skill and productivity of India's manufacturers as well. Meanwhile India's affluent urban consumers have started buying autos, appliances and homes, and they're demanding improvements in the country's roads, bridges and railroads. To stoke Indian manufacturing and satisfy consumers, the country needs cement, steel, and electric power in record amounts... Anxious to revive their moribund economies, the poor but resource rich states of eastern India have given mining and land rights to Indian and multinational companies. Yet these deposits lie mostly in territory where the Naxals operate.

Chhattisgarh, a hotbed of Naxalite activity, has 23 per cent of India's iron ore deposits and abundant coal. It has signed memorandum of agreements worth billions with Tata Steel and ArcelorMittal, De Beers Consolidated Mines, BHP Billiton, and Rio Tinto... And US companies like Caterpillar want to sell equipment to the mining companies....

The naxalites may be the sleeper threat to India's economic power, potentially more damaging to Indian companies, foreign investors and the state than pollution, crumbling infrastructure, or political gridlock. The growing Maoist insurgency over large swathes of the mineral-rich countryside could soon hurt some industrial investment plans. Just when India needs to ramp up its industrial machine to lock in growth and just when foreign companies are joining the party – the naxalites are clashing with the mining and steel companies essential to India's long-term success. The threat doesn't stop there.

The naxalites may move next on India's cities, where outsourcing, finance and retailing are thriving. The CPI-Maoist is partly political, partly insurgent, partly terrorist organisation. It believes in the Maoist strategy of capturing political power with the help of a well-motivated and well-trained army of the impoverished rural masses... As an insurgent organisation it believes in establishing its control over territory 'liberated' by it. As a terrorist organisation, it differs from others. It does not indulge in indiscriminate killings of civilians (non-combatants)... Maoist terrorism is a totally indigenous phenomenon motivated by domestic grievances and a domestic political agenda.

Naxal Threat

Yet it makes it sharp and clear that the primary responsibility for the 'problem' lies with the government and it has some startlingly strong words to say about it. It asserts that the government is squarely to be blamed for the "*criminal* neglect of the rural economy" and following a "*scorched earth policy*" in the rural agrarian sector with feudal lords in command ". Thus the conditions that prevail in vast areas of the Indian countryside are "mature for waging a people's war by the Maoists". Such high abundance of natural resources in the areas under Maoist influence, its benefits are far from reaching local populations. Thus, going by their past experience with 'development', the tribals are rightly apprehensive of the mining and construction activity and plans. It concedes that the tribals are supposed to get a fair compensation for the land given for business, but the "*state's record in this area is patchy at best*".

It further blames the local vested interests and corruption, the alliance of contractors, money lenders, politicians, etc., for lack of effective delivery of development goods to the local population. It even has scathing comments for programmes like NREGA that, according to the task force, "suffer from appalling levels of corruption". Thus "government policy of offering doles, unemployment allowances, rural employment grants, etc. have made about 35 per cent of the rural population to look up to the political rulers as *gods raining occasional manna*." Through this process people in such areas, "gradually start looking up to the

Maoists for protection..." and "they start living on the hope that the changed system as promised by the Maoists would one day deliver the *dream world that would glitter like the cities and homes of the affluent*.

They rapidly lose confidence in the State and any coercive action implement(ed) by the State further alienates the(m)." Another aspect which is repeatedly emphasised in the report is the inadequacy of the security apparatus of the state. It stresses continually on the capabilities of the Maoists in mounting large-scale surprise attacks on 'hard targets' in vast area under their control. And it bemoans the poor state of policing (including paramilitary) and intelligence set-up to such an extent that they fail to "inflict even a moderate level of attrition" on the Maoists – "(i)n the vast operational areas from Bihar to Andhra Pradesh with most active hubs in (remote tribal areas of) Orissa, Jharkhand (and) Chhattisgarh... the Central and State intelligence apparatus is appealingly inadequate." The report is at pains to bring out the fact that the primary problem is "infirmity of the state" and not really the strength of the rebels. Thus "inadequacy of State response makes the Maoists look bigger than life." It even warns that, "in the absence of supplementing administrative, economic, and security reforms, mere application of force by isolated police actions (is likely to) alienate the people more, resulting in (further) erosion of state's (authority)."

THE BLOODY NETWORK OF INDIAN MAOISTS

Continuous attacks by the Nassaliti rebels in the Indian states of so-called "red corridor". The exploitation of the claims of tribals and peasants, confrontation with the Marxist Communist Party that governs West Bengal, links with the rebels in Nepal. Indian Maoists continue their standoff with New Delhi and will not let go of 13 of the 28 states where they are present. On the night of November 24th a group of 55 Maoist rebels have blew up a government office in Kharakpur in Munger district of Bihar state. It was the latest in a series of attacks by insurgents along the so-called "red corridor" that runs through the states of Maharashtra, Andhra Pradesh, Chhattisgarh, Orissa, Jharkhand, Bihar and West Bengal. The Maoists have spread to 13 of the 28 Indian states and are considered the most serious threat to the country's internal security.

The historic and strategic epicentre of the red revolt that has been sending shock waves through India for decades is West Bengal. For 32 years the *Communist Party Marxist* (CPM) has been in government in the state bordering Bangladesh, and has become a symbol of power. The opposition has been monopolized by the Maoists who are deeply rooted in tribal villages and forests. The legal opposition, of course, is in the hand of the National Congress of Sonia Gandhi and the Trinamul Congress of Mamata Benerjee, but the defence of the most poor and needy tribals had been hijacked by the Maoists and many times in a violent way. Since November 2007, 69 CPM workers and 10 villagers had been killed in West Midnapore district alone. In June this year the Maoist raided the police station and kept under control the town of Lalgarh. Eleven companies of Central Reserve Police Force (CRPF) had been deployed against state government's demand of 50. There is no week without news of some ambush by the Maoists.

On November 20 the Maoists threaten to kill Bihar ministers' kin since the Bihar police machinery are letting loose a reign of repression against the families of the top Maoist leader Arvind Kumar. On the same day the Tata-Bilaspur passenger train was derailed after the Maoist blew up rail tracks near Goelkera railway station. The Naxalite movement started in the sixties when Majumdar and Kanu Sanyal of the CPI (Marxist) inspired by Mao Zedong lead a violent Santhal uprising in West Bengal Naxalbari village. In 1969 the Communist Party of India (Marxist-Leninist) was born. The history of the communist movement in India went through a fragmentation that produced three communist parties.

In 1977, when the Congress Party lost control of the central government in New Delhi the Communist Party went to power in Calcutta (West Bengal) and is still in power now. For 25 years the mythical figure of Jyoti Basu held the reins of power, but his style of governance kept changing. When Deng Xiaoping in China embraced successfully the capitalist mode of development, the communist government of West Bengal follow suit, but the most poor of the poor felt betrayed and reorganized themselves in the jungle. After Jyoti Basu, came Buddhadeb Bhattacharjee who open up to many industrial houses and started expropriating agricultural land to build industrial estates alienating the farmers. "Calcutta runs after Shanghai" writes Federico Rampini. That was the occasion when the Maoists jumped in to the fray, organized the farmers and resisted the take-over. That is what happened in Singur and Nandigram. The Tatas had to shift their Nano plant to Gujarat. This success emboldened the Maoists who multiplied their attacks. But the presence of Maoists is not confined only to the state of West Bengal.

The red belt cuts across India, starting from Nepal in the North, through West Bengal, Bihar, Jharkhand, Chhattisgarh, Orissa, west Maharashtra and Andhra Pradesh in the South. They put their training camps on the border regions so that they can easily escape from the police of one state crossing over the border. Recent reports in the press give the origin of the supply of their arms from Nepal, Bangladesh and China. At least 30 different groups are active across the country with a combined membership of around 50.000 activists. But their differences over their perceived revolutionary roles often result in bloody battles.

Many groups are accused of land grabbing and extortion. In 2004 the Maoist Communist Centre and People's War join hands to form the Communist Party of India (Maoist), which is now the biggest armed group ever to challenge the very existence of the Indian state. An estimated 20.000 are bearing arms, one fifth of India's forest is under their control. And they are active in 165 districts of the 604. Now the central government is in a fix. The state governments ask assistance from the centre and request also the help of the army particularly for military aerial survey.

The helicopters are vulnerable also to small arms, but the central government does not allow to return fire. The centre has extended its full support to the Left Front government in Bengal to combat Maoist terror in the state. The move could spark fresh tension between the Congress and UPA ally Trinamul Congress whose leader, Mamata Banerjee is keen on a dialogue between the state and the Maoist Red brigade. But the Interior Minister, Chidambaram and the Bengal Chief Minister Bhattacharjee agreed that there should be "no talks with the Maoists, unless they agree to completely surrender their arms and come for a dialogue under the constitutional framework". Bhattacharjee requested the Centre to start operations in the neighbouring Jharkhand as well, where the Naxals, on rum from Bengal, are taking shelter only to return later. But the Centre can not intervene unless it is called by the State.

But a day after Chidambaram's tough talk Maoists kill 17 cops in Gadchiroli district, at Laheri, in the neighbouring state of Maharashtra, 18 km from the border, on 8 October. Early this year, Maharashtra state cops lost 15 men in Maekegaon and 16, including 5 women, at Hattigota, both in Gadchiroli district. According to sources, the Maoist numbered more than 300 and comprised mobile military dalams that have recently moved from Chhattisgarh.

Police said there were many from Nepal among attackers who were equipped with sophisticated weapons and ammunition. In two days the Maoists struck three attacks, beside Laheri, they set on fire a gram panchayat building in Irupdhori village, and killed a farmer, Suresh Halami suspected to be a police informer. These three attacks have shattered the morale of the district police. The Maoists are very vindictive with police informers.

On the 5 October, in Taliban-style execution, they beheaded a special branch inspector, Francis Indwar, and threw his body on a branch road leading to National Highway 33 that connect Patna to Jamshedpur, 20 km from Ranchi.. The officer was abducted few days before and held hostage demanding a swap for arrested Maoist ideologues Kobad Ghandy in New Delhi and Chhatradhar Mahato in Kolkata and another captured leader Chandrabhusan Yadav. On 21 Settember, Maoists launched a massive attack on CPM party office at Enayetpur, 15 km from Midnapore, triggering a gunfight that left at least 15 people dead. Witness say that at least 10.000 tribals took part in the assault. Going back in time the list of attacks is very long:-on July 12, twenty-three cops, including a DSP, were killed in ambush in Rajnandgaon in the state of Chhattisgarh;-on May 22, sixteen cops killed in Gadchiroli; on Feb 1, a party of policeman walk into trap laid in Dhanora, Gadchiroli district, to probe arson and 15 were killed; June 29 2008, 38 specially trained Greyhounds were killed in Malkhangiri in the state of Orissa.

There are, of course, successful police operations against the Maoists. On 16 September 8 Maoists had been gun down and a gun factory destroyed in Chinta Gufa of Dantewada district in Chhattisgarh state. But a real undeclared war is going on with success and defeat on both sides. Also on the political scene accusations and contra-accusations are hurled at each other. The Trinamul Congress chief, Mamata Banerjee accused of being sympathetic with the Maoists returned the fire suggesting that the

Maoists an the Marxists of the government were two sides of the same coin. "They are working together" she said. Mamata's outburst came a day after chief minister Buddhadeb Bhattacharjee asked her party to "sever links with the rebels". CPM veteran leader Jyoti Basu, too echoed his words, charging the Trinamul with joining hands with the Maoists to unleash violence in the state. "Everyday our workers are getting killed. Our party offices are burnt. The Trinamul Congress an the Maoists are doing this together. They are taking law into their own hands" said Basu.

At the beginning of November, after being in the denial for months, the Nepalese Maoists admitted that they are extending "full support and cooperation" to the Naxals in India. A senior standing committee member of the Unified Communist Party of Nepal Maoist (UCPN-M) CP Gajurel, was quoted in a daily as saying: "We have extended our full support and cooperation to the Indian Maoists, who are launching armed revolt." The same newspaper had also earlier carried a report that a Maoist leader had met Indian leader Kishenji at an undisclosed place in October.

Faced with the Maoist menace the Left Front government in Bengal is now planning to spend Rs 1.600 crore for the development of the three Naxal-hit districts of West Midnapore, Bankura and Purulia. The chief minister of West Bengal, Buddhadeb Bhattacharjee, at the beginning of November paid a visit to Jangalmahal in Midnapore district. In sheer defiance of the huge police bandobast for the chief minister visit, the Maoists ambushed a patrol party 50 km from Midnapore town and just 30 minutes after the CM left, killing four soldiers. Eyewitness said the Maoists sprayed bullets from AK-47 rifles, looted arms from the vehicle, and walked away without any resistance.

On 27 October, tribal activists, backed by armed Maoists, under the name of local outfit People's Committee against Police Atrocity (PCPA) seized the Bhubaneswar-Delhi Rajdhani Express in West Midnapore district and detained it for five hours before security forces could free the hostages. The railways continue to be a vulnerable target. What is shocking is that in these states where the Maoist revolt is burning the local governments are only busy rewarding their own cadres and forgetting the large populations.

So it is with the CPM in West Bengal and also in Chhattisgarh a recent scandal has revealed that a former tribal chief minister,

Madhu Koda, in four years as chief minister, has increased his declared assets of 20.000 Euro in 2005 to an estimated 60 million Euro today, with illegal investments allover the world. Before becoming a deputy he was a daily wages earner. Corruption and police atrocity seem to be the upsetting causes.

NAXALITE/MAOIST MOVEMENT TODAY

Compared to the Naxalbari movement of the earlier phase, the (CPI Maoist)-led armed struggle is seen by observers to be at a more advanced level. It has spread over a larger area and has survived for over two decades. The strongest guerilla zone remains the Dandakaranya forest region in central India covering eleven districts across the four states of Andhra Pradesh, Maharashtra, Chhattisgarh and Madhya Pradesh. The Maoist Communist Centre (MCC) of Bihar and Jharkhand claims that its influence in the region extends to a population of about 12 million people of tribal origin. Even though more widespread than the earlier Naxalite movement, the Maoists of today have not yet been able to build powerful country wide political movements. The overall picture is one of a relatively strong militant outfit with popular support in its strongholds in the south, central and eastern regions. Outside its core areas, the Indian state has been able to prevent Maoist entry into the national political arena.

During the 1980s, the MHA was not just a law and order ministry but was responsible for the important subject of the development of the Scheduled Castes (SCs) and Scheduled Tribes (STs). Initiatives such as Special Component Plan for the former and the Tribal Sub-Plan for the latter were started and implemented on the ground through the state governments. The ministry also took a keen interest in the increasing violence against the SCs and STs in the country and initiated effective measures to stop the violence and to punish the offenders with 'deterrent rapidity'.

The Civil Rights Cell monitored the trends of violence and prepared reports for the Cabinet and Parliament. The MHA was a strong and powerful ministry with funds and police forces to compel the state governments to follow the central guidelines and instructions on issues of violence, development and social justice. The creation in the subsequent period of the Ministry of Social Justice and Empowerment and the allocation of the subject of the development of Scheduled Castes and Tribes to that ministry along with the issue of socio-political violence against these communities reduced the MHA to a purely law and order apparatus. As a consequence, the annual report of the ministry for the year 2005-06 reads like a strange document devoted entirely to Naxalite violence with nothing to say on the increasing number and intensity of violence against the SCs and STs in the recent period. Such a juxtaposition of the naxalite violence with the increasing violence against the SC's and ST's is necessary for appreciation of both 'violence of development' and 'development of violence' and to devise appropriate measures in coordination with the state governments. In this sense, the creation of a separate Ministry of Social Justice and Empowerment was not perhaps an altogether happy development for the Scheduled Castes and Tribes.

The process of commercialization of forest resources has reduced the access of indigenous communities to these resources. Alienation of tribal land to richer non-tribal elements from outside is a significant factor in tribal unrest. Displacement due to the construction of large dams and other industries has impoverishment of these communities, strengthening demands for tribal self governance. Government programs for tribal development have had adverse consequences for tribal communities as documented in several studies including those conducted on behalf of the government of India (GOI, 2008).

The extension of Panchayati Raj Institutions (PRI's) to tribal areas can become an instrument of empowerment only after steps are taken to restore indigenous rights over land and forest. The setting up of the new states of Chhattisgarh, Jharkhand and Uttaranchal to enable tribal participation in governance and decision making at decentralized levels, is largely ineffective due to the unchanged character and mindset of the administrative and police setup. B. Mungekar, Member Planning Commission of India is reported to have prepared a report showing that between 1951 and 1990, 40 million people were displaced as result of development projects. Of these 40 percent were tribal people. Only 25 percent of the displaced have so far been 'rehabilitated'. The adequacy and quality of 'rehabilitation' has come into serious question especially in the context of the recent controversy over the Sardar Sarovar Project. In the light of this, it is not surprising that the naxalite movement has found support among those sections of Scheduled Tribes who became victims rather than beneficiaries of development. The issue was examined in depth by Dr. B. D. Sharma, then Commissioner for Scheduled Castes and Tribes in his 28th Report to the President of India. The report elaborated a Constitutional schema for establishing an egalitarian society with clear provisions for countering simultaneously the inequities of tradition and the 'backlash of modernization' in the nation's development.

The focus was on the dalits and the adivasis. The assessment was that the outcome of the developmental measures taken plus the adverse forces already at work was a negative one as indicated by the accentuation of deprivation and the 'relentless slide back' in the fortunes of these communities notwithstanding some token achievements such as 'reservations' in government jobs. The analysis laid bare the 'omissions, distortions, subterfuges and the studied silence on vital issues' in order to protect vested interests. The people were paying a heavy price for the so-called 'development'. All the institutions of the state, executive, legislative and judicial, had abdicated their constitutional responsibility of safeguarding the interest of the deprived sections. The executive in particular, with its distorted role perception, is working against the interests of those whose wellbeing is its sacred trust. The action taken on the report by the government amounted to undermining constitutional values and trivialization of institutions by those who had the responsibility to protect them. However, the model that was adopted in practice legitimized divestiture of the indigenous people's traditionally recognized rights in the name of 'development'. Not merely were the immemorial customary rights of the tribals ruthlessly violated but they were made to appear as trespassers in their own lands. All this was being done in spite of the concern expressed in the Constitution's Fifth Schedule that the laws of the land should be suitably adapted in their application to Scheduled areas, a responsibility entrusted to the executive as part of its duty for the advancement of the Scheduled Tribes. To accomplish this task, the executive was conferred with special powers. The deliberate non-use of these powers resulted in not just unconstitutional and unjust governance but also in cruel and callous administration.

In the light of this analysis, the Report to the President also examined the issue of self governance at the village level and the disastrous effect of the non-recognition of command over community resources, which had resulted everywhere in disorganization, displacement and destitution of the adivasis. There could be no peace in the Scheduled Areas so long as the confrontation between the people and the state continued on the issue of self governance, particularly on the intimately associated question of the command over resources. A recent paper by Amit Bhaduri and Medha Patkar published in EPW meaningfully carries forward the discussion started by BD Sharma.

The current strategy of the MHA, as spelt out in its annual reports for 2004-5 and 2005-6, appear retrograde and counterproductive in the light of this analysis. The deployment of paramilitary forces on a large scale in the interior tribal areas of the country does not solve the problem but can cause immense misery to the common people. The whole policy of raising and deploying central paramilitary forces for local conflict management is based on faulty thinking and leads to serious internal security disasters. Paramilitary units as India Reserve battalions, which the Centre is encouraging states to raise to deal with internal security problems cannot be effective since their basic military type of training involves no local contact or interaction or understanding of the local population and problems. A recent visit to Chhattisgarh, where a Nagaland based IR battalion has been deployed, indicated emerging tensions between the district police leadership and the Naga battalion leadership since the latter is prioritized over the former, which is basically responsible for law and order management. A similar tension had emerged in Punjab earlier when the National Security Guard (NSG) was deployed over the head of the state DG of Police who was basically responsible for law and order in the state. Similarly, it has been found in the northeast that lack of local knowledge on the part of the central paramilitary forces (CPFs) often led to disasters for the men, who were ambushed because they followed misleading intelligence provided to them by some interested local elements. Further, the induction of CPF's often leads to tensions between them and the local police responsible for law and order and to demoralization of central of the central forces.

8

Maoist Guerrillas

Active Maoist Guerrilla warfare and passive expansion of the ideology of capturing power through the barrels of the gun is swinging imagination of masses living in the fringe areas of the society-the rural have-nots, forgotten forest dwellers and the exploited masses in different parts of the country. Statistically the Maoist headed movement has affected several states right from West Bengal to Maharashtra and Andhra Pradesh.

The units in Kerala, Karnataka and Tamil Nadu are yet to start organized armed violence. Recent visit to certain areas in Punjab-Sangrur, Faridkot and Bathinda etc areas and certain pockets in Haryana educated me about existence of strong Maoist groups in these so called prosperous states also. Delhi, Kolkata, Patna etc cities continue to be the hub of intellectual sympathizers and promoters of the movement.

The speed with which the movement is spiraling has not been analysed in the correct perspective by the political decision makers, intellectuals, intelligence agencies and law and order implementing agencies. The reasons are many, parts of which I had shared with the readers, Maoist Apparatus and Bridging Old Fault Lines, published in this portal. It is proposed to outline some more details in this essay concluding the last essay. It is better to have a peep into the efforts of the Union and State governments in the direction of meeting the menace with approximated correct prognosis.

Some readers of the Part 1 of the essay asked me to explain Mass Control and its cyclic effect. Mass Control is both physical and psychological control on the people in a given area, who look up to the STATE for means of livelihood, basic amenities, protection of lives and properties and ensuring upward movement of the people from poverty to prosperity. In vast areas of rural India, forested areas inhabited by the Advasis (aboriginal tribes) and in mining, industrial areas huge segments of people live under extreme penury.

In certain areas (including prosperous Punjab) peasants commit suicide in large numbers, marginal landholders become landless, forest areas are denuded by timber tycoons, Tendu leaf (for making bidi) cultivation is hijacked by the moneylenders, forest lands are forcibly grabbed for mining purposes and most of the government schemes to help the rural people with monetary help land up in the pockets of politicians, bureaucrats and middlemen. Over period such people lose confidence on the STATE and it is gradually replaced by the revolutionary group who seek emancipation through violence.

This inevitably follows by armed conflict between the STATE and the Revolutionaries; in this case Maoists. Gradually Law & Order takes priority over other mandatory duties of the STATE. Gradually the conflict takes the shape of guerrilla warfare between the STATE and the Maoists.

The STATE tries to retain Mass Control by using police forces and that alienates people to greater degrees. Sometimes the Maoists deliberately attacks police posts located in villages. This invites increased retaliation on the village from the STATE. Under STATE pressure the people surrenders to Maoist Mass Control and the chain of STATE and MAOIST violence continue to haunt the people.

Once small areas are "liberated" by the Maoists they run their own government and paralyze all government establishments including schools, health centres lines of communication and even stoppage of payment of revenue to the STATE. The economy of the area is paralyzed and the STATE continues to depend on force as a multiplier ingredient to smash the Maoist movement. Use of the expression Fringe People is an inclusive exercise for incorporating poverty stricken, landless, jobless, uprooted mass of people. The level of poverty, as per unreliable government data is also alarming. It is estimated that 456 million Indians (42% of the total Indian population) now live under the global poverty line of $1.25 per day (PPP). This means a third of the global poor now reside in India. The Planning Commission of India uses different criteria and has estimated that 27.5% of the population lived below the poverty line in 2004–2005, down from 51.3% in 1977–1978, and 36% in 1993-1994. The source for this was the 61st round of the National Sample Survey (NSS) and the criterion used was monthly per capita consumption expenditure below Rs. 356.35 for rural areas and Rs. 538.60 for urban areas. 75% of the poor are in rural areas, most of them are daily wagers, self-employed householders and landless labourers.

Indian economy has grown steadily over the last two decades. Its growth has been uneven when comparing different social groups, economic groups, geographic regions, and rural and urban areas. Between 1999 and 2008, the annualized growth rates for Gujarat (8.8%), Haryana (8.7%), or Delhi (7.4%) were much higher than for Bihar (5.1%), Uttar Pradesh (4.4%), or Madhya Pradesh (3.5%). Poverty rates in rural Orissa (43%) and rural Bihar (41%) are among the world's most extreme.

The India State Hunger Index 2008, by the International Food Policy Research Institute, Punjab has the best nutritional situation, whereas malnutrition in Madhya Pradesh is worse than in Ethiopia or Sudan. Worse is the condition in tribal areas of Chattisgarh, Orissa, Garhchiroli area of Maharashtra, plain and hill regions of Jharkhand, rural areas of West Bengal and Bihar.

These are areas where the Maoists or Naxals have stepped up their Guerrilla warfare. On a given map the compact area looks like a liberated zone. The State response basically veered around restoration of law & order, battling the guerrillas, decimating them through live action and forcing them out of the "liberated areas." The nucleus of police response is the Police Station. For example Dantewada district in Chattisgarh has 21 police stations and 2 police outposts. Number of Police outposts has gone up during last two years. In addition to state police force a few central police force encampments have also been established. The hill district having 9046.29 Sq kms area has only 478.93 kms tarred road. Police mobility is extremely limited. Average strength of a police station is about 10-15, except on occasions Special Forces are attached to a police station for raiding Maoist hideouts. Previously most of the police stations were located in makeshift or dilapidated structures without any watch tower, perimeter defences and faster communication facilities. The phone lines are unreliable and are generally deactivated by the Maoists. Wireless communication is being improved and in recent times some police officers have been given mobile phones. The problem with mobile phones is that towers are very few and often some existing towers are blasted out by the Naxals.

A police station is supposed to dominate an area of over 450 kms. With the given available strength in a working day (normal average is 7 out of 10), poor motor transport facility, inadequacy of wireless communication and supply of antiquated rifles the presence of normal police force is considered insignificant; not fit for fighting Maoist rebels equipped with modern arms. The inventories of the Maoists include Kalashnikov rifles, Light Machine Guns, 2" mortars and assorted rapid firing weapons. In addition to these they possess several kinds of landmines and IEDs. The Maoists are well trained in guerrilla warfare, jungle warfare and tactics of ambush. Their encampments are mobile. The guerrillas have no fixed HQ. In fact, a given guerrilla group do not spend nights in the same village. The groups are mainly composed of compatible tribe members.

Most of these tribal inhabited areas are extremely poverty ridden. Cultivation, harvesting forest resources etc are main sources of livelihood. In most cases funds provided under Integrated Rural Development Programme, NREG, Sampoorna Gramin Rozgar Yojana and other social security programmes do not reach the real people. For example, if an amount of 300 is sanctioned per family under NREG the fortunate family may get rupees 100, if they are lucky. In most cases out of 100 about 7-9% people actually receive the amount; rest goes to pockets of the bureaucrats, local politicians, leaders of local self government and even petty clerks. The STATE government sanctions the amounts to the district collectors, allocated by the central government. From that point downwards the money develops wings and the real recipients remain where they were. Same is the fate with Anganwadi system introduced in some of the areas. Right from the district office to the lowest governing tool in the panchayat and certain elements in the Anganwadi institutions share the money and the real education and total child development system remain where they were.

We will discuss these aspects in later parts of the essay. Police operations have three basic formats: group patrolling (often in platoon strength, rarely in company strength); village searches, and rare ambush parties. In group patrolling the general trend is to march in a column with 15-20 feet distance between two sepoys. These parties do not have mine sweeping vehicles and mostly they are not equipped with handheld mine detecting devices. This results in frequent mine explosions and police casualties. The information that a police party was planning patrolling in a particular direction somehow or other reaches the Maoists through their information network, interception of VHF radio talks. They plant antipersonnel mines on the likely routes to be taken by the patrol parties.

My experience in Nagaland and Manipur and the experiments conducted by army and paramilitary units indicated that instead of a single column patrol party or area domination party it was safer to send out two other parallel parties (smaller in size); one on both flanks of the main party. This tactics paid good dividends and guerrilla parties waiting in ambush were often taken by surprise.

Village searches are mostly perfidious. Police and Salwa Judum parties often enters homes, violate privacy of women and forcibly take away eatables including fowls, goats etc. Often the villagers are made to assemble in one place and some are tortured to obtain information. Police commanders do not realize that such tactics and illegal plundering and faulty operational methodology alienate the people more and they prefer the Maoists to buy protection.

Deployment of ambush parties are not done on the basis of precise human intelligence. This is the weakest area of anti- guerrilla operations. The tribesmen have basic distrust for State administration; they are alienated by malpractices of timber-tycoons, Tendu leaf contractors, loan sharks, Mahajans (who advance money against crop) and of course against police, whom they consider as ambassadors of State repression. The normal state intelligence outfit and its district detachments are burdened with multifarious-political errands to normal terrorist-jihad activities. They are supposed to keep track of dowry killing, starvation death by agricultural workers, village feuds and most law & order problems. They have no focused training and resource to gather human intelligence (HUMINT) about the Maoists. It is high time the State governments create special intelligence cells for Maoist problems. In a State like Jharkhand a special intelligence cell should consist of minimum 500 officers and men, specially trained by the Intelligence Bureau and other outfits handling commando and guerrilla warfare. Several meetings of the Union Home Minister with the State police chiefs and advisories to the Chief Ministers have not been able to make them understand that without high quality HUMINT it is not possible to carry out successful armed actions against the Maoists. Every district of the affected states should have a contingent of the special intelligence unit. These units should have attached compliments of trained commandos, who can move with lightening speed to intercept the Maoist group informed upon by the human assets. The DG police and the Operations Chief in each district may order immediate planned action without waiting for bureaucratic shenanigans. Unfortunately, in States like Chhattisgarh (despite an efficient DG Police) and Jharkhand such modern anti guerrilla concepts are yet to be implemented. Neither the Union and State governments have looked into the old British model in Malaysia, US model in Vietnam, and the models practiced in Greece and Italy nor they have gone for any other innovations improving upon India's own experiences in insurgency infested areas. The politicians talk for the sake of befooling the people.

Even if some Central paramilitary forces are inducted they cannot operate without help of local police and intelligence. As newcomers they are more vulnerable. Central forces can only succeed if battalions are allowed to dig in the affected areas for years together, build up defences, sanitize the villages and develop their own HUMINT potential. Temporary visiting units are guests; they are not effective operative units. Delhi must understand this and persuade the States to borrow Central forces for at least ten years. Units may change, but CRPF must be replaced by CRPF for the sake of continuity and force-homogeneity. A contingent of CRPF to be replaced by a contingent CISF after three months is a useless exercise. Minimum rotation of forces can ensure better operational capability.

While on Chattisgarh the issue of Salwa Judum is required to be briefly examined. Pro-Maoist intellectuals have painted pictures of "village grouping" by the government in the name of mobilising villagers against the Maoists. "Village Grouping" was successfully tried by the army in Mizoram. The principle was to deny water to the fish and make them vulnerable to lack of oxygen. There is no doubt that the villagers, either out of "Mass Control" factor or fear of decimation provide help to the Maoists. Once the villages are "grouped" (temporarily) the Maoists would be denied the water to swim about freely. Human rights groups and even the judiciary have intervened in the matter. The system of VVF (as in Manipur), Village Guards (as in Nagaland) and Special Police Officers (as in Punjab) for deployment after sustained training by a paramilitary force in guerrilla warfare and handling of medium and heavy weapons.

The Constitution has bestowed rights on the people to defend themselves. No court can rule against this fundamental right. Besides Chattisgarh, the readers to visit Lalgarh, Jangalmahal etc places in West Midnapore of West Bengal. Maoist activities (Naxal) are not new in this district of West Bengal bordering Bihar/Jharkhand. The Naxalite movement in Debra, Gopiballabhpur in mid-1969 had wrought the mass-killing violent movement for over 7 years, before the peak of the movement could be blunted. In fact, Debra, Gopiballabhpur, Jhargram, Shalboni, Jangal Mahal, Lalgarh etc areas are in West Midnapore district. These are most backward areas of Bengal. Except Haldia ports complex, Kharagpur and a few pockets nearer to Kolkata rest of the district is as backward as the adjacent districts of Purulia, Birbhum and Bankura are.

Some efforts were made, too late in the regime of the CPM, to start industrialization in Singur (Nano factory of TATA) and Nandigram (chemical complex of Salim group). Here is another classic case of political rivalry between the CPM and Trinamool Congress feuding over industrialization in agricultural area and politicization of land acquisition on the plea of displacement of the rural people. This feud helped TMC, Jamiat-ul-Ulama-e-Hind and several NGOs, and indirectly the Congress to create severe disturbances. The government had expressed intention of acquisition, the Haldia ports authority had issued a notice about likely acquisition, but no government action had been taken to forcibly occupy the land for the proposed SEZ at Nandigram. The TMC led agitation helped the Maoists to walk into the vortex of tornado created by political rivalry. There is no denial of fact that the issue of acquision of agricultural land for industrial use in Nandigram (Midnapore) and Singur (Hooghly) had kicked off bloody trails of political tornado, but these politicized movements might have had earned a few more votes for the TMC and the Congress, but the momentum had encouraged the Maoists to slip into Jhargram, Shalboni, Lalgarh and even Midnapore Sadar areas with arms and explosives. In Nandigram and nearby Singur area the Bhumi Uchhed Pratirodh Committee and Jami Rakkha Committee etc bodies were organised and were highly infiltrated by the Maoists.

Nandigram and Singur were the stages where TMC and Congress rehearsed political revival and the Maoists initiated a new phase of sustained movement in west Midnapore, basically a forested single crop area, mostly inhabited by the tribal people-Santhal and Oraon, Majhi, Mahato, Ho, Munda etc and sprinkling of lower caste Hindus. Here also a front organisation was floated styled as Peoples Committee against Police Atrocities. This mass organisation was headed by CPM's local committee member Chatrdhar Mahato. Besides this front organisation the Maoists also organised Solidarity Forum for Lalgarh, Shramajivi Swastha Udyog, Utsha Manush, Janaswastha Committee, and Janaswastha Swadhikar Mancha etc. These front organisations received support from Bengali intellectuals, writers and film makers.

The apex social organization of the Santhals, the Bharat Jakat Majhi Madwa Juan Gaonta took up the leadership of the struggle, although the leader of the organization, the "Disham Majhi" Nityananda Hembram openly professed that they were being guided by the people's movement and they had no control on it. The upsurge of adivasis is continuing unabated and is also spreading to newer areas. They laid siege of Jhargram and only after discussion between the Bharat Jakat Majhi Madwa Juan Gaonta and the administration, the siege of was partially lifted. The blockade on the road connecting Jhargram and Dahijuri was lifted on 14th November but the Bharat Jakat Majhi Madwa could not convince the protesters to lift the blockades of the other roads connecting Jhargram. Besides Lalgarh, the movement has now spread to Binpur, Jhargram, Jamboni, Shalboni, Belpahari, Garbeta and Gopiballavpur. People's response to joint State and Central operation was so spontaneous that the movement had spread to the last two blocks of the Jhargram sub-division, Nayagram and Sankrail. Nayagram block was disconnected by piling tree trunks on the roads in Dhankamra and Barpat. Dhankhori, Gajashimul, Mudakati and Kungarda areas of Sankrail block have also been blockaded. On the other hand, all connections to police stations and camps in the Belpahari block of Jhargram sub-division has been cut off. A group of around 500 armed tribal blockaded the Neguriya police camp near Chakadoba in Belpahari. The local shopkeepers and traders have declared that they would not supply anything to the policemen in the camps.

The West Bengal government cannot deny its responsibility for neglecting the area. While Below Poverty Line index in the state is 27% in West Midnapore areas the index is 43% to 37%. There are about 12 government aided schools in the tribal area, but hardly any teacher is available, The Health Centres are almost nonexistent. There is no regular doctor, least speaking of free medicine supply. Some sample study was made about a few central funded welfare projects in the Jhargram-Lalgarh areas. People have not even heard about Sampoorna Gramin Rojgar Yojana (SGRY), Rural Housing, Self Employment Programme, Berozgar Bhatta (unemployment allowance), and National Rural Employment Guarantee (NREG) etc schemes.

A sample study of Belpahadi indicated that the CPM leaders offered some NREG facility to their cadre. Only 7% of rest of the tribal people received some NREG support. Some sampling was made of Anganwadi (rural school) scheme in Sankrail and Nayagram areas. It was found that only 5 to 7% benefit reached the targeted people. Rest of the money was misappropriated by the village authorities, Block officials and even top notches of the Aganwadi scheme. A sample study of the Integral Rural Development Programme (IRDP) was made in Belda area. The findings were disheartening. The amount received by the district and Block authorities and the Panchayats were distributed amongst the political sharks. The real tribal people received nothing (CPM supporters excluded). It is not possible for one person to study the entire developmental activities. But the if samples are any indicator, it must be said that the governmental tools were misused and the benefits offered by Delhi were either eaten by the political-bureaucratic cartel and very little trickled down to the deserving tribal population.

The magnitude of the national problem of sharks eating up the smaller fries was horribly exemplified in a publication of the Times of India (Nov. 26, 2009) about 22,853 ghost employees drawing pay for decades from the Municipal Corporation of Delhi to the tune of Rs. 17 crores per month. Statistics about only one agency has been dug out. There are about 10 such departments under Delhi government which maintain ghost employees costing the tax payers about Rs. 50 crores per month.

What is happening in the rural areas and in the forested tracts as well as in vast mining tracts in different parts of the country, where India's shining global economy is yet to shine even for fractions of days in any given year. Nearly 30% of India's population goes to bed in empty stomach and about 40% can barely manage two square meals in any given day. In Lalgarh area the same misfortune of the people was noticed by non-partisan observers.

Militarily the government of West Bengal failed miserably to control the Maoist movement. Local formations of the CPM (notoriously known for motor cycle groups) dominated the area and maimed all political opposition and even reasonable ventilation of genuine grievances. They were, at many places, supported by the local police. The ordinary people lost touch with the administration and the administration was blissfully ignorant about the Maoists building up local committees, arming the people, bringing in improvised explosive devices and building up comprehensive people's fronts. Obviously, these fronts received support from Trinamool Congress and Congress, who thought of Nandigram like exploitation of the Maoists for retrieving political ground. This was a miscalculation. The Maoists are very active in adjacent Jharkhand, Orissa and Bihar. The borders are open. When chased the Orissa and Jharkhand Maoists slip in Midnapore and Purulia districts of West Bengal. Similarly, the Maoists also recruit their cadres from West Bengal tribal population. The intellectual brains of Bengal, Andhra Pradesh and Orissa guide the movement. Local leaders are also emerging in Jharkhand, Chattisgarh and other parts of the country.

Let us look into the military formation in Lalgarh and Jangal Mahal area of West Midnapore. The Maoists have organised village level squads for cutting of road connection, planting IED or anti-personnel and anti-tank mines (to hit mine proof vehicles). These village committees are also assigned the task of attacking isolated police posts. Major police stations are at West Midnapore Kotwali, Sankrail, Jhargram, Lalgarh, Shalboni (also EFR headquarter) Manikpara (near Kalaikunda airbase) etc. Besides the District HQ the average strength of police stations were (before joint operations)

10-15. The police were armed with.303 obsolete rifles. One jeep per police station was the only means of communication. Phone lines were unreliable and cell phones were not in profuse use because of lack of towers. Wireless communication was also generally absent. The police depended on muscle support from the CPM cadre.

Once the organised Maoist activities started in Lalgarh, Jhargram, Shalboni, and Jangal Mahal etc areas police resistance evaporated. The State did not deploy sufficient numbers of the crack Eastern Frontier Rifles (EFR) and other State Armed Police Battalions. Kolkata depended on ramshackle police forces and party cadre. Once these efforts were blunted by the front organisations the trained Maoists' reserve arms caches in the hill areas were brought in. This is proved by the daring attack on Sankrail police station by 100 Maoists and kidnapping of the officer in charge. The Maoists have attacked government establishments in West Midnapore Sadar (planting of mine), Jhargram sub-divisional HQ, Shalboni, Nayagram and other places.

The joint Central and State police operations (seen on TV) were mainly conducted in plains areas of Lalgarh, amidst populated segments and in some cases under pan of TV cameras. My enquiry with local people, not connected with the Maoist movement, mostly apolitical, some owing allegiance to CPM, revealed that the State government first tried to augment ridiculously low strength in the police stations. They also depended on the trained party cadre to build up local resistance. However, backed by other tribal organisation, Trinamool Congress and Congress the Peoples Committee against Police Atrocities (PCPA) organised sustained opposition to police incursion. The main Maoist guerrillas provided support by planting mines and opening fire on the Central and State forces under cover of deep forested areas. The joint operation was limited to regaining government control on the Lalgarh tract and no sustained and planned operations were conducted in the hills adjoining Jharkhand and Orissa. The hardcore Maoist cadres infiltrated from Jharkhand and Orissa and revived the Naxal movement in West Midnapore areas along with pockets in Birbhum and Bankura. If a bird's eye view is taken of the compact Maoist affected areas in this region it would seem that the belt between Birbhum (home district of Union Finance Minister), Bankura, West Midnapore, Jharkhand and Orissa is painted either red or pink.

This is what the Maoists call "liberated zone." What are the preparations of the West Bengal government? It is a sad and shady story. Without going into the political skullduggery it can be safely concluded that the CPM and other Left partners had built up groups of Banditos, often armed with lethal weapons and homemade bombs. After about 25 years other political groups, such as the Trinamool Congress and its passive partner the Congress have also started organizing groups of Banditos, who gradually gathered the courage of physically clashing with the Left opponents. Both the sides made West Bengal into a political killing field. The Maoists are known for taking advantage of such mass chaos and side with one or the other to progress in their planned advance in selected pockets. Working in conjunction with the violent political forces they establish their own bases.

Historically the CPI (ML), the hardcore Charu-Kanu-Jangal faction was against the CPM line. My personal experiences in Naxalbari operations gave me impressions that Charu Majumdar was vehemently opposed to any negotiation with the Left leaders like Hare Krishna Konar. However, later in 1972 elections elements of the Naxals supported the Congress in districts like Midnapore, Bankura and Birbhum, Jalpaiguri, Burdwan and Hooghly etc. Besides the Bangladesh war effect support from the Naxals also resulted in resounding victory for the Congress. That CPI (M) should crash from 113 in 1971 to 14 in the 1972 was totally unexpected so was the Congress party's tally of 216 seats. The point made is that the Maoists are not averse to side with political parties of their choice to augment their own agenda. They enter a new area as tails of political parties and later establish bases of their own. If it were Congress in 1972 to seemingly exploit the Maoists, it is Trinamool Congress and its appendage, Congress in 2011. Political parties forget the universal lesson that the tiger they often ride devours the rider sooner than later.

The State government's dependence on local police and party cadre misfired. The Maoists initially took advantage of anti-SEZ proposals of the government and often violent agitation started by TMC and its allies. Nandigram to Singur to West Midnapore was not reached in one lap. It took the Maoists and their political allies (tactical allies only) to build up movement in West Midnapore around the Union and State government's proposal to allot 4,500 acres of land near Shalboni to Jindal Steel Works SEZ factory. The chain of events started after the 2nd November, 2009 land mine explosion targeting the convoy of West Bengal chief minister Buddhadeb Bhattacharjee and union steel and mines minister Ram Vilas Paswan as they were returning from the inauguration of the Jindal Steel Works SEZ. It was alleged by the Maoists and their political allies that the land in question belonged to the government and was earmarked for distribution among the tribals. The chain of events resulted in violence between CPM cadres on the one hand and Trinamool cadres supported by Maoist front organisations on the other. Unable to resist the "occupation" of Lalgarh, Jangal Mahal etc areas the State government requested for central forces and they seemingly "reoccupied" the tract from the Maoists.

The fact is that the government of West Bengal still does not have any plan to build up forces to fight the Maoist guerrillas. They, in collaboration with guerrillas from Jharkhand and Orissa have started hitting at targets even in the heart of the district head quarter. Some semblance of law and order is being maintained by the State police and the Central forces deputed to help the local authorities. There are plans to start another combing operation. But the holes in the government nets are so big that small Maoists Pisces swim in the area unhindered. The State governments in West Bengal, Jharkhand and Orissa are yet to prepare a joint blueprint for fighting the guerrilla forces. The Central governments often announce certain offensive joint actions. However, except deputation of certain elements of central forces in the affected States no Joint Command has been conceived as yet. There is no intelligence coordination between the State governments and the central intelligence agencies. Police stations are the best bases from where local intelligence is collected for tactical operational purposes. The intelligence networks in the rural and urban police stations have dried up. The area chowkidars, dafadars, lower revenue officials, gram sevaks, and other rural government employees have ceased to feed the police stations. Human intelligence is appallingly poor. Even the central intelligence agencies have not been able to build up HUMINT resources in the affected areas. Anti-Guerrilla warfare cannot be fought by wild goose's chase. Forces have to act on precise intelligence.

As the Maoists often use cell phones it is not impossible to locate the GPS coordinate of the phone under use. Once located helicopter borne forces can raid the area and neutralize the target. This aspect of coordination between signal intelligence (SIGINT) and airborne attack has not been conceived as yet. On the other hand the Maoists have excellent HUMINT assets from amongst the villagers and even educated sympathizers. Villagers not cooperating with the Maoists and suspected to be informers of the police are mercilessly punished. Recent incidents of cruel killing of police officers and innocent villagers prove that Mass Control mechanisms of the Maoists are near complete.

It is understood that the Maoists in Chattisgarh, Jharkhand. Orissa and West Bengal have obtained VHF communication sets from former LTTE members. These are used for communication between the Command with the Squads. VHF communications are able to transmit to shorter distances. If transmitted from a higher location the signals can be received even at a distance of 40 kilometers. Often the desired height is achieved by hanging an antenna on high rise trees. The State police are yet to install array of VHF monitoring instruments to pick up signals from the sophisticated VHF transreceivers used by the guerrilla forces. The police forces often use VHF sets in analog mode and not in automatic digital encryption mode. These can be easily intercepted either by identifying the frequency or by scanning the frequency logs. Police forces have not taken security precaution while using VHF sets during operations. These limitations are required to be attended forthwith.

The government agencies have just started thinking in terms of using Unmanned Aerial Vehicle (UAV) to survey the affected areas, locate hideouts and send the live broadcasts to the nearby forces to mount counter attack. Use of UAV in forested terrains may not yield expected results, unless the government acquires infrared equipped cameras for the UAVs to enable these flying machines to look down at precise targets through thick foliage and often mist covers.

Sample studies in Chattisgarh and West Bengal (broader study in all affected areas is necessary) it is found that the State police in Chattisgarh is better prepared and their mechanism of operations are more scientific. There has been marginal increase in HUMINT assets, but paucity of force prevents the State from comprehensive area domination. In West Bengal the police forces are yet to wake up to the reality that the Maoists of today are not ragtag Naxals of seventies and eighties. These guerrillas are well trained, well armed and indoctrinated. They follow the Maoist principles of guerrilla warfare scrupulously. Bengal police forces, paralyzed by political pressure, have not been exposed to anti-guerrilla warfare.

The thin police forces are so inadequate that they are not enough in numbers to take on sustained anti-guerrilla warfare, they lack in weaponry and training in anti-guerrilla warfare. Even the Central forces are not trained to fight the guerrillas by organizing them into effective counter-guerrilla forces. Some States have designated certain numbers of policemen as Special Forces with fancy names like Cobra Force etc. The Centre and the States may like to consider assisting each affected State to raise minimum 7 battalions of anti-guerrilla Special Forces trained in the army's anti-insurgency warfare school. The present model of training some policemen in the model of National Security Guard (NSG) training manual may sharpen the efficiency edges. But the NSG is basically a static operations force for tackling static incidents like Mumbai incident of 26/11. It is not meant for deployment in anti-guerrilla warfare. The specially trained anti-guerrilla warfare police forces, like the VVF mentioned earlier live on and in the ground divided into strike squads coordinated by the battalion and higher commands. To fight guerrillas the forces have to adopt guerrilla ways of life.

The Central government often announces coordinated joint operations. This constructive idea can better be enforced if the entire mobilized forces (from different colours) are fused into a single operational force put under command of a Special Divisional Command (like the army) and operationalised in allocated territories for specializing in that territory till they are successful to retrieve the given territory from the Mass Control and military control of the Maoists.

However, it must be added that police action cannot alone eradicate the Maoist problems. An integrated and balanced approach and inclusive action plan is necessary to implement developmental works, providing employment, remodeling rural economy, education, health care and agricultural activities. Mushrooming of enrooted corruption in different welfare schemes, as discussed in this essay are required to be probed. The government must ensure that minimum 70% of the welfare funds and yojanas benefit the people. At present only 10-15% benefits reach the real affected people. Combating Maoist guerrillas require total attention of the political decision makers and bureaucrats at macro and micro levels. Otherwise, present efforts would prove to be a war exercise between the State and certain segments of the people, who may ultimately be 25-35% of the population in the affected areas. The Guerrillas accrue new territories trough continued mass action. The present red and pink map may get enlarged sooner than later if corrective measures are not adopted NOW and NOW.

9

Mao's Legacy and the Future of Maoism

It's time then to talk of Mao's legacy. As we have seen, Maoism has a definite view about how to get to socialism, and about what needs to be done to meet the basic needs of everyone in a poor country. Development is to be on an egalitarian basis — we are all in it together and everyone rises together. What then of Mao's legacy, Maoism? Surely, this is open to all who share his Weltanshuuang, his method of analysis — materialist dialectics — his values, his vision, and choose to embark together on the long march to socialism, knowing before hand, that the journey is fraught with considerable peril. What then of Maoism in India, one might ask? Maoist China did its best to feed, clothe and house everyone, keep them healthy, educate most of them. Contrast this with the deplorable conditions in India at the end of the 1960s and even today — the tragedy of India ruled by her own big bourgeoisie — and one gets wind as to why there are some in India who look to the Maoist model of development as the way to a richer and fuller life for all. Anu — whom we started this article with — was one of them.

However, while one may have deep respect for such people, one needs to ask the question: Are the basic path and strategy of revolution that were necessary in China in the 1930s and 1940s right for India in the 21st century? Well, India differs very significantly from the China of those times, more so in its history, geography, class and social structure, traditions, and in the nature of its "semi-feudalism"/backward capitalism, the accommodation of the big bourgeoisie with imperialism, the strength of the repressive apparatus of the state, the nationalities question, and so on. And, importantly, while Chinese history is replete with periodic widespread peasant uprisings, Indian history, in a comparative sense, is scarce of such rebellions, which perhaps can be explained in terms of caste – it is fundamentally antithetical to any meaningful unity of the exploited and the oppressed. Recall that Mao adapted his Marxism-Leninism to the realities of China's history, China's potentialities; "learn truth from practice" was his message. Surely a party [CPI (Maoist)] that stems from a political tendency that, over the last 40 years, has done its best to take the Indian revolution forward might like to take a hard re-look into the abyss that is India – its history, its potentialities.

The Maoists must keep in mind that the scientific validity of the Maoism they uphold will be judged in the first instance in India by its contributions to correctly explaining Indian social reality. There is a lot they have had a hand in this respect, for instance, in emphasising the parasitical reliance of Indian capital on the state for its self-expansion, expressed in the notion of *bureaucrat* capital. Or, in stressing the powerful role of the state in the very making of the Indian big bourgeoisie (of course, the "state's" fostering of the ruling classes more than the other way round, going back to ancient times, is an insight from the eminent historian D D Kosambi). The Maoists have also helped us to see the post-1956 official "land reforms" as having led to the partial amalgamation of the old rural landowning classes into a new, broader stratum of rich landowners, those not setting their hands to the plough, including an upper section of the former tenants, all of whom, despite the various markets, have yet to rid themselves of various "semi-feudal" practices and pre-capitalist elements of culture. Also, it is the Maoists who, in their practice, correctly do not even try to differentiate the rural poor into "agrarian proletariat" or "landless peasantry", knowing very well that the same very poor household can be categorized in one or the other at various points in time. And, in organising the "agrarian proletariat"/ "landless peasantry" along with the poor and middle peasants, and a section of the rich peasants, they insist on factoring in the caste question, despite their knowing how highly problematic and painfully difficult such a getting together can be. Also, it is the Maoists more than others who first grasped the brutal character of the dominant classes and the leaders of the political parties they have co-opted, the very same categories whose forebears had taken power in the name of Gandhian non-violence. All this is knowledge essentially derived from their practice; and, needless to say, in keeping with Mao's legacy, the content of practice and knowledge has to go on continuously rising to a higher level.

The party [CPI (Maoist)] has come in for a lot of condemnation for its violent activities, including killings. The violence however has to be viewed in the context of the undeclared civil war that is underway in the areas of its influence, for instance, in Dantewada in the state of Chhattisgarh (PUDR 2006). The government is implementing a barbaric counter-insurgency policy, which includes the fostering of a network of informers and combatants among the civilian population, right from the village level upwards — a state-supported, state-sponsored, and even state-organised so-called people's resistance [called Salwa Judum (SJ)] against the Maoists. Entire villages have been evacuated and the villagers forcibly dumped into relief camps, and this, in the circumstances of large-scale acquisition of land by private corporations in what is a mineral-rich region. The last four years have witnessed violent attacks, loot, destruction, intimidation, rape and killing on an unprecedented scale principally by the SJ; indeed, the latter has even forcibly mobilised the displaced into its ranks. Undoubtedly, the killing is by both sides, but the big difference is that the Maoists, generally when they target specific state representatives, or even informers, they first warn them to desist from the anti-people activity they are undertaking. Those guilty of rape, torture, deaths in custody, or responsible for "encounter" killings are singled out so that others may, out of fear of such reprisals, desist from acting thus. As far as the SJ representatives are concerned, any person who joins them is targeted, not because of any personal enmity, but because of the role that the SJ has been playing in the undeclared civil war.

More generally, the violence also has to be seen in the context of the close de facto nexus between economic and political power at the local and regional levels; the dominant classes, through various means, exercise a degree of control over the police and the judiciary, which increases the chances of violent confrontation between the contending classes.

Those who deliberately, falsely depict the Maoists as "devotees of violence", choose to suppress the fact that the violence of the oppressed (and the Maoists who now lead them) has been always preceded and provoked by the violence of the oppressors (and the state and private forces that back them). To claim, as some liberals do, that the violence of the oppressed is "morally equivalent" to that of the oppressors, is to endorse the reactionary state, which backs the oppressors. And, in this age of the management of public opinion, the "programming" of what the public thinks, sees and reads, the "facts" that are disseminated are artificially separated from a whole host of other relevant facts, never allowing the public to discern the "real" present.

But, while acknowledging that antagonistic contradictions between hostile class-based organisations will lead to violence, it is a Maoist tenet that guerrilla actions ought to be subordinated to "mass-line" politics — the Maoist guerrillas should give precedence to winning over the mass of the people in their base areas and, in consequence, in the surrounding areas — and work towards a better balance ("proportionality") than ever before between means and ends. Regarding the resort to violence in the revolution, to the extent that I have absorbed their writings, it would be fair to say that Marx and Engels might not have disagreed with the use of violent methods by the revolutionary forces in India today. The dominant classes could never be expected to give up their control without employing all the repressive power at their command. It is useful perhaps to recall that Marx's response to the "crimes and cruelties alleged" against the "insurgent Hindus" of 1857 was to set out an account of the daily violence "in cold blood" of British rule in India (Marx 1857).

As to the false claim that the Maoists have no mass support in their areas of influence, one has only to listen to perceptive yet sensitive, independent observers who know the situation on the ground. The state forces are much stronger (as far as armaments and numbers go) than the Maoist guerrillas, and yet the tribal peasants support the latter. Why do these peasants take the risk of supporting the underdogs, even when they know that when the guerrillas are vanquished, they, as their supporters, will be at the mercy of the state forces, and will most probably perish? If, at the risk of death itself, the peasants choose the guerrillas, surely there must be something more significant going on over here.

Besides India, Maoism is a political force to reckon with in Nepal, the Philippines, and Peru. The Nepali Maoist leaders have been imaginative — their ideas of some combination of the "Chinese" (triumph in the countryside and spread to the cities) and the "Russian" (victory in the cities and spread to the countryside) models of revolution, and of "21st century democracy" (multi-party competition as long as all agree by the goals of "new democracy") are appealing. But these theories are being put to a severe test in practice. The Unified Communist Party of Nepal (Maoist), given its relative strength vis-a-vis "the enemies" of democracy and their friends and masters outside the borders of that small country (above all in India), seeks to utilize the bourgeois republic as a stage in mustering the force of the impoverished masses and nationalist intermediate strata to proceed towards NDR.

What then of the future of Maoism and the renewal of socialism that it promises? Frankly, "whatever chance there may have been that the revolutions of the 20th century could or would provide successful working models of socialism" have long since been extinguished; "socialism, we are told, has been tried and failed". But, as Marx was the first to show, the obstacles to a better future cannot be meaningfully addressed within the framework of capitalism. The challenge then is to revive and renew the legacy of socialism. In this, can Maoism illuminate the way?

Maoism has its roots in Marx who was, above all, a *radical* democrat — he demanded the reincarnation of community and mass solidarity; he dreamed of the communion of human beings with nature; he stressed the dialectic of liberation; he looked forward to a just society alongside "rich individuality"; and, as Paresh Chattopadhyay (2005) reminds us, he insisted on the removal of commodity exchange, the division of labour, the state,... But, then, Lenin too, in his *State and Revolution* appeared as a thoroughgoing democrat, though he introduced into his conception of socialism elements that are antithetical to the "association of free individuals" — wage labour and state (Ibid).

Mao and the Chinese Maoists too gave the impression of being revolutionary democrats, that is, if one were to go by the 20 million people marching through the streets of various Chinese cities in the last week of May 1968, the demonstrators mainly chanting the slogan: "long live the revolutionary heritage of the great Paris Commune". Indeed, Marx's interpretation of the Commune was then deemed relevant to the revival of the revolution in China, something that found a place in the famous "Sixteen Points" of 8 August 1966. "Let a hundred flowers blossom, let a hundred schools of thought contend" was not merely intended policy for the promotion of progress in the arts and sciences, but one of ushering in a flourishing socialist culture, at least that was the claim.

Thus, given the *radical* democratic streak running from Marx to Mao, the best thing that Maoism could do is to commit to the promise of *radical* democracy; after all, while it is true that there cannot be liberty in any meaningful sense without equality, for the rich will certainly be more "free" (have more options) than the poor; so there also cannot be equality without liberty, for then some may have more political power than others.

THE IRONIES OF INDIAN MAOISM

A rough periodisation of the Maoist movement in India might read as follows: (1) The seminal years of "Naxalism" from the late 1960s to the end of 1972 were defined by a split from the Communist Party of India (Marxist) [CPI (M)] in 1967 when a large-scale exodus began, and by mass upsurges in various parts of West Bengal, in largely tribal-dominated districts, and in Srikakulam along the Andhra coast, construed by the split-away "Marxist-Leninists" as uprisings of the peasantry and struggles for state power. (2) A period from the main part of the 1970s to the 1980s, when the movement reassembled itself outside Bengal, chiefly in central and southern Bihar and in the Telangana region of Andhra Pradesh. Here two major "armed-struggle" tendencies survived with substantial continuity through the whole of the 1970s: the Chandra Pulla Reddy group and a group around Kondapalli Seetharamaiah. (3) A dramatic escalation of conflict from 1985 that would lead eventually to a wholesale militarisation of the movement in the 1990s and to the civil war that is currently raging in the tribal heartlands of the formerly undivided district of Bastar in the state of Chhattisgarh.

If the party launched by Charu Mazumdar in April 1969 had disintegrated by 1971 and fragmentation remained a characteristic of the Maoist groups throughout the 1970s and 1980s, the most recent phase has seen a series of mergers and a more consolidated Maoist movement. Today the two major currents of Indian Naxalism are the CPI (Marxist-Leninist) (Liberation) which is a more or less open party that has contested elections since the late 1970s, and the CPI (Maoist), which is waging the guerrilla war in Bastar and parts of Orissa. When the Indian government describes Maoism as the country's biggest "internal security threat", it is referring not to all the various Maoist parties, which are still numerous, but specifically to the CPI (Maoist) which emerged in 2004 as a merger between People's War (PW) and the Maoist Communist Centre of India (MCCI). PW was itself the outcome of a merger between the People's War Group (PWG) founded by Seetharamaiah and a Bihar-based party, Party Unity. Unlike Liberation, the PWG had been banned (on and off) for most of its history, and so of course is its avatar, the CPI (Maoist).

Andhra Pradesh has always been the true backbone of Indian Maoism. It was the only state in the country where the Maoists were in a majority in mid-1967, when a series of state-level coordination committees revolted against the CPI (M) leadership, egged on by the Chinese Communist Party's (CCP) call for a fight against "revisionism". "The party lost 60 percent of its membership in the state," with Nagi Reddy carrying 11 of the 14 district committees with him. But the Andhra Maoists stayed out of the All India Co-ordination Committee of Revolutionaries in November 1967. When the dissidents either left or were forced out of the CPI (M) and the coordination of state committees renamed itself the All India Coordination Committee of Communist Revolutionaries (AICCCR) by the middle of 1968, it had more or less committed itself to forming a separate party.

Yet, as Mohan Ram wrote, "there was intense confusion in the AICCCR about the priorities towards building a party and about the kind of party to be built". For Charu Mazumdar "the primary condition for building such a party was to organise armed struggle in the countryside". "The major task of revolutionaries was to plunge into work among the peasant masses and set up revolutionary bases". Mazumdar "had nothing to say about the role of mass organisations and the accent was on a secret party".

The divisions within the AICCCR were essentially on the issue of mass work and whether a party formed in this way, with middle class youth being sent out to "rouse the peasant masses in the countryside" to "wage guerrilla war" and "build rural base areas", would be in a position to sustain armed struggle. Brushing these differences aside, the Communist Party of India (Marxist-

Leninist), or CPI (M-L), was formed on 22 April 1969 and launched at a May Day gathering that year, and had more or less disintegrated by 1971, with a section led by Bihar's Satya Narayan Singh dissociating itself from Mazumdar. Singh (or "SNS", as he was called) had described Mazumdar's line as "individual terrorism" as early as July 1970. By November that year "a majority of the CPI (M-L)'s 21-member Central Committee withdrew support from Mazumdar", and he was *expelled from the party in 1971*.

The CCP had come down heavily on Mazumdar, denouncing his conception of annihilation as "secret assassination", claiming he had no agrarian programme, and describing his "policy" as "wrong". Most substantially, it argued, "Without mass struggle and mass organisation, the peasants' armed struggle cannot be sustained." "Regarding the formulation that if a revolutionary does not make his hands red with the blood of class enemies, then he is not a Communist; if this be the yardstick of a Communist, then that Communist Party cannot remain a Communist Party". Top leaders like Kanu Sanyal, in jail by 1972, referred to their "great disappointment, regret and disgust" at the fact that Mazumdar had refused to learn any lessons from the "valuable suggestions" of the CCP.

CLASS ROOTS OF REVOLT

Naxalbari in the north of West Bengal became a template for the Indian revolution and gave the Naxalites their name. But there was no serious attempt by the Maoist leadership to look at the nature of the struggles there or in Midnapore (Medinipur) or Srikakulam or Kondamodalu. For example, Duyker notes that in the Santal-inhabited areas of Debra and Gopiballavpur (in Midnapore) the Naxalites succeeded in "mobilising large numbers of landless labourers and sharecroppers". There was widespread landlessness among the Santals of districts like Midnapore and Birbhum, and it was essentially these landless tribals who formed the backbone of the mass agitations that the new party led in 1969, in harvesting campaigns that Mazumdar himself was opposed to! The rural upsurges in Midnapore and Birbhum coincided with the monsoons when "the landless could least expect to gain work".

In Naxalbari, in the Siliguri subdivision of Darjeeling in the north, the land occupations that mushroomed between March and May 1967 involved Santal tea garden labourers who worked as sharecroppers on the excess land of the estates. The local leadership here, Kanu Sanyal and Jangal Santhal, did not subscribe to the strategy of small squad actions and concentrated on mass agitation. The agitation (on issues like eviction of sharecroppers and recovery of excess land) was given the character of a nascent insurgency because the Santals were armed with bows and arrows and remained "poised for attacks on police parties", as the CPI (M)-led United Front government decided to break the movement with large-scale arrests and hundreds of tribals fled to the forest where they formed ill-armed and inexperienced guerrilla units besieged by a massive police force. By August wholesale surrenders began to take place—the government had succeeded in breaking the movement by force.

In the Srikakulam Agency Area the bulk of Adivasis (or Girijans, as they were called here) were agricultural labourers. Andhra Pradesh accounts for the highest incidence of tribal land alienation in the country, with non-tribals owning more than half the land in the scheduled areas. Thus here landlessness stemmed from a widespread process of dispossession that had occurred on a larger scale in the coastal tracts of Andhra where primitive accumulation by the state and by moneylenders involved the suppression of customary rights like *podu* and the appropriation of large tracts of land either as "state forests" or land seized by non-tribals. In Srikakulam the Communists had built a broad-based organisation of tribals by the late 1950s, and the land occupations and crop seizures that exploded in 1968 were directed as much against those forces as against any abstract "feudalism". In Kondamodalu in East Godavari "the first demand that was taken up [by the party] concerned the indebtedness of the tribals and their exploitation by the moneylenders", but "the issue on which the movement really picked up was farm wages". Here the land seizures of 1969 targeted land that had been alienated to the non-tribals or mortgaged to moneylenders and did *not* include "the 'self-cultivated lands' of the landlords over which the tribals as yet felt they had no claim".

The movement in Srikakulam was crushed by the middle of 1970 and a period of decline set in. Mazumdar died in custody in July 1972. On one estimate, by March 1973 there were some 17,787 Naxalite prisoners in West Bengal alone. Shock attacks on the class enemy had had disastrous results. In Andhra, Nagi Reddy's group, the Andhra Pradesh Revolutionary Communist Committee (APRCC), argued, "Some persons, forming themselves into groups and without any relation to the mass movement, attack the landlords and other exploiters. We want to make it clear that these attacks carried on without any relation to a mass revolutionary movement cannot enable us to dissolve feudalism". Annihilations would not "annihilate the system or the forms of exploitation". The CPI (M-L)'s "methodology made the people feel that someone else and not they were the liberators".

The setback was so severe that the CPI (M-L) fragmented rapidly and was badly divided in the months leading up to the state of emergency declared by prime minister Indira Gandhi in June 1975. During the emergency of 1975-7 some ten Maoist groups were banned and an estimated 40,000 cadres were in jail. But within the Maoist mainstream the disintegration of the Central Committee spawned repeated attempts at reunification. Nagi Reddy, who had been opposed to the formation of a centralised party and had repeatedly emphasised the need for a longish period of mass work, teamed up with Parimal Das Gupta (one of Mazumdar's earliest critics) and others nationally to form the Unity Centre of Communist Revolutionaries of India (Marxist-Leninist). This more or less disintegrated when Nagi Reddy died in 1975. In Andhra itself Nagi Reddy's group was the weakest of the three groups that existed there in the 1970s. The Andhra Pradesh Revolutionary Communist Party led by Chandra Pulla Reddy, the strongest group in the state in the 1970s, defended the armed defence of the cadres in the face of repression, but combined this with mass struggles or at least the need for an active mobilisation of masses in struggle.

Despite this, CP Reddy supported SNS's drive to regroup the CPI (M-L) and was part of the "Provisional Central Committee", till he split in 1980. Thus the C P Reddy group absorbed very different sorts of influences. It would abandon the boycottism of the CPI (M-L) and start contesting elections from 1978, even winning a seat in the Andhra Assembly elections. It was also the C P Reddy group that was first active in forming the Ryothu Coolie Sanghams or agricultural labour unions. These spread rapidly in the late 1970s and were a key factor in creating substantial popular support for the Naxals in Andhra. The third Maoist group in Andhra was in some ways the most orthodox, since its leader,

Kondapalli Seetharamaiah, had joined the AICCCR early in 1969, and when the Central Committee disintegrated Seetharamaiah was the Andhra face of the "pro-Charu" Central Organising Committee (COC). These coordinations meant little in practice, since the Andhra Maoists were largely independent in their evolution.

In the general retreat and disintegration of the CPI (M-L) that dominated the early 1970s, both CP Reddy and the Andhra COC retained the elements of a squad organisation in north Telangana, and again the issues were less those of a peasantry than of the purely landless and Scheduled Caste labourers and farm servants in districts like Karimnagar and of tribals and other working people in the Godavari valley region. Unlike the insane putschism that had controlled and destroyed the party under Mazumdar's leadership, Telangana in the late 1970s and early 1980s saw major developments that laid the groundwork for the "people's war" of the 1990s and 2000s. The PWG, formed in 1980, had substantial control of Telangana by the end of the 1980s, and it is crucial to see why.

The reason, as the late human rights acivist K Balagopal explained, was that "unlike the rest of [Andhra] where the Naxalites spread through the armed squads, in northern Telangana there was a clear period in the late 1970s and early 1980s…when it was the mass organisations, mainly the agricultural labourers' associations and the student and youth fronts, that were the instrument for the spread of Maoism as an ideology and a political practice". That phase "was soon to pass and the people would start depending on the armed squads for justice". But Seetharamaiah, who attracted the younger generation to his group in large numbers, saw no conflict between mass organisation and armed struggle, and their combined impact was to strike "fatally at the power relations of rural Telangana society" and endow "the poor, the Dalits and the tribals with a voice of their own and the courage to speak out". For all the violence they unleashed, their own and the even worse, more widely spread violence of the state in Andhra, it was possible for Balagopal to maintain that "there is this fear that if the Naxalites go away, 'the poor cannot survive'."

If the PWG emerged as the dominant group in Andhra, even more so when the CP Reddy group split in 1984, in Bihar the field was equally divided between Liberation, Party Unity and the

Maoist Communist Centre (MCC). A key factor in the survival of the PWG was its expansion into the largely tribal districts of Telangana, where the cadre encouraged tribals to cut down and cultivate reserved forests, forced a substantial increase in the wages paid by tendu leaf contractors, and put an end to the harassment Adivasis suffered at the hands of forest officials and the police. In Bihar the oppression of the rural poor took a different form. Though called "zamindars" by the labourers, the Bhumihars of districts like Bhojpur were in fact a substantial peasantry (kisans) and the suppression of the rural poor was as much a struggle for dignity (izzat), that is, for freedom from violence and caste oppression, as a struggle over wages and land rights. The violent colonial repression of the military labour markets of North India had done little to modify the warrior ethos of zamindars and peasants alike in states like Bihar, and the Dalits who formed the bulk of labourers (mazdoors) knew that "any open challenge to upper and middle caste domination would eventually and inevitably result in armed violence".

One student claimed that in the village he studied most Dalits "wanted the Maoist armed squads to remain in the area as they feared that the landlords would re-establish their dominance" if the Maoists withdrew. Another was told, "Because we have arms, the zamindars have shrunk with fear". Thus all of the main Bihar groups were committed to "armed struggle" to one degree or another. The Naxalites who were brought into Bhojpur in the late 1960s would later split from the CPI (M-L) (pro-Mazumdar, pro-Lin Piao faction) led by Mahadeb Mukherjee without gravitating to S N Singh's Central Committee at the other end of the pro/anti-Mazumdar spectrum. Liberation was the outcome of the new Central Committee formed in July 1974 by Subroto Datta alias Jowhar, the young leader of this "third" tendency, and of the three Bihar parties was the one that showed the most substantial evolution in terms of seeking strategies for both survival and growth.

In an extraordinary combination of legal and illegal work, Liberation floated a front organisation, the Indian People's Front (IPF), that contested 50 seats in the Bihar Assembly elections of 1985, even as its armed squads pulled off over 60 "annihilations" between 1980 and 1984! Much of this violence was part of the titanic struggle the Bihar groups were engaged in against the caste-based private militias formed by the Bhumihars, Kurmis and other landed castes in their drive to exterminate Naxalism from the plains of Bihar. This warfare dominated the whole of the 1980s and much of the 1990s, and while the CPI (M-L) was successful in fighting the smaller militias, it was drawn inexorably into a caste dynamic that shaped the nature of the movement and its struggles.

Party Unity, formed in 1982, successfully fought the Bhoomi Sena in Jehanabad, but by the 1990s it drew much of its support from the Kurmis, and its Dalit supporters (all of them workers) felt deserted and betrayed. The MCC, which had evolved from Dakshin Desh, one of the Maoist groups that had stayed out of the AICCCR and eventually built its base in Jharkhand (then south Bihar) had a large following among Yadavs, and became deeply embroiled in caste vendettas that involved horrific massacres on all sides. The MCC had no interest in open organisations of any sort; Party Unity's style of politics effectively drove its one open front, the Mazdoor Kisan Sangram Samiti, underground (it was banned in 1986); and Liberation had to disband the IPF in 1994, worried that its popularity was actually a threat to the "identity of the party"! Finally, not the least of the problems with this total absorption in left wing militarism (less true of Liberation which seems to have dismantled its squads by the late 1990s) has been the armed clashes between the various Naxal groups, involving the liquidation of each other's cadre.

MILITARISATION OF THE STRUGGLE

The late 1980s saw a dramatic escalation of conflict once the PWG took the fateful decision to target the state directly by mounting attacks on the police, inaugurating a spiral of violence that has not abated till today. "It was in July 1985 that the first incident of deliberate murder of a policeman by the Naxalites took place; that was in Jagtial, a 'disturbed area' of Karimnagar, where the police in collusion with armed BJP landlords had been subjecting Naxalite youth to repeated and savage torture". Balagopal himself referred to these escalating levels of violence as a "new" phase. They would transform the conflict into a full-scale war, with sizeable paramilitary forces converting Telangana and the adjoining forest areas into a "vast police camp" and with a profound militarisation of the PWG itself. By the end of the 1980s "whole tribal hamlets were set on fire to teach them a lesson not to harbour Naxalites". By 1997 Balagopal could write that "the 1990s have seen an unprecedented escalation in the magnitude of the killings. More than 60 percent of the encounter killings of the [last] three decades have taken place in the last six years".

Since then, over the period 1997 to 2007, the Andhra Pradesh Civil Liberties Committee has recorded roughly 1,800 "encounter" killings by the police. It is crucial to note that the vast majority of the victims of these extra-judicial killings are Dalits and tribals, many of them with no direct connection to the Naxalites. The culture of impunity extended to the police establishment by the two dominant parties in the state has left a pall of fear hanging over large parts of Telangana, and though it has driven the PWG into the forests of Bastar and the border districts of Orissa, spawning the delusion that Andhra has solved its Naxalite problem, the sheer incoherence of the state's strategies (repeated banning of the PWG, repeated legalisation and unmitigated repression) has left a legacy of substantial underlying support for the CPI (Maoist) (or former PWG) leaders in Andhra itself. For the radical left, the key issue is whether the armed struggle that has now been displaced to the adjoining districts in Chhattisgarh and Orissa is truly the form of a movement for socialist emancipation and the kind of political culture it wants and sees as viable in a country as vast and complex as India. Before coming to this, we should look briefly at the latest phase of the conflict.

Bastar is today the frontline of the "explosive Naxal battle" that is retailed to millions of households in India through the news channels. PWG's expansion into Bastar and Gadchiroli began in the early 1980s, fleeing early waves of repression in Andhra, and by 1989 the party felt strong enough to form a mass "peasant" front called the Dandakaranya Adivasi Kisan Mazdoor Sanghatana, backed by a series of armed squads that contained something under 200 cadres. These expanded rapidly in the early 1990s, a period when Seetharamaiah was hounded out of the party and a new, younger leadership consolidated its hold. In fact, the 1990s threw up an explosive conjuncture. As state governments began dreaming of the fabulous sums of money to be made from the mineral-rich tribal districts they had abandoned to decades of oppression and misery, the PWG rapidly militarised itself, with major increases in lethality (vastly more sophisticated weaponry including the extensive use of landmines), an elaborate organisation of platoons, battalions and military commands, and new expansion into the tribal districts of southern Orissa. By 2001 the party (now called People's War) decided to intensify the war in ten states, and in 2004 PW and the MCCI merged to form the CPI (Maoist).

With police forces too demoralised to handle the insurgency, in Chhattisgarh the BJP government secretly funded and armed a "private" lynch mob called Salwa Judum ("Purification Hunt" in Gondi) that has since emptied hundreds of villages by forcing inhabitants into internally displaced persons camps where they can be easily controlled. "Large swaths of Dantewara are now abandoned. Villages in Salwa Judum-controlled areas that refuse to cooperate are deemed 'Maoist' villages, and are then attacked". On one count, some 40,000 tribals have been herded into these camps and others have fled deep into the forest or across the border into Khammam. Meanwhile, in the last year the Maoists have inflicted major losses on the CRPF (the official military operation in Chhattisgarh), forcing the central government to take control of counterinsurgency operations. The wholesale militarisation of the movement since the 1990s has culminated in a vanguard war trapped in an expanding culture of counterinsurgency, with tens of thousands of civilians caught between them.

THE CRITIQUE OF ARMS

In 2006 K Balagopal wrote, "Nothing justifies the tendency in democratic circles to talk as if all that is relevant for understanding the role of the Maoists in the area (Bastar region and Dantewara in particular) is the poverty and general backwardness of the tribes living there". What he meant by this was that ultimately the kind of militarised Maoism that has emerged in India would have to stand or fall in terms of a critique from the left itself. The dispossession and oppression of tribals and the redoubled drive to open their districts to exploitation by large industrial capital, with the displacement and impoverishment this causes, have been major sources of the tenacity of Maoism in India, a movement to which tribal support has always been crucial. But it is pure naivety to reduce one to the other or identify the tribals and the Maoists as if their agendas were the same or the victory of one would mean the emancipation of the other. Responses, critical or otherwise, from the left can be classified broadly into four categories. Maoists and Maoist sympathisers abstract from the profound deformities of the movement to engage in solidarity with it at any cost. They posit an almost mystical identity between the Maoists and "the people" and do precisely what Balagopal advised democratic circles not to do, namely use the poverty and general backwardness of the tribal areas as an excuse for not engaging with the CPI (Maoist) politically.

A second line of response has been the CPI (Marxist)'s savage repression of all popular movements that challenge their own agendas for the state of West Bengal, using the machinery of the state to crush both the Maoists and much wider layers of the population (again largely tribal) they see as sympathising with them or opposing their own policies. Thus, whereas the CPI (Maoist) sabotaged a struggle like the one in Lalgarh by infiltrating the People's Committee Against Police Atrocities and eliminating all political rivals, the CPI (Marxist) fell back on its own vigilante groups and on state counterinsurgency forces to quell the movement there. Both parties (and large parts of the state apparatus, of course) have an interest in branding what began as and was for months a democratic popular upsurge as "Maoist". And, of course, the two "Marxist" parties have been slaughtering each other's cadre.

Sharply different from both the above has been the civil liberties critique that was largely represented in the writings of the late Balagopal through most of the 1990s down to his death in 2009. Balagopal's critique recorded features that displayed an unmitigated authoritarianism on the part of a movement he had been closely associated with, features he saw as undermining its sources of support. He referred to the "ruthlessness" of the party (the PWG) that had evolved by the early 1990s, to the calculated use of terror as a political instrument, the "medieval forms of violence" that characterised the so-called People's Courts, the lack of possibility of any opposition to the party "so long as the police are taken care of", the "new" culture that had "permeated the Naxalite organisations" as they recruited large numbers of new cadres "more attracted by its weapons than its politics", and the "recognisable deterioration of quality" this had brought with it. More substantially, he saw the movement in Andhra culminating in "stagnation" by the 2000s and forced to sidestep the crisis by expanding into new territory, failing to consolidate a second generation of support. And finally, there were clear elements of a critique of the substitutionism of a vanguard struggle where most decisions were "taken and implemented over the heads of the people but justified in the name of the people", a politics that had simply "corrupted the masses into receivers of justice rather than fighters for it".

These are among the most political criticisms that have been made of the obsessively violent forms Maoism has come to take and they are profoundly more significant for any future left movement in India than the uncritical solidarity of fellow travellers. The indiscriminate killing of village headmen, the widespread laying of landmines, the recruitment of minors, the sabotage of all means of communication, the ban on employment-generating public works have all started to drive a wedge between the party and its tribal sympathisers precisely in the "liberated" zones.

A fourth sort of response would have to come from Marxists who have never identified with any of the Stalinist political traditions in India and do not see revolutionary movements developing in a class vacuum, in complete isolation from industrial workers and the more organised groups of wage earners and employees in the economy at large. The bulk of the Indian labour force remains unorganised into unions, and it is stupefying to imagine that a revolution against capitalism can succeed while the mass of the workers are in a state of near-complete atomisation. The impoverished notions of democracy that either reduce it to a battle for electoral supremacy or dismiss it as a fraud, the failure to encourage and develop a culture of working class organisation and debate, to encourage forms of intervention that contest capitalism in concrete ways, and build a movement that can address the widest possible range of issues starting from the desperate struggle for survival of the millions of landless in India, are all part of the legacy of a left that was moribund intellectually and deeply conservative in its culture.

Shankar Guha Neogi (murdered in 1991) and AK Roy of the Marxist Coordination Committee (expelled from the CPI [M] in 1973), both charismatic union leaders, stood in sharp contrast to that political tradition. They drew their popular support precisely from the landless tribals employed in the iron ore and coal mines of Chhattisgarh and Jharkhand. The CPI (Maoist)'s conception of the working class is a rhetorical one, since it is the party that embodies the "leadership" of the class and conducts the class struggle on its behalf, unelected, unaccountable and never subject to recall. This has been a consistent feature of the Naxalite groups since the late 1960s.

Secondly, the Maoist grasp of theory is unbelievably primitive, a collage of abstractions that bear little relation to reality at any level (analysis or strategy). "Semi-feudalism", "comprador bourgeoisie", "four-class alliance", "protracted people's war", etc are all slavishly copied from Mao's theorisations for China that will soon be almost a century old! For example, a leader of Liberation defends the label "comprador bourgeoisie" by saying it refers to the "increasing organic integration between Indian big business and imperialist capital". But "organic integration" between capitals across national boundaries is precisely what defines capitalism, unless one is going to see the latter as an aggregation of national economies.

Third, even the mass organisations fail to be truly democratic as long as they are "controlled by a secretive and hierarchical party". Yet "parties like the CPI (Maoist) require secrecy not just from the state, but also to penetrate democratic mass movements" to gain control of them, as Santosh Rana showed for Lalgarh. And finally, of course, the Marxist critique will have to be able to absorb the civil liberties one, not simply ignore it. As Balagopal's colleague, Andhra's most distinguished civil rights lawyer, noted years ago, no political movement working for the overthrow of an exploitative order "has any right to reproduce the brutalities practised" by that order.

THE RUMOUR OF MAOISM

In his classic *Elementary Aspects of Peasant Insurgency in Colonial India,* Ranajit Guha outlined certain methodological imperatives for the historian who wanted to 'get in touch with the consciousness of [peasant] insurgency' when access to it is barred by the discourse of counter-insurgency that structures official records. How does one look beyond this discourse of the state that frames the archives in order to gain access to the voice of the rebels? Guha's solution was relatively simple: Counter-insurgency, he argued, derives directly from insurgency and is so determined by the latter that 'it can hardly afford a discourse that is not fully and compulsively involved with the rebel and his activities.'

Unlike British Marxist historian E.J. Hobsbawm who had tried to track the story of 'social bandits' through a somewhat problematic reading of folklore, Guha warned that 'folklore relating to peasant militancy can be elitist too', for many singers and balladeers belonged to upper-caste families who had fallen on hard times and were, therefore, often suspicious of the revolt of the lower castes or tribals. Guha underlined that though the records of the colonial state and its police officials registered the voice of those hostile to the insurgents – including landlords and usurers – they could not avoid being shaped by the will of the insurgents. His conclusion therefore was that the presence of rebel consciousness could be read *in the body of evidence produced by the discourse of counter-insurgency itself*.

The burden of Guha's argument was that in order to decode the language of counter-insurgency, it was often enough to simply reverse the values in the terms used by the official discourse: thus 'badmashes' simply meant peasant militants and not 'bad characters'; 'dacoit village' would indicate an entire village involved in the resistance and 'contagion' would most likely refer to the solidarity generated by the uprising.

Those were happier days from the historian's point of view. For the peasant and tribal insurgencies that Guha was discussing were organic struggles which drew their leadership from amidst the peasants or tribal communities themselves. Whether it was Sidhu-Kanoo, Birsa Munda or Titu Mir – the leadership of the movements and their 'ideologies' derived directly from the world of the tribals. The context of colonial India was also, in a significant sense, quite clearly polarized and the possibility of written records being produced from a multiplicity of sources was simply out of the question. It may, therefore, be possible to follow Guha's suggestion and merely reverse the values in order to get a sense of that other discourse.

In contrast, the methodological challenge for a scholar of contemporary India seems insurmountable. And if any future historian were to explore the Maoist movement of our times, say a hundred years later, she is likely to be completely misled if she decided to follow in Guha's footsteps. For not only would she or he be confronted with the official discourse of counter-insurgency, there would also be a 'Maoist discourse' to contend with – which is almost certainly not the voice of the 'insurgent peasant' (or the adivasi). What this future historian will find in the archives, apart from the standard genre of documents produced by the state and its officials, will be a whole range of writings that claim to speak *in the voice of the peasant/adivasi*, produced by the state-in-waiting: the Maoist vanguard and their intellectual spokespersons. Among these will be actual party journals, pamphlets and statements, but they will also include a large body of writings produced by academics, journalists, human rights activists and other supporters of the movement.

For our historian-scholar, it will be relatively easy to deal with the documents and reports produced by the state and its officials. The real challenge lies in finding ways of decoding the mass of materials that are produced by the partisans of the movement. For one of the myths being endlessly reiterated in this genre of writings is that of virtually complete identity between the poor adivasi or peasant and the insurgents – a sub-sumption of the adivasi voice into the voice of the Maoist vanguard.

Unlike early colonial India, twenty-first century India is a world saturated by the media – it is indeed a world of media explosion; a world where the media is no longer captive to either the state or corporate elites. We live in an era where public discourse is framed by a multiplicity of voices. And yet, it might well be impossible for our future historian to find even one unfiltered voice of the adivasi – unfiltered, that is, through elite discourse.

The adivasis cannot represent themselves; they must be represented, it would seem. They must be represented either by the agents of the state – the Salwa Judum and Mahendra Karma for example – or by the revolutionaries. Unlike Karma who at least is himself an adivasi, the voice of the revolutionary is almost always that of a Brahman/upper caste Ganapathy or Koteswara Rao or their intellectual spokespersons.

So we have a Maoist-aligned intelligentsia vicariously playing out their revolutionary fantasies through the lives of adivasis, while the people actually dying in battle are almost all adivasis. Take the following killed in West Bengal in recent months: Rajaram Mandi, Lakhinder Mandi and Gopinath Soren on the side of the Maoists and Sadhan Mahato, Tapan Mahato, Barendranath Mahato and Gurucharan Mahato on the CPI(M) side. It will be hard to find a single Bhattacharya, Banerjee, Mukherjee, Basu or such like among the dead. On the face of it, the list of dead would seem to suggest that the Maoist story is correct and that the entire battle is being fought by and among the adivasis. But as a matter of fact, we do not even know whether the peasant or the adivasi in question is really the 'insurgent' we are looking for. I say this in a deliberately provocative vein because a point being repeatedly made by the Maoist-aligned intelligentsia is that to deny that the peasants or adivasis themselves are rising in arms, is to deny 'them' agency.

There is a definitional fiat at work here: you are by definition not an agent if you are not a Maoist. Claims like these abound in almost all writings of intellectuals sympathetic to the Maoists. And the only time we hear an actual adivasi voice (filtered, no doubt) is when an Arati Murmu, one of the endlessly harassed people of Lalgarh, assaulted by the police, says: 'Whenever there is a Maoist attack the police raid our villages and torture our women and children. For how long will we suffer this oppression by the police? *All of us are Maoists, let the police arrest us*. Today we have come out.'

Statements like these have been endlessly retailed by the Maoist-aligned intellectuals in support of their argument that all adivasis are Maoists, as though the meaning of Arati Murmu's statement is quite so transparent. It is possible that she is actively involved in the Maoist movement, but it is also possible that she is making this statement in exasperation. If Arati Murmu is who she says she is, an ordinary adivasi woman whose fellow-villagers have repeatedly been bearing the brunt of police repression and harassment, then the statement can be read more as an expression of defiance of the police and not necessarily as a true and valid claim that *all villagers* are now Maoists.

It is indeed true that many adivasis in Lalgarh, Chhattisgarh and many other parts of the country have become Maoists in the face of continued police harassment. However, to conclude from this that the only way adivasis become or can become agents is to completely misrepresent the situation.

A related question is that of the 'organicity' of the Maoists' relationship to the adivasis. One of the ways in which Maoist-aligned intellectuals have been countering the charge of appropriating the voice of the adivasis is by claiming that the Maoists *are* the adivasis, that they are *not* an external factor in adivasi life – at least in areas of their influence.

Take for example, the following argument which takes historians Sumit Sarkar and Tanika Sarkar to task for criticizing the Maoists. According to the author, they argue that 'the movement in Jangal Mahal had been going quite well until the Maoists entered the scene from outside and derailed the movement... [and] it is the violent activities of the Maoists that brought joint forces into the scene.'

The author counters this position by asserting that '(T)he reality... is that the Maoists did not fall from the sky; the Maoist Communist Centre and the CPI(ML) People's War had been active there from the 1980s and 1990s and fought over day to day issues by the people's side and suffered persecution, molestation and incarceration for years together.'

This apparently is 'proof' enough of the Maoists' deep roots among the adivasis, for the author then proceeds:

'Their social roots lie in the soil of Jangal Mahal, however disturbing this may sound to these historians and sections of "learned personalities". *Thus the statement* that the Maoists are external to the movement, that they have entered the scene all of a sudden and taken control of it, *does not have any factual basis at all.*'

I have emphasized the phrases, 'thus the statement' and 'does not have any factual basis', in order to underline the structure of the argument. The only 'facts' that Bhattacharyya refers to is that the MCC and PWG have been active in the area since the 1980s and 1990s and from this it is supposed to follow that they have 'deep roots' among the local populace. By that reckoning the RSS and Vishwa Hindu Parishad also must have 'deep roots' among the adivasis (often in the same areas!). Let us leave aside the minor possibility that different kinds of political forces can be active in an area without managing to get any significant support from the local population.

The writer then goes on to charge intellectuals like the Sarkars with 'portraying the masses in a way that these 'ignorant people are devoid of any initiative of their own, that they are unthinking, unfeeling robots, which can only follow, but cannot lead".'

There are a number of issues here that are worthy of consideration. First, the author's own rendering of the Sarkars' position indicates that according to them, a movement was already on, and in pretty good health before the Maoists took it over. How is this a 'denial of agency' to the adivasis? It would not have been possible for them to hold that position if they had been inclined to 'portray the masses' as 'ignorant', 'devoid of initiative' and 'robots' as Bhattacharyya alleges. It is also worth mentioning that the Sarkars' account is based on the evidence of an active sympathizer of the Lalgarh movement (an activist of the Lalgarh Andolan Sanhati Mancha) who was by no means hostile to the Maoists. My point is that for Maoist-aligned intellectuals, adivasi agency can be recognized *only* as long as they are the foot soldiers of the Maoists.

Second, the question of agency as it is routinely posed in a number of such writings assumes a simple and unproblematic relationship between the adivasi who becomes Maoist and the Maoist vanguard, i.e. the CPI (Maoist). The fact is that this is precisely where matters are considerably more complex and interesting. Those who pick up the gun and ally themselves with the Maoists are, indeed, not mere unthinking robots or 'ignorant' fools – they are agents in more complicated ways than simplistic Maoist-inspired accounts would allow us to see.

In the first place, to merely reassert a commonplace of much historical and political research of recent decades, most people (adivasis and peasants, as opposed to middle class intellectuals) who 'become Maoists' do not do so because they agree with their politics, their 'ideology' or their programme. They do so because 'Maoism' performs some function in a very immediate sense in their lives.

Take the story of Jagadish Mahato – one of the abiding legends of the rise of the Naxalite movement in the Bhojpur region in Bihar. A school teacher by profession, Jagadish Mahato was born into a poor peasant family in the now well-known village of Ekwari. He began his sojourn in politics in the context of the most vicious and unimaginable economic, social and sexual oppression of the local dalit people by upper caste landlords. Till 1968, he was an Ambedkarite of sorts and also published a short-lived newspaper by the name of 'Harijanistan'. He and his friends also organized demonstrations to raise the demand for Harijanistan but to no avail.

Peaceful struggle against the armed might of the landlords turned out to be utterly ineffective. Then he heard about the

'Naxalites' and their activities in Kolkata, in Siliguri and Medinipur. He and Rameshwar Ahir sought them out and established contact with the CPI(ML). Thus began the drama of one of the most important segments of the Naxalite movement outside West Bengal. 'Naxalism' became the weapon in a battlefield of caste-class conflict. Jagadish Mahto died soon thereafter but the CPI(ML) Liberation struck roots in that region.

There are innumerable stories of similar kind in the history of social and political movements. The 'movement' first appears as a rumour in a situation of ongoing battle. To return to our earlier example, Jagadish Mahato could hardly have been an Amebedkarite in the sense we know Amebedkarism today, for the very name Harijanistan gives away the fact that his own self-identity was still being defined within an inherited Gandhian vocabulary. Ambedkar too was little more than a rumour – the rumour of a leader of the 'depressed classes' about whom, possibly many legends were in circulation. And Jagadish Mahato did not have to wait for the 'real' Ambedkar or the Naxalites to materialize before he became an agent. He sought out the Naxalites and Charu Mazumdar. Both Ambedkar and Naxalism played the role that he assigned them in his life. The partnership can then carry on or not, depending upon a variety of factors. Mahato died too soon and we do not know what would have happened to his relationship with the CPI(ML). It is possible that he might have refashioned himself completely in order to become a party leader, but that is another story.

It is also well worth bearing in mind that agency is not always about noble struggle. If vanguards are instrumental in 'using' people for their purposes, ordinary people who choose to join them can be no less instrumental. Thus for instance, Bela Bhatia's field work revealed how, 'There have been instances where individuals have misused such power [as comes from wielding a gun] for private gain.' 'Attraction for armed power,' she found, 'may lead unprincipled individuals to join the movement.' Some of them, she went on to observe, 'formed gangs after running away with the party arms and turned against the party itself (e.g. Jagnandan Yadav group in Bihar).'

It has been argued that exclusive focus on 'armed struggle' for 'capture of state power' 'involves intense paranoid secrecy and a normalization of a wartime mentality.' It is worth considering what happens when such a situation combines with the ways in which wielding of technologically sophisticated arms shapes subjectivity as suggested by Bhatia's account. It is also worth considering how it can radically alter the dynamic of ongoing caste/class struggles. Take, for instance, the following report, once again from Jharkhand:

'The Maoists have not been immune to that fundamental and all-pervasive characteristic of Indian society – caste. Tussles over sharing money, as well as inter-caste clashes between Yadavs and Ganjus, a dalit community, have led to the formation of splinter groups like Tritiya Sammelan Prastuti Committee (TPC) and the Jharkhand Prastuti Committee (JPC). This has come as delightful news to the local administration which often supports one group against the other, and seeks to extract information by providing protection.'

Thus to make the argument that whoever joins the Maoists becomes an agent is certainly true if we bear in mind that it is not the agency of a Maoist revolution that is in question here but rather, agency in its precise social-theoretic sense – as belonging to a person who thinks and takes decisions and acts according to them in whatever way possible. S/he is, in that sense, always-already an agent – even if decisions are always implicated in a web of power relations.

It is also clear from many independent accounts that from the late 1980s, resentment has been brewing against the Maoists in Chhattisgarh. There is independent corroboration from different quarters that the rise of the Salwa Judum as a state-sponsored counter-insurgency was preceded by a rising discontent against Maoist activities in May-June 2005.

Versions differ as to the reasons for the resentment: In one version, villagers decided to resist the Maoists who had come to take a young girl away from her family as a recruit – this forcible taking of one member from every tribal family being a standard practice of the Maoists. (What this does to the question of agency is best left to the reader to ponder.) Another version points to the Maoist-enforced boycott of trade in *tendu* leaves against the backdrop of a drought, as the main precipitating factor behind the resentment. These are complicated questions but it is possible to sift through various contending accounts to get a sense of what is actually going on as far as the relationship between the adivasis/ peasants and the Maoists is concerned. In this one sense, our historian is much better placed than Ranajit Guha. And here in these accounts of resentment against the Maoists, we get a glimpse of yet another dimension of adivasi agency, especially in Chhattisgarh but also in some other parts of the Maoist area of influence.

The most recent instance of the complex dynamic that the adivasi-Maoist relations embodies comes from the Jangal Mahal area – precisely the area about which Bhattacharyya (cited earlier) makes his claims against Sumit Sarkar and Tanika Sarkar. This is the story of Gurucharan Kisku alias Marshal, from all accounts an important tribal leader of the Maoists. Kisku reportedly joined the MCC as far back as in 1988 and had arms training in handling all manner of sophisticated arms, including laying and detonating mines. It is clear from Kisku's statements that his main grouse centres on the 'tribal question':

'I decided to quit the party when I realized that it does nothing for the adivasis. In fact, the party is using them as instruments... Kishenji is an outsider who does not know anything about tribals here... Tribals are a social entity with distinct customs, religion and language. The party is destroying this tribal system and way of life in Jangal Mahal and other areas.'

It is possible that Kisku is particularly bitter at this moment of his break-up with a party and movement he has been involved with for two decades, and this articulation of his complaints could be an exaggerated overstatement. What is undeniable, however, is that in order to express his angst, he draws on an existing discourse among the adivasis populace where certain adivasi cultural practices are seen to be under threat from the Maoists.

Of course, this does not mean that 'Maoism' has no social support among the adivasis and peasants and is simply a fantasy of the revolutionary intelligentsia. Maoism exists and indeed, its area of influence has been expanding. It is impossible to reduce the growth of this 'Maoism', which arises out of an unstable compact between the political party – the CPI (Maoist) – and the ordinary peasants or adivasis, to any single factor. There are a number of different factors and indeed, different histories, that lie behind the phenomenon. At a superficial level, this difference can be located in the very different histories of the different components that went into the making of the party in its present form, namely the CPI(ML) People's War (better known as the PWG), the CPI(ML) Party Unity and the Maoist Communist Centre – all of whom had different styles and different kinds of social base.

The history of the PWG goes back to the post-Emergency mass upsurge of the poor peasantry of Karimnagar district and other parts of Telengana in Andhra Pradesh. The primary issues were those of land, wages and vicious forms of caste oppression. 'The organizational centre' of this struggle, writes K. Balagopal, 'was the agricultural labourers union or Raythu Coolie Sangham (generally known as the Sangham), and not the underground armed squads, known as *dalams*.' The struggle was mainly of the unarmed poor, though the Naxalites did kill a few particularly vicious landlords.

Sympathetic critics have noted that this mode of operation continued till well into the 1980s – in the struggles in Adilabad against food shortages where common villagers would loot granaries and shops and redistribute food. By 1985, however, as the state's retaliation, mostly on behalf of the rural rich, began, PWG strategy itself underwent a transformation. Gradually, mass struggles receded to the background and increasingly, their place was taken over by the dalams. However, it is not correct to say that this shift was entirely in response to state retaliation. It was increasingly becoming a short cut, for as the Naxalite legend spread, it struck fear among sections of the landlords – another form in which Naxalism then, as Maoism now, existed as rumour. Often then, mere putting up of the posters demanding a rise in wages, for example, could lead to a rise in wages. The rumour did its work.

The armed intervention of the Naxalites on behalf of the poor provided a counter, a backdrop against which the mass struggles were fought as the movement spread in other parts of Telengana. The arms of the Naxalites fulfilled a social function here that must be clearly recognized: they were a foil to the armed might of the upper/dominant caste landlords and local arms of the state that functioned, always in the interests of the former.

As distinct from the land and wage struggles of this period, the more recent growth of the Maoists, in say Northern Karnataka, was among tribals who were at the point of displacement with the formation of the Kudremukh National Park. Though many other organizations and movements have also been agitating in the area, holding road blockades, 'storming the forests', organizing human chains and satyagrahas, the attraction for the Maoists at least among a section of the poorest seems to have been quite evident.

Here the conflict was not with the immediate oppressor, namely the landlord. Rather, the perceived threat was from a distant and impersonal force – the state and its officials – and the impending displacement that stared the adivasis in the face. Violence at least had the potential to make news and attract attention to their situation, where satyagrahas, nonviolent actions and human chains have been made completely ineffective and delegitimized by the state and the media.

In places like Lalgarh or in some other parts of Jharkhand too, the prospects of Maoist violence have often seemed liberating in the face of the most vicious nexus of forest contractors, local police and business interests. Elsewhere, I have written about how the state's repression of all legitimate democratic struggles has made the Maoist option look so attractive that it has ended up eliminating all intermediate spaces of mass politics.

In the Dandakaranya region, which includes Gadchiroli and the districts of Dantewada, Bastar and Kanker – the current 'war zones'– there is yet another kind of state and state-sponsored violence that is destroying adivasi life. Little surprise that the influence of the Maoists has phenomenally increased over the years. Here the most recent conflicts have been around the renewed drive by the state to industrialize and throw open the mineral rich forest areas to corporations. This clearly involves large-scale displacement of the tribal population from their traditional habitats. Important steel companies like Essar Steel and Tata Steel have been in the process of acquiring prime agricultural land in the area.

Independent reports have testified to the fact that the entire process of land acquisition was being conducted at gun point. Gram sabha meetings, ostensibly meant to discuss and give or withhold consent to land acquisition, were a farce: instead of meetings, individuals were being called in to a room and made to sign their consent – or so the villagers felt. Held under heavy armed guard, these meetings were a farce in another sense. Legally, no outsiders are allowed to attend gram sabha meetings but the interested parties, namely Essar Steel officials – in the case of the report cited above – were inside, overseeing the process. As a reporter put it, the same procedure was being followed in other places: Gram sabha 'meetings' were held under the shadow of Section 144, while all outspoken critics of the acquisition would be under arrest.

Such stories have been filtering in from researchers in the field for some years now and it was clear that in this new phase of neo-liberal industrialization, a new kind of violence was being unleashed on people who were to be dispossessed in order to make room for mining and industry. In many such cases (for example, Kashipur, Kalinganagar, Singur, Nandigram, Goa, Pen tehsil in Maharashtra), mass struggles have been ongoing for some time.

Even apart from these well-known, emblematic names, there have been innumerable mass struggles throughout the country which have resisted the frenetic drive towards industrialization and mining through displacement, often successfully.

However, it is equally true that often, in the face of the darkest state violence, the prospect of a counter-violence holds great attraction for many people. Maoism seemed to provide precisely such a possibility.

Bibliography

Barmé, Geremie R. *Shades of Mao: The Posthumous Cult of the Great Leader.* Armonk, N.Y.: M. E. Sharpe, 1996.

Bottomore, Tom: *A Dictionary of Marxist Thought,* New Delhi, Maya Blackwell, 2000.

Breslin, S. G. *Mao: Profiles in Power.* London and New York: Longman, 1998.

Chalmers, Johnson. *Autopsy on Peoples War*. Berkeley: University of California Press, 1973.

Dasgupta, B.: *The Naxalite Movement,* Bombay: Allied Publishers, 1974.

Debray, Regis. *Revolution in the Revolution*. New York: Grove Press, Inc., 1993.

Duyker, E.: *Tribal Guerrillas: The Santals of West Bengal and the Naxalite Movement,* New Delhi: OUP, 1987.

Geoffrey, G.: *Development and Underdevelopment: A Marxist Analysis,* London, Macmillan, 1975.

Ghosh, Suniti : *The Historic Turning-Point: A Liberation Anthology,* Calcutta, 1992.

Kay, Geoffrey: *Development and Underdevelopment: A Marxist Analysis,* London, Macmillan, 1975.

Meisner, Maurice J.: *Marxism, Maoism, and Utopianism : Eight Essays.* Madison: University of Wisconsin Press, 1982.

Mukherjee, Arun Prosad : *Maoist 'Spring Thunder' : The Naxalite Movement (1967-1972),* K P Bagchi and Company, Delhi, 2007.

Muni, S.D. : *Maoist Insurgency in Nepal : The Challenge and the Response,* Rupa, Delhi, 2004.

Pomeroy, William J.: *Guerrilla Warfare and Marxism*. New York: International Publishers, 1996.

Prakash A. Raj: *Maoists in the Land of Buddha : An Analytical Study of the Maoist Insurgency in Nepal*, Nirala, Delhi, 2004.

Rajendra Singh Yadav, *Bhojpur: Naxalism in the Plains of Bihar*, New Delhi, 1980.

Ray, R.: *Naxalites and their Ideology*, New Delhi: OUP, 1988.

Regis, D.. *Revolution in the Revolution*. New York: Grove Press, Inc., 1993.

Robert Sir: *War In Peace: Conventional and Guerilla Warfare Since 1945*. New York: Harmony Books, 1982.

Rothermund, D.: *A History of India*. Totowa, New Jersey: Barnes and Noble, 1986.

Schram, Stuart: *Mao's Road to Power: Revolutionary Writings, 1912–1949*. 5 vols. Armonk, N.Y.: M. E. Sharpe, 1992–1999.

Sharma, A.N. : *Bihar: Stagnation or Growth*. Delhi: Spectrum Publishing House.

Snow, Edgar. *The Long Revolution*. New York: Random House, 1972.

Sumanta, B.: *In the Wake of Naxalbari: A History of the Naxalite Movement in India*, Calcutta: Subarnarekha, 1980.

Suniti, G. : *The Historic Turning-Point: A Liberation Anthology*, Calcutta, 1992.

Thapa, Deepak : *Understanding the Maoist Movement of Nepal*, Centre for Social Research and Development, Delhi, 2003.

Thompson, Robert Sir: *War In Peace: Conventional and Guerilla Warfare Since 1945*. New York: Harmony Books, 1982.

Tom, B.: *A Dictionary of Marxist Thought*, NewDelhi,Maya Blackwell, 2000.

Tse-tung Mao: *Mao and the Nepali Revolution*. London: Oxford University Press, 1965.

Wheatcroft, Andrew. *The World Atlas of Revolution*.New York: Simon and Schuster, 1983.

William J.: *Guerrilla Warfare and Marxism*. New York: International Publishers, 1996.

Yadav, Rajendra Singh : *Bhojpur: Naxalism in the Plains of Bihar*, New Delhi, 1980.

Index

□□□